Write Now!

THE PRACTICAL APPROACH TO LEAVING CERTIFICATE ENGLISH PAPER 1

Mary Ó Maolmhuire

GILL & MACMILLAN

Gill & Macmillan Ltd
Hume Avenue
Park West
Dublin 12
with associated companies throughout the world
www.gillmacmillan.ie

© Mary Ó Maolmhuire 2002
0 7171 3367 2

Print origination in Ireland by O'K Graphic Design, Dublin
Colour reproduction by Ultragraphics, Dublin

The paper used in this book is made from the wood pulp of managed forests.
For every tree felled, at least one tree is planted, thereby renewing natural resources,

All rights reserved.
No part of this publication may be copied, reproduced or transmitted in any form
or by any means without written permission of the publishers or else under the terms of any
licence permitting limited copying issued by the Irish Copyright Licensing Agency,
The Writers' Centre, Parnell Square, Dublin 1.

CONTENTS

Introduction	vii

Unit 1 Youth and Identity
Section A Comprehending
Introduction: four texts	1
Genres	2
Text 1: 'My Daughter Smokes' by Alice Walker	3
Text 2: 'Statistics give lie to war zone image' by Patrick Smyth	6
Text 3: 'Young men in a hurry' by Tim Blair	9
Text 4: Images of Youth and Identity	12

Section B Focus on ... the Language of Narration   15
Fictional Narrative	15
Non-Fictional Narrative	17

Section C Composing   22
Planning the Composition	22
Writing the Composition	23
The Titles – Theme: Youth and Identity: seven essay titles with notes on genres	26

Section D Language Skills   30
Efficiency of Language Use 1	30
Punctuation	30
Spelling	34

Unit 2 Race and Racism
Section A Comprehending   35
Introduction: four texts	35
Text 1: 'What do people think' from *Amnesty Ireland*	36
Text 2: 'Australia experiences surge of nationalism' by Conor O'Clery	38
Text 3: 'Death be not proud' by Robert Badinter	41
Text 4: Images of Race and Racism	44
Sample Answer	46

Section B Focus on … the Language of Argument	48
Examples	49
Section C Composing	57
Starting the Essay	57
The Titles – Theme: Race and Racism: seven essay titles with sample openings	58
Section D Language Skills	65
Efficiency of Language Use 2	65
Syntax: structure, sentences, phrasing, paragraphs	65
Punctuation	70
Spelling	72

Unit 3 Man and Nature

Section A Comprehending	75
Introduction: four texts	75
Text 1: 'They've got it sorted' from *Irish Times* magazine	76
Text 2: Hitting the wall: first ascent of a Baffin Island peak by Greg Child	81
Text 3: 'We May Be Brothers After All' by Chief Seattle	85
Text 4: Images of Man and Nature	88
Sample Answer	90
Section B Focus on … the Language of Information	92
Newspapers	93
Reviews	100
The Internet	105
Section C Composing	108
Engaging with the Text	108
The Titles – Theme: Man and Nature: seven essay titles with notes on engaging with the text	110
Section D Language Skills	120
Efficiency of Language Use 3	120
Register: formal and informal use	120
Vocabulary: synonyms and spelling exercises	122
Punctuation: apostrophes	125
Spelling	127

Unit 4 Power and Powerlessness

Section A Comprehending   129
   Introduction: four texts   129
      Text 1: 'Ain't I a Woman?' by Sojourner Truth   130
      Text 2: 'Turning good people to evil acts' by Derek Scally   133
      Text 3: 'The power of writing' by Joel Swerolow   136
      Text 4: Images of Power and Powerlessness   141
   Sample Answer   143

Section B Focus on … the Language of Persuasion   144
   Advertising in the Media   145
   Political Speeches   149
   Satiric Text   156

Section C Composing   158
   Concluding the Essay   158
   The Titles – Themes: Power and Powerlessness: seven essay titles
   with notes on concluding your essay   159

Section D Language Skills   172
   Efficiency of Language Use 4   172
   Expanding your Vocabulary Base   172
   Grammatical Patterns: adjectives and nouns, adverbs and verbs   175
   Punctuation: quotation marks   177
   Spelling: homonyms and homophones   183

Unit 5 Journeys and Change

Section A Comprehending   186
   Introduction: four texts   186
      Text 1: 'Four island students a class apart' by Lorna Siggins   187
      Text 2: 'Travels with an elephant' by Teresa Nerney   190
      Text 3: 'Last Days' from *Cider with Rosie* by Laurie Lee   193
      Text 4: Images of Journeys and Change   196
   Sample Answer   198

Section B Focus on … the Aesthetic Use of Language   199
   Fiction   200
   Poetry   205
   Drama   213

Section C Composing	222
Bringing It All Together – The Exam Essay	222
The Titles – Theme: Journeys and Change: seven essay titles	224
Section D Language Skills	226
Efficiency of Language Use 5	226
Avoiding Repetition	226
Writing More Concisely	228
Grammatical Patterns: active and passive voices	229
Punctuation: extracts from five novels on the course	232
Spelling	239
Last Words: range of quotations on various themes	242
Glossary of Terms Used in the Exam	245
Marking Criteria for Leaving Certificate English	247
Acknowledgments	248

INTRODUCTION

To the student

So. You need to tackle Paper 1 of the revised Leaving Certificate English syllabus and you find the prospect daunting. You know that it carries half of the marks for the exam, but you are uncertain about how to approach the comprehending and composing tasks. Not to worry. My own students are facing the same challenge. My aim in writing this book is to help you to gain confidence in your use of English, by giving you the language skills necessary for the task. In the process you will be reading many interesting, challenging and informative texts, encountering some powerful images, and composing in a variety of genres. My hope is also, that these will give you a taste for reading and composing for life, and not just for the exam.

Paper 1 of the revised Leaving Certificate English Exam consists of four texts linked by a common theme and seven composition titles loosely connected to that theme. You are required to answer one Question A and one Question B from two different texts. You must also write a composition in a particular style or 'genre'. Initially, the term 'genre' may cause you some concern. However, simply defined, it merely seeks to classify language under five general headings. These are:

- the language of information
- the language of argument
- the language of persuasion
- the language of narration
- the aesthetic use of language

In line with these headings, this book comprises five units. As reflected in the format of the paper, each unit contains four main texts linked by a general theme and seven composition titles. In Section A of each Unit (Comprehending), you will find pre-reading exercises designed to help you to approach these texts intelligently, in order to write better answers to those A and B questions. You will also find a sample A or B answer in Units 2–5.

Section B of each Unit will concentrate on one of the five 'genres'. For example, Unit 1 defines the language of narration, lists its sources and gives you some short text examples of this genre and a commentary on its individual features. This will help you to become familiar with the genre, and identify it more easily.

Section C in each Unit (Composing) offers you a choice of seven titles for composition – loosely connected to the overall theme of the reading texts. Here, you will learn the skills of pre-writing, drafting and re-drafting material, starting the composition, engaging with the texts and concluding. You will also study the criteria for assessment in the exam, how marks are allocated and what this means in practice when you tackle the comprehending and composing tasks.

Finally, Section D of each Unit (Language Skills) will heighten your awareness of how language is used to convey meaning. There are opportunities to expand your vocabulary base, to practise grammatical patterns appropriate to the task, to learn about syntax and paragraphing. You will also exercise the 'mechanics of language', i.e. punctuation and spelling. These exercises are designed to give you a greater variety of expression, and more control and power over the language you use. This is one of the fundamental aims of the revised syllabus.

Remember that acquiring good language skills for Paper 1 will also be invaluable when writing answers to questions on Paper 2. Being careful with the bones and brickwork of the language will make you a better writer *and* reader.

If you work at language, and give it a reasonable amount of time and effort, you will succeed.

Good luck to you in your exam and in your future life and career.

Mary Ó Maolmhuire

Unit 1 Youth and Identity

SECTION A COMPREHENDING

Introduction
This section contains four texts on the general theme of *Youth and Identity*, including a set of pre-reading exercises on Texts 1–3.

Text 1
'My Daughter Smokes' is an extract taken from a collection of essays, entitled *Living by the Word*, by the black American writer, Alice Walker. Her provocative prose explores feminist, environmental and political issues and sheds new light on racial debates. This extract is primarily an example of the language of **narration**, but with strong elements of the languages of **argument** and **persuasion**. There are moving and powerful images which are also examples of the **aesthetic use of language**.

Text 2
'Statistics give lie to war zone image' by Patrick Smyth is an article from the *Irish Times*, 'Education & Living' supplement, 6 March 2001. It focuses on the issue of violence in American schools in the period 1983–99. The article is mainly informative, and is therefore an example of the language of **information**. However, the text may also be perceived as arguing a particular point of view, in relation to the subject matter, and as such contains elements of the language of **argument**.

Text 3
'Young men in a hurry' by Tim Blair is a feature article (edited) from *Time* magazine, dated 5 March 2001. It profiles the emergence of young, inexperienced racing drivers onto the Formula 1 circuit. The article quotes facts and statistics on the subject of young Formula 1 racing drivers, and is, therefore, largely **informative**. However, the article also presents the contrasting attitudes of those in the racing industry itself, each of whom seeks to **persuade** the reader to a particular point of view. Be prepared to find examples of the language of **argument** and of **persuasion** here.

Text 4

Text 4 consists of a series of photographs depicting different facets of the theme *Youth and Identity*. There is no written text, but you are required to study the images, and respond to them in a variety of ways.

To the student

'All attempts at reading are attempts to **make meaning**. Comprehending is a meaning-making activity and must always be approached in that way.'
('Revised Leaving Cert. English Syllabus')

Note: The comprehension tasks in Paper 1 focus on perspectives of meaning. The **context** of a text is important, as is your interaction with it. Reading is intended to be a **purposeful** activity, with you as the student engaging with the text, responding to it and its possibilities of **interpretation**. This is far more exciting and challenging, than merely regurgitating information.

New style comprehending questions are designed to elicit a more thoughtful and thought-provoking response from you, the reader. It is more demanding, certainly, but will lead to an increased awareness of how language works and how the whole meaning of a text is revealed.

Genres

Do not be unduly concerned at this stage about the mixture of language 'genres' or styles in these texts. It *is* important that you understand and are familiar with each of them separately, but with reading and practice you will identify them more easily. In addition, Section B in each Unit of this book focuses on a particular genre, e.g. the language of **narration** in Unit 1. Remember that genres are described in the syllabus as '*means*, not masters'. Language itself is constantly evolving and genres too are changing and developing all the time. Writers, moreover, are not bound by any one style of writing. They are simply concerned with rendering their experiences into words. You should see genres simply as the means by which a writer *shapes* and *orders* his experience.

Indeed, this concept of language as a powerful means of shaping and ordering experience is central to the philosophy of the revised syllabus.

'Students should develop an understanding of how the language a person uses *shapes* the way that person views the world.'

Furthermore, the syllabus states that a wide range of encounters with language in its many *shapes* will be 'reflected in the assessment and examination of students'.

Text 1 My Daughter Smokes by Alice Walker

Stage 1 Pre-Reading
Aim: To focus on the particular subject matter of the text, i.e. smoking in adolescence and its consequences in Text 1, and to provide stimuli for the composing tasks in Section C.
Task: In pairs or small groups, discuss some or all of the questions below for ten minutes, then report back to the class.
OR
Your teacher may choose to discuss the questions with the whole group. The most important thing is that you take *notes* of other students' points, for use later in one of the *composing* tasks in Section C.

Questions
1. At what age, and why, do young people start to smoke?
2. According to statistics, adolescent girls smoke more than boys. Why is this, do you think?
3. Are young smokers influenced by older family members who smoke?
4. Why do adolescents ignore the well-documented health risks associated with smoking?

Stage 2 Reading

My Daughter Smokes by Alice Walker

> My daughter smokes. While she is doing her homework, her feet on the bench in front of her and her calculator clicking out answers to her algebra problems, I am looking at the half empty package of Camels tossed carelessly close at hand. Camels. I pick them up, take them into the kitchen, where the light is better, and study them – they're filtered, for which I am grateful. My heart feels terrible. I want to weep. In fact, I do weep a little, standing there by the stove holding one of the instruments, so white, so precisely rolled, that could cause my daughter's death. When she smoked Marlboros and Players I hardened myself against feeling so bad; nobody I knew ever smoked these brands.
>
> She doesn't know this, but it was Camels that my father, her grandfather, smoked. But before he smoked 'ready-mades' – when he was very young and very poor, with eyes like lanterns – he smoked Prince Albert tobacco in cigarettes he rolled himself. I remember the bright-red tobacco tin, with a picture of Queen

Victoria's consort, Prince Albert, dressed in a black frock coat and carrying a cane.

The tobacco was dark brown, pungent, slightly bitter. I tasted it more than once as a child, and the discarded tins could be used for a number of things: to keep buttons and shoelaces in, to store seeds, and best of all, to hold worms for the rare times my father took us fishing.

By the late forties and early fifties no one rolled his own anymore (and few women smoked) in my hometown, Eatonton, Georgia. The tobacco industry, coupled with Hollywood movies in which both hero and heroine smoked like chimneys, won over completely people like my father, who were hopelessly addicted to cigarettes. He never looked as dapper as Prince Albert, though; he continued to look like a poor, overweight, overworked colored man with too large a family; black, with a very white cigarette stuck in his mouth.

I do not remember when he started to cough. Perhaps it was unnoticeable at first. A little hacking in the morning as he lit his first cigarette upon getting out of bed. By the time I was my daughter's age, his breath was a wheeze, embarrassing to hear; he could not climb stairs without resting every third or fourth step. It was not unusual for him to cough for an hour.

It is hard to believe there was a time when people did not understand that cigarette smoking is an addiction. I wondered aloud once to my sister – who is perennially trying to quit – whether our father realised this. I wondered how she, a smoker since high school, viewed her own habit.

It was our father who gave her her first cigarette, one day when she had taken water to him in the fields.

'I always wondered why he did that,' she said, puzzled, and with some bitterness.

'What did he say?' I asked.

'That he didn't want me to go to anyone else for them,' she said, 'which never really crossed my mind.'

So he was aware it was addictive, I thought, though as annoyed as she that he assumed she would be interested.

I began smoking in eleventh grade, also the year I drank numerous bottles of terrible sweet, very cheap wine. My friends and I, all boys for this venture, bought our supplies from a man who ran a segregated bar and liquor store on the outskirts of town. Over the entrance there was a large sign that said COLORED. We were not permitted to drink there, only to buy. I smoked Kools, because my sister did. By then I thought her toxic darkened lips and gums glamorous. However, my body simply would not tolerate smoke. After six months I had a chronic sore throat. I gave up smoking, gladly. Because it was a ritual with my buddies – Murl, Leon, and 'Dog' Farley – I continued to drink wine.

My father died from 'the poor man's friend,' pneumonia, one hard winter when his bronchitis and emphysema had left him low. I doubt he had much lung left at all, after coughing for so many years. He has so little breath that, during his last years, he was always leaning on something. I remember once, at a family reunion, when my daughter was two, that my father picked her up for a minute – long enough for me to photograph them – but the effort was obvious. Near the very end of his life, and largely because he had no more lungs, he quit smoking. He gained a couple of pounds, but by then he was so emaciated no one noticed.

Question A

(i) Based on your reading of the whole text, what is the attitude of the author towards her daughter's smoking? Support your points by quotation or reference. (20)

(ii) What are your impressions of the writer's *father* as you encounter him in the extract? (15)

(iii) 'By the late forties and early fifties no one rolled his own anymore ... hopelessly addicted to cigarettes.'

This is one example of the language of *narration**, as used by the writer in this text. Can you find one other example of this genre in the text? Justify your choice. (15)

(*See Section B Focus on ... Language of Narration.)

6 Write Now!

Question B
Imagine that you are the daughter in this essay. Write a letter to your mother, in which you attempt to explain your own feelings and experience of smoking, as an adolescent. (50)

Text 2 *Statistics give lie to war zone image by Patrick Smith*

Stage 1 Pre-Reading
Aim: To focus on the particular subject matter of the text and to provide stimuli for possible use in one of the composing tasks in Section C.

Task: In pairs or small groups, discuss some or all of the questions below for ten minutes, then report back to the class.

OR

Your teacher may choose to discuss the questions with the whole group. The most important thing is that you take *notes* of other students' points, for use later in one of the *composing* tasks in Section C.

Questions
1. What are your preconceptions of violence in American schools? Are they largely based on TV and film depictions or on actual knowledge?
2. How significant a factor is the availability of firearms to American youth when considering this issue?
3. Is Ireland experiencing a problem with violence in our schools? If so, *how* and *why*?
4. Are gang memberships and/or drugs an issue in terms of violence in our schools?

Stage 2 Reading

Statistics give lie to war zone image by Patrick Smyth

Statistics give lie to war zone image

The truth about violence in US schools is not straightforward.

Perceptions of war zones are profoundly wrong. A student is 100 times more likely to be killed outside his front door than in school. And in school, he or she is ten times more likely to be killed in a gang or drug-related incident than a mass shooting.

The United States suffered an epidemic of violence in the decade from about 1983 to 1993. Arrest rates of young people for homicide and other violent crimes skyrocketed, with three factors contributing significantly: gangs, drugs and guns. Since then, arrests and victims' reports of violence have declined, returning in 1999 to rates only slightly higher than those in 1983.

In a study published last week, 'Indicators of School Crime and Safety 2000', researchers from the US departments of justice and education said violent crime in schools dropped between 1992 and 1998 – from forty-eight crimes per 1,000 students to forty-three crimes per 1,000.

Yet several other leading indicators of violence remain high. Young people tell surveys that their own involvement in violence has not declined at all. Arrest rates for aggravated assault remain quite high. Some estimates of gang membership indicate that this problem remains close to levels at the peak of the epidemic.

But today's youth violence is less lethal, largely because of a decline in the use of

Grieving parents and students following the massacre at Columbine High School

8 Write Now!

firearms. Homicides at school are declining. Violent confrontations are less likely to result in killing or serious injury, and the police are less likely to be called.

And yet violent behaviour is just as prevalent today as it was during the violence epidemic. Some ten to fifteen per cent of high school seniors reveal in confidential surveys that they have committed at least one act of serious violence in the past year. This prevalence rate has been slowly yet steadily rising since 1980.

Of the 177 students age five to nineteen who were killed at school in the five years to June 1999, the vast majority of the homicides (eighty-four per cent) involved firearms. During that period, school-associated homicides remained at less than one per cent of all homicides among students, but the frequency of homicides involving more than one victim increased.

The three school years from August 1995 through to June 1998 saw an average of five multiple-victim homicides or homicide-suicides per year. An average of one such event occurred in each of the three years from August 1992 through July 1995.

The National Crime Victimisation Survey found that between 1992 and 1998, the rate of serious violent crimes at school remained relatively stable at about eight to thirteen per 1,000 students. However, recent findings regarding students carrying weapons (a gun, knife, or club, for example) at school are encouraging. In 1999 a survey found that about seven per cent of all high school students reported carrying a weapon on school property within the last thirty days, down from twelve per cent in 1993.

(Irish Times, 6 March 2001)

Question A

(i) What general conclusions do you draw, from this article, on the state of violence in US schools? Outline your view in 150–200 words, illustrating the points you make by reference to the text. (25)

(ii) 'The truth about violence in US schools is not straightforward. Perceptions of war zones are profoundly wrong.'

What arguments* does the writer make in support of his viewpoint in this article? Consider all of the text in your answer, supporting your points by quotation or reference. (25)

(*See Unit 2, Section B Focus on ... Language of Argument.)

Question B

Violence in our schools – what effect does it have on young people? Write an article for a local or national newspaper expressing your views on this question (150–200 words). (50)

Note

1. Your article should be ***informative*** – supported by facts and/or statistics relating to this topic.
2. If you wish to make an argument, study the style and layout of the newspaper article, and attempt to write one in a similar style.
3. Make your points clearly, and avoid using slang or accusatory language. Stay ***objective*** at all times, as is the writer Patrick Smyth in the *Irish Times'* article.

Text 3 *Young men in a hurry by Tim Blair*

Stage 1 **Pre-Reading**

Aim: To focus your thinking on the particular subject matter of this text and to provide some starting points for one of the *composing* tasks in Section C.

Task: In pairs, or small groups, discuss some or all of the questions below for ten minutes, then report back to the class.

OR

Your teacher may choose to discuss the questions with the whole group. The most important thing is that you take *notes* of other students' points, for use later in one of the *composing* tasks in Section C.

Questions

1. What is the *attraction* of racing for young male drivers, and why is it exclusively male?
2. Can Grand Prix racing be regarded as irresponsible and dangerous? What about the numbers of drivers who have been badly injured or killed in recent years?
3. How much of the popularity of Formula 1 racing has to do with image, and commercial greed, rather than the sport itself?
4. Do you think anyone under twenty-one should be awarded a permit (superlicense) to race in Formula 1? If so, why? If not, why not?

Stage 2 **Reading**

Young men in a hurry by Tim Blair

Too fast to be denied, a new band of motor racing prodigies are taking their places on the grid, confounding Formula One's old guard.

Schoolboy Lewis Hamilton is a dutiful student. His grades in math and English have always been high, and this year the fifteen-year-old from Hertfordshire, England, expects an 'A' in French. Typical of many boys, Lewis dreams of becoming a Formula One driver; he has a collection of Grand Prix videos and reads car racing magazines. In Hamilton's case, however, these are just as much study guides as his algebra and language textbooks. In 1998 Hamilton, a champion racer of tiny, motorcycle-engined go-karts, signed a contract with Formula One powerhouse McLaren to shape and develop his racing career. He has been headed for the 340-km/h world of Formula One since he was just thirteen.

Hamilton is among the youngest of a battalion of youthful speedsters who are charging at F1's gates. Some have already burst through: this Sunday in Melbourne, Australia, nineteen-year-old Fernando Alonso will compete in an F1 Grand Prix race for the first time, alongside twenty-one-year-olds Jenson Button and Kimi Raikkonen, and Enrique Bernoldi, twenty-two.

Mosley's main worry leading up to the Australian Grand Prix is Raikkonen, a former kart champ with only eighteen months' experience racing cars. Swiss F1 team Sauber signed Raikkonen for the 2001 season after noting the Finn's astonishing speed in junior racing, but the FIA – citing rules that require demonstrated expertise in lesser cars – balked at awarding a permit (called a superlicense) that would allow Raikkonen to compete. In December, Raikkonen drove flat out for hours at Spain's Jerez circuit while twenty-five members of the FIA commission, made up of F1 teams, sponsors, manufacturers, promoters and tire makers, looked on. His superlicense was granted by a vote of twenty-four to one. The only 'no' vote came from Mosley, who told the London *Times* the decision was 'irresponsible and potentially dangerous.'

The FAI president isn't alone in his concerns. Jaguar driver Eddie Irvine was dismissive of Raikkonen's test, and of subsequent rapid times the Finn set during practice in fine weather. 'It's all well testing in sunshine,' he said. Button, after competing in only seventeen F1 races himself, surprised F1 observers by saying the Finn 'may have difficulties competing on a packed grid. It is a big step up and he will have to be careful.' Even schoolboy Hamilton is dubious. Raikkonen, he says, 'is making a big mistake.'

Age and guile no longer cut it for F1 teams driven by enormous commercial need – large outfits such as Ferrari and McLaren run on $500 million annual budgets – to unearth the next new star. 'Young and sexy are great for marketing,' says Graham Jones, communications manager for Italian-based F1 team European-Minardi, for which Spanish teenager Alonso will drive this year. 'In coming years', he says, 'drivers as young as sixteen or seventeen may compete in Grand Prix': 'Young drivers can help a team's profile and attract new sponsors. They tend to be quick. And, if you're lucky, they won't be accident prone.'

The FAI is hedging its bets on at least one 'kid.' Raikkonen's superlicense is valid for only four races, after which it will be reviewed. Tim Schenken, clerk of course for the Australian Grand Prix, says a review and license revocation may come sooner: 'It is extremely unlikely, but if Raikkonen spun several times or had accidents (in Melbourne), it could be over for him after one practice session.'

Last year, Button – whose level of experience was only slightly higher than Raikkonen's – provoked similar alarm. Dual world champion Mika Hakkinen predicted that the newcomer was in for a 'nightmare four or five years' while he adapted to F1; ex-driver turned commentator Martin Brundle said Button had joined F1 at least two years too early. By the end of the season, however, Button was regularly qualifying ahead of established stars, and is now tipped to one day become a title winner. Many observers of Raikkonen's brief career deliver equally glowing predications.

In Hertfordshire, the hype over youthful F1 contenders hasn't led to panic. 'My ambition isn't to get to F1 early,' says Lewis Hamilton. 'It's just to get there.' And he's prepared to bide his time. According to Hamilton, he might not be ready for F1 until he is twenty-two or twenty-three. There is such a thing in racing as moving too fast.

(*Time* Magazine, 5 March 2001)

Question A

(i) To what extent are young drivers making significant inroads into Formula 1 racing, according to this article? How powerful an influence are they exerting on the industry as a whole? Support your points by detailed reference to the text. (20)

(ii) From your reading of this article, what, in your view, is the most powerful argument made by the writer **in favour** of young racing drivers participating in Formula 1, (15)
AND
the most powerful argument **against** their participation at such a young age? (15)
Support your point of view by detailed reference to the text.

Question B

You have been asked by your teacher to give a two-minute talk to the class on the subject of 'Young drivers and their obsession with speed'. Write the text of the talk you would deliver (150–200 words). (50)

Text 4 *Images of Youth and Identity*

1.

2.

Youth and Identity 13

14 Write Now!

Note: Text 4 requires a different approach. You are asked to 'read' a series of images with usually no written text. You should study each of them closely before attempting to answer the questions. Be especially attentive to detail in the photographs – the setting, the personalities/characteristics of people and/or objects, their gestures, facial expressions and body language. Look, too, at colour, light and shade, and for the underlying message or intention inherent in each image in terms of the overall theme of *Youth and Identity*.

Question A
(i) What are the different impressions of contemporary youth suggested by the images in Text 4? (15)
(ii) Which image of youth do *you* identify with most? Explain your choice. (15)
(iii) Select *one* of the photographs in Text 4 for inclusion in the school magazine. Write a *headline* for the picture and a short text to accompany it (100–150 words). (20)

Question B
Imagine you have been asked by a local newspaper to compile a series of pictures/images of youth in the twenty-first century.

Write a brief letter to the editor in which you outline the kinds of image you would include and giving reasons for their inclusion. (50)

SECTION B FOCUS ON ... THE LANGUAGE OF NARRATION

> 'We live immersed in narrative ...' (Peter Brook)

To the student
You will be familiar with many forms of this genre.

Anecdote, for example, in the shape of gossip or scandal is central to our conversations, and is a very basic form of narrative. Similarly, you regularly encounter this genre in romantic novels, science fiction, thrillers, soaps on the box, etc. Almost certainly, you will have read fairy tales, folk tales and fables as a child, and have written stories as part of your English classes since primary school. So, you already have some knowledge of the language of narration that can be built on and developed.

The Revised Syllabus
The Department guidelines tell us that '<u>students should encounter a wide range of texts, which have predominantly a *narrative function*</u>. This should involve students in encountering narratives of all kinds, e.g. short stories, novels, drama texts, autobiographies, biographies, travel books and films.'

Note: Narrative can be **fictional** – as in short stories, novels, drama texts, or **non-fictional** – as in autobiographies, biographies and travel books. It may also include letters, diaries, and some forms of journalism, i.e. news features and stories. These may also be fictional or non-fictional, e.g. *The Secret Diary of Adrian Mole* is written in the form of a diary, but is entirely fictitious. However, *The Diary of Anne Frank* is factual or non-fictional and narrates the actual life experiences of a young Jewish girl during World War Two.

Here are some short text examples of the language of narration with a brief commentary on those characteristics that shape the individual narrative.

Fictional Narrative
The Novel
An extract from *The Faloorey Man* by Eugene McEldowney.

> Sarah's stories always had happy endings. I remember as a little boy in short pants sitting with my mother at the kitchen table, the big picture book spread out

> before us. I recall even now the smell of the ink and the shiny texture of the pages, and Sarah's finger slowly tracing the words as she drew me inexorably into that innocent world where virtue was rewarded and everyone lived happily ever after. Those tales always ended well. All except the story of the *Titanic*.

Comment

This is the opening paragraph of the novel. It immediately establishes the *context* (childhood), 'a little boy in short pants'; the *setting* (the kitchen), introduces one of the main characters (Sarah), and the key element of the story, 'Sarah's stories always had happy endings'. Note too, the *atmosphere* of that childhood moment of storytelling, its significance *recalled* to mind, '... the big picture book spread out before us. I recall ... everyone lived happily ever after'. And finally, there is the lovely touch of *humour* in the innocence of the child's remark about the *Titanic*. 'Those tales always ended well. All except the story of the *Titanic*.'

Short Story

An extract from *First Confession* by Frank O'Connor.

> All the trouble began when my grandfather died and my grandmother – my father's mother – came to live with us. Relations in the one house are a strain at the best of times, but, to make matters worse, my grandmother was a real old countrywoman and quite unsuited to a life in town. She had a fat, wrinkled old face, and, to Mother's great indignation, went round the house in bare feet – the boots had her crippled, she said. For dinner she had a jug of porter and a pot of potatoes with – sometimes – a bit of salt fish, and she poured out the potatoes on the table and ate them slowly, with great relish, using her fingers by way of a fork.

Comment

This is from the beginning of a very famous short story by the writer, Frank O'Connor. The opening lines instantly express the attitude of the narrator towards the character of the grandmother, and also his relationship with the reader. Here, the *tone* of the narrative is established. It is intimate and good-humoured and the writer draws the reader into his world immediately, in a gossipy manner, '*all* the trouble ....' The actual 'trouble' is taken very seriously by the boy narrator, who is embarrassed by his grandmother's behaviour, and who exaggerates it, as children often do. Again, the *innocence* of childhood is evoked, with the revelation of personal details about the grandmother, 'For dinner she had a jug of porter ... using her fingers by way of a fork'. In this, the narrator displays a childlike trust in the reader, and in doing so, gains our sympathy. This intimacy of tone becomes a predominant feature throughout the story.

Non-Fictional Narrative
Autobiography

An extract from an essay called 'Aging', from Maya Angelou's book of essays entitled *Even the Stars Look Lonesome*.

In the crisp days of my youth whenever I was asked what I thought about growing old, I always responded with a nervous but brassy rejoinder that hid my profound belief that I never expected to live past twenty-eight. Tears would fill my eyes and bathe my face when I thought of dying before my son reached puberty. I was thirty-six before I realised I had lived years beyond my deadline and needed to revise my thinking about an early death. I would live to see my son an adult and myself at the half century mark. With that realisation life waxed sweeter. Old acquaintances became friendships, and new clever acquaintances showed themselves more interesting. Old loves burdened with memories of disappointments and betrayals packed up and left town, leaving no forwarding address, and new loves came calling.

Comment

'I write about being a black American woman, however, I am always talking about what it's like to be a human being. This is how we are, what makes us laugh, and this is how we fall and how we somehow, amazingly, stand up again.' Maya Angelou

Maya Angelou has written five volumes of her autobiography. The most famous one is the first volume, and it's on your Leaving Cert. course list – *I Know Why The Caged Bird Sings*. The above extract is taken from a more recent book of essays published in 1998, by Virago

Press. It is an example of her particular style of writing – which is **narrative**, in that it tells a story, her own story, but always with wit and wisdom. Note the **philosophical tone** of this piece, a hallmark of her work, its self-mockery, 'I was thirty-six before I realised I had lived years ... early death'. Her writing is personal and revelatory. We learn much about her life's experiences and traumas, but her observations are never self-pitying or morbid. There is an inherent optimism everywhere. She seeks to uplift the human spirit, to celebrate life in its fullness, no matter what age we are. There is a constant reappraisal of her life, and relationships, 'old acquaintances become friendships ... new loves come calling'. The relationship too, between the narrator and the reader, is an intimate and intelligent one. We are drawn into her life. She allows us to experience her world and to reflect upon it, as she does – but as a writer/narrator, she is never patronising or apologetic. She presumes an intelligent, reflective response from the reader.

Biography

An extract from *Remembering Eilis Dillon* by Patricia Donlon.

> My definition of a friend is someone who accepts me absolutely for what I am and who does not crowd me with too much togetherness, seeking to be what my grandmother graphically called 'a pocket to my hip'. Eilis was a friend who never grumbled when you had not phoned or made contact for weeks or even months and who took up with you as if it was only yesterday that you had talked. I admired her strength, her ability to bow under the many seemingly endless personal blows in her life and in the lives of those she loved and not be beaten or bitter. She would sigh a quiet sigh, shrug her shoulders and get on with life. I loved her ability to party long into the night, to entertain disparate and odd groups of people and to weave us all into her personal fabric of friendship ...
>
> If I were an artist and could paint, I would want to show Eilis as an Indian Chief, wrapped in shawl, sitting centre with her pipe of peace and passing on her stories to the tribe, in communion with the spirits, leaving her gifts. Her last gift to me was the most precious. She showed me how to say 'goodbye'.
>
> She was facing death and knew it and knew how its manifestations would be. She chose to do it her way. She called together friends and family and we celebrated her life with a Mass, the celebrant being the gentle Enda McDonagh. It was the last time I saw her. I was in Galway when the news of her death came and watching the birds wheeling above the Corrib I could not help thinking how she had challenged in her life something the Chinese understand: how she could not

> stop the birds of sorrow from flying overhead but she never, ever let them nest in her hair.
>
> (Courtesy of resource materials, Dept. of Education and Sciences)

Comment

The *narrative viewpoint* is interesting here. It is clearly different from autobiography in that the writer of this piece is commemorating a fellow writer – Eilis Dillon, and it is therefore clearly *biographical*. Yet there are elements of autobiography in this extract too, in the sense in which Eilis Dillon's life impacted on the writer's own 'Eilis was a friend ... talked'.

However, Patricia Donlon's main intention is to highlight facets of Eilis Dillon's personality and philosophy, 'I admired her strength ... get on with life'. Note, too, the colourful *imagery* in Donlon's vision of Eilis Dillon as an 'Indian chief, wrapped in a shawl, sitting centre with her pipe of peace ... leaving her gifts'. At all times, the *tone* is respectful, tender, and admiring – but never becomes maudlin. Even the *anecdotal* account of her death is simply told, without sentimentality, 'I was in Galway when the news of her death came ....'

Patricia Donlon herself said of this piece, 'I like the fact that it paints pictures.' The last image of this tribute does just that, '... how she could not stop the birds of sorrow from flying overhead but she never, ever let them nest in her hair.' A lovely philosophical note on which to end this narrative, or 'story', of Elis Dillon's life.

Travel Book

An extract from *Under the Tuscan Sky* by Frances Mayes.

> I am about to buy a house in a foreign country. A house with the beautiful name of Bramasole*. It is tall, square, and apricot-colored with faded green shutters, ancient tile roof, and an iron balcony on the second level, where ladies might have sat with their fans to watch some spectacle below.
>
> The way we have potatoes is the way most everything has come about, as we've transformed this abandoned Tuscan house and land over the past four years. We watch Francesco Falco, who has spent most of his seventy-five years attending to grapes, bury the tendril of an old vine so that it shoots out new growth. We do the same. The grapes thrive.
>
> To bury the grape tendril in such a way that it shoots out new growth I recognise easily as a metaphor for the way life must change from time to time if we are to go forward in our thinking.
>
> Italy is thousands of years deep and on the top layer I am standing on a small

plot of land, delighted today with the wild orange lilies spotting the hillside. While I'm admiring them, an old man stops in the road and asks if I live here. He tells me he knows the land well. He pauses and looks along the stone wall, then in a quiet voice tells me his brother was shot here. Age seventeen, suspected of being a partisan. He keeps nodding his head and I know the scene he looks at is not my rose garden, my hedge of sage and lavender. He has moved beyond me. He blows me a kiss. 'Bella casa, signora.'

(*Bramasole: from the Italian 'bramare', to yearn for, and 'sole', sun. Something that yearns for the sun.)

Comment

Travel books are, of their nature, factual and informative, but they are much more than that, as you may observe from this extract. It opens with a simple yet momentous event in the writer's life, 'I am about to buy a house in a foreign country'.

The **setting** of the book is immediately established, and the house acquires a **character** in its naming (Bramasole*), and in the meaning of that name.

The description of the house, the **imagery** of light and colour transcends mere information. The beauty of this place is evoked, '… tall, square, and apricot-coloured with faded green shutters', and its links with the past, with history, '… where ladies might have sat with their fans to watch some spectacle below'. Much of the language of this extract, although narrative in form, is also poetic, and an example of the aesthetic use of language. (You can see how genres mix and meld in good writing!)

We are introduced to the character of Francesco Faldo, who has 'spent most of his seventy-five years attending to grapes'. We begin to realise that this narrative is not simply an account of the restoration of an old house in Tuscany, but also the story of the complex and resilient people who inhabit the land itself.

The **tone is philosophical**, '... to bury the grape tendril ... a metaphor for the way life must change'. A meaning for life emerges, the connecting forces that bind man and nature, their interdependence. The element of *storytelling* too, becomes predominant in the narrative '... his brother was shot here. Aged seventeen, suspected of being a partisan.'

The narrator respects and acknowledges the old man's 'apartness', his unique and separate place in this landscape, '... I know the scene he looks at is not my rose garden ... He has moved beyond me.'

N.B. You will find more examples of the language of narration in other Units of this book. Refer back to the above notes, for clarification when you need to.

SECTION C COMPOSING

Planning the Composition

To the student

The new syllabus requires you to write a composition from a choice of seven titles, linked closely to the overall **theme** of the paper. The pre-reading exercises in Section A of this Unit gave you the opportunity to take notes, which may now be used as a springboard for your composition. Question B in the comprehending section also required you to compose a shorter piece of writing, based on the overall theme of *Youth and Identity*. Before you begin to write your composition, however, you should ask yourself this question: <u>how can my reading of the comprehending texts help me in my own writing</u>?

You must keep firmly in mind the **purpose**, **audience** and **register** appropriate to this task.

1. What do these mean exactly? Here are some brief definitions:

   The **purpose** is the aim or the intention of the essay.
   - Do you wish to *inform*? (Language of Information)
   - To *argue* a point of view? (Language of Argument)
   - To *persuade* someone to your point of view? (Language of Persuasion)
   - To tell a story? (Language of Narration)
   - To move? (Aesthetic Use of Language)

2. The **audience**: who are you writing this essay for?
   - Your peers?
   - The readers of a popular magazine?
   - For those who read serious newspapers/journals?

   Each of these will expect a different response. Always be conscious of your audience.

3. The **register**: what *style* of language will you use for the task being set?
   - Is a *formal* or *informal* approach more appropriate? Remember that a serious article should respect the intelligence of the reader, but that humour is very attractive in a popular article, whose purpose is to entertain.
   - You can write passionately, with daring, and in a variety of genres, but the *register* you use should be appropriate to the task and you should take care with **punctuation**, **spelling** and **grammar**.

The Length of the Composition

'<u>How long should my essay be?</u>' This is the question I am asked most often by my students!

The fact is that you should not be overly concerned with the length of your composition. Exam candidates write essays that vary considerably in length, but this is not, in the main, an issue of concern for examiners. Anything from three to five pages of the A4 exam booklet is acceptable, as handwriting varies in size. Achieving high marks depends on **how you engage with the spirit of the task set** (the one printed in bold type on the exam paper). This is of much greater significance to the examiner than the number of pages you write. The *quality* of your writing, in terms of the assessment criteria (outlined below), is what counts most.

> Your composition will be assessed on the basis of your ability to do the following things:
> 1. Engage with the set task (clarity of purpose, 30 marks).
> 2. Sustain your response over the entire answer (coherence of delivery, 30 marks).
> 3. Manage and control language to achieve clear communication (efficiency of language use, 30 marks).
> 4. Spell accurately and use patterns of grammar that are right for the task (accuracy of mechanics, 10 marks).

Writing the Composition
The Process

You may be one of those students who dreads this section of the paper. You never know where to start ... You don't like writing ... Ideas don't come easily to you ... Indeed the very prospect of filling three to five A4 pages with intelligent thoughts makes you want to run away and hide! Not to worry. You just have to believe that writing a decent essay is not entirely impossible, but that it does require patience and good preparation. **Planning** is the key. You will have been told this by your teacher many times, but now you really must begin to *practise* it. There are no quick fix, short answer solutions here, no sample essay to cover all eventualities, no magic formula. However, the revised English syllabus does recommend some simple but practical steps to writing the composition. And they *do* make sense. So let's look at them.

Stage 1 Pre-Writing
What to do – here are some suggestions:

1. **Consider all of the comprehending texts as a resource**. The revised syllabus actively encourages you to 'engage with the texts'. They contain information that will be useful to you; and will certainly give you some ideas that you can use. They may also *clarify*

your own thoughts on the topic you have chosen.
2. Use your notes from the *pre-reading* exercises in Section A (Comprehending).
3. Have a *brainstorming* session in class for 15–20 minutes only – an open discussion of one of the topics – with you gathering ideas and stimuli from your fellow students and teacher. *Jot them down*!
4. In addition, your teacher may allow you a few days to *research* some material for a particular topic. You will be required to produce some written evidence of this in class. Your research should centre on the challenge posed by the essay title, and the particular *writing genre* appropriate to it.

Stage 2 Drafting (First Draft)
Writing sequence
1. Write freely at first, in order to get a flow of ideas. Be innovative and fearless at this stage. Write down everything that comes to mind, fill as many pages as you can. Don't worry about the sequence of thought too much at this point. The aim here is to *rough draft* the essay, no more.
2. *Write a series of viewpoints* of the composition title – contrasting attitudes, questions that may occur to you, incidents from novels, TV, film, etc., that are relevant to the title. Consider what *quotations** you might use, e.g. the lyrics of songs, poems, speeches, novels, magazines, plays, TV, film, advertisements, news items – any memorable moments.
(*See 'Last Words' at the end of Unit 5, and Section C in Units 2 and 4.)
3. *Scan the reading texts* for specific details and points relevant to your chosen title. You are free to refer to, quote or draw ideas from any or all of the texts and their accompanying illustrations. Jot examples down for development later in Stage 3 (Re-drafting).
4. Try expressing your thoughts in a variety of *genres*, i.e. the informative approach, the narrative, the persuasive, the argumentative, the aesthetic. You will soon realise which genre is appropriate to the title, and which one you feel most comfortable with in your own writing.
5. Having followed the sequence outlined in 1–4, you should now attempt to *arrange* your thoughts – in other words, to *structure* this essay.
You should now decide:
   (a) the number of *paragraphs*, e.g. two or three per A4 page
   (b) where you wish to *begin*
   (c) which points you wish to explore more fully
   (d) an opening *question, quotation,* or *short dramatic statement,* and
   (e) a concluding question, quotation or statement.

Stage 3 Re-Drafting (Second Draft)

By now, you will have written the bones of a very good essay. But it needs a *final shaping*, a coherent structure and form.

Writing sequence

1. You must now decide **the predominant genre** you are writing in, and then be consistent in your use of that genre throughout the composition. This will be important for coherence.
2. Decide on your opening – and your stance (viewpoint) in the first paragraph.
3. Keep a sense of continuity and **clarity of purpose** from the first paragraph to the next.
4. Retain your *strongest* points from the first draft stage. Dump everything else. Otherwise your essay will be unbalanced and unsure.
5. Keep on track by frequently glancing back at the *title*. Irrelevancy is a major fault in Leaving Cert. essays.
6. Avoid a tendency to use slang or unsuitable language. Respect the notion of **register**, i.e. an appropriate language *tone* in your writing. Is it critical, informative, humorous, serious or argumentative? If you adopt a serious stance at the beginning of your essay, for example, it seems appropriate to continue in that vein. Try very hard not to mix registers – as this is confusing for the examiner, and irritating too. *Management and control of language* is essential to clear communication.
7. Keep your reading **audience** in mind at all times. Do I intend this composition to appeal to my peers only, or to society in general? Is the *purpose* of my writing to *persuade* the reader to my point of view, or to simply *present* a variety of viewpoints, leaving the reader free to come to his or her own conclusions?
8. Finally, try to end on a strong note. If you do, the examiner may forgive some weaknesses in the body of your essay. A good *ending** is always impressive, so put time into this vital stage of your writing. Bad essays just seem to trail off at the end, to run out of steam. You want to leave the examiner thinking that this is a truly interesting essay, which raises some challenging questions and which held his/her attention from start to finish – in short, your best essay.
(*See Unit 4, Section C.)

Stage 4 Proofreading (The Final Task!)

Read your completed essay again, in order to check **your punctuation, spelling** and **grammar**. This is not a trivial or unimportant task. Care and clarity are essential elements in good writing. Think about it for a moment. Have you ever read a novel on your Leaving

Cert. course that was badly punctuated, with a host of spelling errors and a total disregard for correct grammar? Of course not. You expect meticulous care in a published work. Try to view your own written work in this light, as you will be penalised for carelessness in this area. 'Accuracy of mechanics' is one of the assessment criteria for the exam, and accounts for ten per cent of your marks.

Moreover, the Department guidelines for the new syllabus insist that 'all students will be expected to be assiduous in their attention to paragraphing, syntax, spelling and punctuation.' So, don't spoil the examiner's final impression of an otherwise fine piece of writing, by a lack of regard for the finished product.

Now let's look at the seven essay titles for this Unit. You will find notes on *genre* for each one. The titles also reflect the format of the exam.

The Titles – Theme: Youth and Identity

Write a composition on any one of the following. Each composition carries 100 marks. The composition assignments below are intended to reflect language study in the areas of information, argument, persuasion, narration and the aesthetic use of language.

Essay 1
Language of Narration/Aesthetic Use of Language

'I do not remember when he started to cough.' (Text 1)

Write a story of the relationship between the father and daughter from this point onwards, up to and including a conclusion of your own imagining.

Note on genre(s): The examiner will expect a sense of story, a beginning, middle and end. Focus on the two central characters, a defining moment in their relationship, the setting. Don't be afraid to attempt the aesthetic use of language*, as this is an important characteristic in narrative writing.

(*See Unit 5, Section B. Focus on … The Aesthetic Use of Language.)

Essay 2
Language of Argument

'There is such a thing in racing as moving too fast.' (Text 3)

> Write an article for the sports section of a serious newspaper in which you challenge or support the view expressed above by the author of Text 3.

Note on genre(s): The examiner will expect you to address clearly the view expressed by the author in the original article. The purpose here is **to argue*** your case clearly. You must adopt a particular stance, i.e. supportive or oppositional (challenge). Shape your arguments in a thoughtful manner that reflects the *register* of a serious sports article. You will be presenting a personal viewpoint, but it should be written with a certain formality. You can employ some of the conventions of a newspaper layout, for example a headline and subheading, if you wish.
(*See Unit 2, Section B Focus on ... The Language of Argument.)

Essay 3
Language of Information

> Write an article for a newspaper in which you outline your views on the levels of violence in Irish schools and how they compare with the American experience. (Text 2)

Note on genre(s): Your purpose here is **to inform***/educate the reader/audience. Your views should be expressed in an objective manner, using the appropriate register, i.e. a serious, informed one. You will be expected to refer to the information contained in Text 2, and to compare and contrast the experiences of both countries. Use factual information for accuracy and clarity, and to support your views. Some research on the levels of violence in Irish schools is clearly needed before you attempt this composition.
(*See Unit 3, Section B Focus on ... The Language of Information.)

Essay 4
Language of Persuasion/Information

The writer in Text 1 argues that 'the tobacco industry coupled with Hollywood movies in which both hero and heroine smoked like chimneys, won over completely people like my father ...'

> Write a composition in which you attempt to persuade your readers that the tobacco industry and Hollywood combined are, *or are not*, a more powerful force than the anti-smoking lobby worldwide.

Note on genre(s): Your target audience (readers) will determine the register here. If you choose to write for your peers, the language register might be informal, sensational even. The purpose is **to persuade***, remember, and you may model your writing on elements of Text 1. Your aim is to bring the reader round to your point of view. Clearly some research is needed here too, on the tobacco industry worldwide, and the anti-smoking lobby.
(*See Unit 4, Section B Focus on ... the Language of Persuasion.)

Essay 5
Language of Narration/ Persuasion/ Aesthetic Use of Language

> Imagine that you are in the world of one of the young people in Text 4. Tell your story.

Note on genre(s): As with Essay 1, the examiner will expect *a sense of story or narrative*. Make use of the *details* in the picture of your choice. Concentrate on the *image*, on narrating the *moment* perhaps captured by the photographer, and the *events* which followed it. Clearly the aesthetic use of language and the language of narration are appropriate to this task. You may allow for various time lapses in your narrative, in order to create a sense of tension and mystery, for example.

Essay 6
Language of Information/Argument

Write an informative article for the school magazine in which you consider some of the implications of a career in Formula 1 racing for young Irish drivers. (Text 3)

Note on genre(s): As with Essay 3, your primary purpose here is **to inform***, but you may wish to argue some points relevant to the topic. So, the language of argument or persuasion may be appropriate here also. However, consider the register carefully. You are writing for your peers – a teenage audience, so this will determine the language style, e.g. thoughtful or sensational. You may *shape* your writing in the convention of a magazine article, i.e. separate paragraphs, headings, subheadings. You may use the material from Text 3, as appropriate.
(*See Unit 3, Section B Focus on ... the Language of Information.)

Essay 7
Language of Narration/Aesthetic Use of Language

Write a narrative that establishes a *link* between two or more of the images in Text 4.

Note on genre(s): This type of composition allows for an imaginative, personal response, with a broad parameter of possibilities in terms of purpose, audience, and register. However, the key point here is that you must establish a *link* between two or more of the images in Text 4. That link should be *clear* in your writing. Focus on the images – while retaining that sense of narrative, as outlined in the notes on Essay 1 and Essay 5. Language registers will mix and mingle here, but the aesthetic use of language is an important characteristic of narrative writing, and appropriate to this task.

SECTION D LANGUAGE SKILLS

Efficiency of Language Use 1

> 'The limits of my language are the limits of my world.'

To the student

The revised syllabus for Leaving Cert. English emphasises some important points about language. Here are some of them.

1. Each person lives in the midst of language. Language is fundamental to learning, communication, personal and cultural identity, and relationships.
2. Language is the chief means by which we make sense of our experience. Language gives us a sense of personal and cultural identity …
3. Developing control and power over language is the most essential educational achievement for all students …

   In order to acquire this desired '*control* and *power* over language', you must, as a student of English language, work on your language skills.

   The aims of the new syllabus are to develop in you, the student:

(a) 'a respect and appreciation for language used accurately and appropriately and a competence in a wide range of language skills both oral and written', and
(b) an ability to interpret and control the 'textual features (grammar, syntax, vocabulary, punctuation, spellings, paragraphing) of written and oral language to express and communicate'.

   In this first unit, I want you to concentrate solely on two of the basic 'mechanics' of good writing – **punctuation** and **spelling**. Here are some activities designed to focus your mind on these areas. As with all of your writing, *care* is essential here. Remember that forty per cent of the marks overall for both comprehending and composing are allocated to 'Efficiency of language use', which includes punctuation and spelling.

Punctuation

'Students need to develop an awareness of how punctuation works in written texts, that stops, commas and apostrophes should not be flung about like confetti but should be used to help the reader to understand the text.'
('Resource Materials for Teaching Language', Dept. of Education & Science)

To the student

In Activity 1, which follows, you will be asked to punctuate an extract from a novel. You will see that *without* punctuation, the text appears disorganised and incoherent, not to mention difficult to read! When you have finished the exercise, it might be useful to discuss the problems you encountered that prevented you from making sense of the text.

Activity 1

Here is an extract from *Cat's Eye** by Margaret Atwood. I have removed all the **full stops**, **capital letters** and **commas**. In addition you will find **ten words spelled incorrectly**.
(a) **Re-write** the passage, replacing the punctuation where necessary.
(b) **Circle** the words spelled incorrectly, and **write down the corrected spellings in a list**, for use in Activity 2.
(c) Consult the original text for comparison, if you wish. (*From Chapter 5, 'Wringer', No. 22. Page 118, Virago edition.)

> this is how it goes it's the kind of thing girls of this age do to one another or did then but i'd had no practise in it as my daughters approched this age the age of nine i watched them anxiously i scrutinized their fingers for bites there feet the ends of their hair i asked them leading questions: "is everything all right are your friends all right?" and they looked at me as if they had no idea what i was talking about why i was so anxious i thought they'd give themselves away somehow: nightmares mopeing but their was nothing i could see which may only have ment they were good at deception as good as i was when there friends arrived at our house to play i scanned their faces for signs of hypocricy standing in the kitchen i listened to thier voices in the other room i thought i would be able to tell or maybe it was worse maybe my daughters were doing this sort of thing themselves to someone else that would account for their blandness the absense of bitten fingers their level blue-eyed gaze
>
> most mothers worry when their daughters reach adolesence but i was the opposite i relaxed i sighed with relief little girls are cute and small only to adults to one another they are not cute they are life-sized

Activity 2

<u>Write one sentence for each of the ten words</u> – now spelled *correctly* – from Activity 1. Each sentence should clearly demonstrate the *meaning* and usage of the word, in a particular context, e.g. practice (noun).

Language exercises provide practice in the correct use of English.
OR
Write a *paragraph* on the theme of *Youth and Identity* (70–100 words) in which each of the ten words is used once only. It should have a sense of *story* – a narrative.

Activity 3
Here is another extract from *Cat's Eye** by Margaret Atwood. This time I have again removed all the **full stops**, **capital letters** and **commas**, but there are no spelling errors. Punctuate the passage carefully, being conscious also of *clear handwriting*. You may then consult the original text for comparison, if you wish. (*From Chapter 10, 'Life Drawing', No. 47. Page 263, Virago edition.)

there are several diseases of the memory forgetfulness of nouns for instance or of numbers or there are more complex amnesias with one you can lose your entire past; you start afresh learning how to tie your shoe-laces how to eat with a fork how to read and sing you are introduced to your relatives your oldest friends as if you've never met them before; you get a second chance with them better than forgiveness because you can begin innocent with another form you keep the distant past but lose the present you can't remember what happened five minutes ago when someone you've known all your life goes out of the room and then comes back in you greet them as if they've been gone twenty years; you weep and weep with joy and relief as if at a reunion with the dead

    i sometimes wonder which of these will afflict me later; because i know one of them will

    for years i wanted to be older and now i am

Activity 4
Punctuate the following article from the *Irish Independent*. You will need to replace capital letters, full stops, commas, apostrophes, inverted commas and two question marks. Re-write the article, again being conscious of the importance of *clear* handwriting.

So You Think You're Funny

ciara dwyer falls for channels 4s latest irish comic recruit graham norton
i saw him on stage in edinburgh it was love as first sight he is graham nor-

ton camp comedian

he was wearing a persil-white suit his brown eyes twinkled and he had the most divine beauty spot he swished onto the stage divilment written all over him do you like the suit he started it was skin-tight and spotless then he gave us that look a sidewards glance a bulging of the eyes and a raised eyebrow all at once we howled

in nortons world its the little frivolous things that count he took of his jacket folded the arms together and hung it on the microphone stand a tidy stage is a happy stage we loved him

he singles out nora from the audience a middleaged greyhaired woman wearing glasses nora looked a bit like a civil servant or someones mother at least

graham norton is the sort who can sanitise a curse word the sort who can be as camp as michael barrymore julian clary and kenneth williams in one and still be good clean fun

nora was not offended

with his gaudy kittycat phone norton collected messages from the advertisement he had placed in a singles column he ordered a pizza and when the delivery man appeared graham leered at his leathers whats your name norton asked neil the leathered one replied what a lovely name norton squealed that look was back

norton didn't do anything extraordinary on stage but his ordinary world was very funny

graham nortons new comedy show so graham norton started on channel 4 last friday night its supposed to be chat showish norton revealed weve come up with other things and now theres less room for guests

born in dublin and brought up in bandon graham studied speech and drama in london most of us know him as noel the youth worker priest in father ted but the boy has brains when ned sherring was on holidays norton hosted radio fours loose ends no mean feat

now we venture into grahams world every friday the show wont be about issues of world importance unless its in a very superficial way it sounds like a line out of noel cowards private lives lets be superficial and pity the poor philosophers lets blow trumpets and squeakers and enjoy the party as much as we can coward would be mad about the norton boy

Spelling
Most frequently misspelled words

> 'My spelling is wobbly. It's good spelling but it wobbles, and the letters get in the wrong places.' (A.A. Milne, *Winnie the Pooh*)

To the student
Winnie the Pooh may get away with bad spelling, but, unfortunately, you won't! The examiner will take a dim view of 'wobbly spelling', so it's worth spending some time on improving it.

Activity 5
Here are ten words that you will use constantly in your writing, and a simple strategy for learning them. (You will find a similar list at the end of Section D in each Unit of this book.) I have underlined that part or letter of the word that is most often spelled incorrectly.
(a) **Learn the spelling**.
(b) **Cover** it. Write the word in pencil in the 'Spell it' space.
(c) **Check to see if it's correct**. If it isn't, rub it out and relearn it, before writing it again.
(d) **Write a *short* sentence** containing the word, in the space provided.

Word	Spell it	Short sentence
1. advertisement	....	....
2. arg<u>u</u>ment	....	....
3. bel<u>ie</u>ve	....	....
4. chara<u>c</u>ter	....	....
5. critici<u>s</u>m	....	....
6. d<u>e</u>scription	....	....
7. exa<u>gg</u>erate	....	....
8. fas<u>c</u>inating	....	....
9. gover<u>n</u>ment	....	....
10. hum<u>o</u>rous	....	....

Unit 2 Race and Racism

SECTION A COMPREHENDING

Introduction
This section contains four texts on the general theme of *Race and Racism*, including a set of pre-reading exercises on Texts 1–3.

Text 1
'What do people think?' is an article from the May 2001 edition of *Amnesty Ireland* magazine. It focussed on Irish attitudes towards racism. It is primarily an example of the **language of information**, but it does raise issues that may evoke a response requiring the **language of argument and/or persuasion**.

Text 2
'Australia experiences surge in nationalism' is an article by Conor O'Clery from the *Irish Times* of 30 September 2000. In it, he reflects on the impact of the Olympic Games on Australia, and its implications in terms of race and self-image. The text is mainly **informative**, but also raises questions about certain elements of Australian nationalism. As such, it employs the **language of argument**. Look, too, for examples of the **language of narration**, in the form of *anecdote,* in this article.

Text 3
'Death be not proud' by Robert Badinter is an article (edited) from *Time* magazine of 21 May 2001. It is an excellent example of the **language of argument**. The writer, a French senator and former Justice Minister, is arguing against capital punishment in the USA, which he regards as both racist and inegalitarian. I have provided a **sample answer** to Question A (i).

Text 4
Text 4 is a series of photographs depicting race and racial pride, but also the disturbing reality of racism in Ireland today. There is no written text. You are required to study the images and respond to them in a variety of ways and genres.

Text 1 *What do people think? from* Amnesty Ireland

Stage 1 Pre-Reading

Task: In pairs, or small groups, discuss some or all of the questions below for ten minutes, then report back to the class.

OR

Your teacher may choose to discuss the questions with the whole group. In either case, the most important thing is that you *take notes* of other students' points, for possible use later in one of the *composing* tasks in Section C.

Questions

1. How would you define *race*? What does it mean to you?
2. How widespread is racism in Ireland today? Is it present in your local community or in your school?
3. There are Irish people of colour, born and raised in Ireland. How do you think they feel when they are confronted by racial slurs and physical attacks from their fellow Irishmen and Irishwomen?
4. Is Ireland ready for a multiracial, multicultural society? As teenagers how can you accommodate change and foster tolerance and acceptance among your peers?

Stage 2 Reading

Question A

(i) What conclusions do you draw about the extent of racism in Ireland from the attitudes expressed in the whole text? Outline your views in 150–200 words, illustrating the points you make by close reference to the text. (30)

(ii) What do you think of the letter beginning 'Mrs Wog' received by the black woman living in Dublin and the anti-torture leaflet returned with the swastikas stamped on it? (20)

Question B

Basing your answer on all of Text 1, draft a brief set of guidelines for a more just and tolerant attitude towards race in Ireland, one that welcomes and embraces all cultures.

(50)

N.B. Write your guidelines clearly and objectively, appropriate to the language of argument. Read Section B (Focus on … the Language of Argument) before attempting Question B.

May 20001   Amnesty

What do people think?

There has been a small flurry of studies surveying opinions about racism in Ireland recently. Here is a selection of attitudes they found ...

The African Refugee Network Survey of 1999 questioned 40 refugees about their experiences.
- 30 said they were denied service because of skin colour.
- 11 said they had been verbally abused.
- 4 claimed physical abuse.

The most commonly-cited sources of racism were landlords and security personnel.

In April 2000 *The Star* newspaper commissioned a survey conducted by Landsdowne Market Research. Over 1100 people aged 15 and over were questioned in 60 places around the country.

It found that:
- 27 per cent of people said they were disturbed by the presence of minority groups.
- 33 per cent said too many minorities live in Ireland.
- 23 per cent said immigrant status should not fully guarantee rights.
- 7 per cent said Ireland should not grant political asylum to those escaping human rights violations.

In March of this year, the Union of Students in Ireland (USI) published a survey of 500 third-level students.

Among its key findings:
- 39 per cent claimed they would find it difficult accepting a Traveller as a sibling's spouse.
- 6 per cent said they would not find it difficult to accept a minority of any kind as a sibling's spouse.
- 20 per cent said all illegal immigrants should be deported without exception.
- 94 per cent agreed that society benefits from diversity.
- 80 per cent said authorities should improve the situation of minorities.

When Amnesty sent out leaflets for our anti-torture campaign, one was returned with swastikas stamped on it. A black woman living in Dublin showed us this letter she received last month.

> MRS WOG
> I NOTICED ON WEDNESDAY, A MEMBER OF YOUR LITTER, A YOUNG BLACK BASTARD, NOSTRILS WIDE APART, APE-LIKE LIPS, CRAWLING AROUND ON THE FLOOR. I ASK THAT YOU HAND OVER THAT ANIMAL FOR THE PURPOSE OF VIVISECTION, SO THAT THE WHITE RACE MAY BE ABLE TO COME UP WITH A CURE FOR HIV, TB, RUBELA, VD AND ALL THE OTHER DISEASES THAT YOU BLACK BASTARDS HAVE SPREAD +++

Text 2 *Australia experiences surge of nationalism by Conor O'Clery*

Stage 1 Pre-Reading

Task: In pairs or small groups, discuss some or all of the questions below for ten minutes, then report back to the class.
OR
Your teacher may choose to discuss the questions with the whole group. The most important thing is that you *take notes* of other students' points for possible use later in one of the *composing* tasks, in Section C.

Questions
1. What does the word 'nationalism' mean to you? Do you equate it with the Word 'race'?
2. What impact, if any, did the 2000 Olympic Games have on you, as an Irish teenager? Did you feel a sense of pride, or were you indifferent to our participation in the Games?
3. In what way do you think a country benefits (other than financially) from hosting the Olympic Games? How does it affect that country's self-image?
4. What do you know of the Aborigines and of their place in Australian history? Who is the most famous Aboriginal athlete to emerge from the Sydney 2000 Games?

Stage 2 Reading (pages 39–40)
Question A
(i) In your opinion, what aspects of Australian nationalism emerge most strongly from the article? (15)
(ii) What impact has Cathy Freeman's success in the 2000 Olympic Games had on Australia, and on its perception of the Aboriginal people as a race? (15)
(iii) 'There is a strain of anti-intellectualism in Australia,' said a teacher. 'This means bright kids are often mocked for being studious, and kids from immigrant families devote all their energies to sport as a way of being accepted.'
Could this teacher's argument apply to Ireland also? If so, why? If not, why not? Write your own response to this viewpoint. Refer to the article to support your points. (20)

Question B
Imagine your school is expecting a visit from an Australian student basketball or football team. Your job as school captain is to welcome them to Ireland and your school. Write out the text of a short welcoming speech (150–200 words) in which you attempt to give them a flavour of Ireland and Irish people, especially its youth. (50)

Australia experiences surge of nationalism

Phillip Dye, an Australian musician, came to Ireland some years ago and experienced pub nationalism in the form of everyone singing *Amhrán na bhFiann* after a night's drinking in a bar in Doolin. This would never happen back home, he thought to himself.

But one night last week, after a gig at a pub in the Rocks in central Sydney, the singer thought he

The Olympics have made Australians proud and may help revive talk of a republic. Conor O'Clery in Sydney sums up the socio-political impact of the Games

would have a go at playing the Australian national anthem, *Advance, Australia Fair*.

'After three lines there was no one left sitting,' Phillip Dye wrote in yesterday's *Melbourne Age*. 'Many had hands on their chests. Everyone was singing.' The Olympic Games, he concluded, had given Australians a sense of personal and national pride to match that of the Irish and Americans.

Australian patriotism has never been overt. The national style is a mixture of mute stoicism and mocking irreverence. But since the dazzling Olympics opening ceremony, the country has been swept by nationalist fervour.

In Australia high achievers have traditionally suffered from begrudgery, or what they call the 'tall-poppy' syndrome, i.e. the poppy that grows highest is cut down.

Australia has now spent a fortnight tending its tallest poppies, honouring the achievements and successes of its hero-athletes. Of them all, Cathy Freeman has become the purest embodiment of excellence and diversity.

No one objected when the Aboriginal runner attached the red, black and ochre Aboriginal colours to the Australian flag to make her lap of honour after win-

Cathy Freeman: the Prime Minister, John Howard, has described her as a role model for all Australians

ning gold in the 400 metres. She represents reconciliation, not black power militancy.

Reconciliation is being taught in primary schools this year for the first time. The Prime Minister, John Howard, who has refused to apologise for the Aborigines' 'stolen generation', described her as a role model to all Australians.

'Cathy has helped define Australia at a time of change,' said a diplomat in Sydney. 'She was able to because she is non-threatening'.

Australia has discarded many racist attitudes. No newspaper would today print the headline which greeted a rare defeat for an earlier Aboriginal athlete. Evonne Goolagong Cawley, twice Wimbledon singles tennis champion: Evonne goes walkabout, it said, borrowing an Aboriginal term.

There was, however, a touch of paternalism in the order by Australia's Channel Seven that there should be no replays of Cathy's comment that her brothers were delighted after her win 'and they aren't even drunk'.

Intended to avoid playing into stereotypes of drunken Aborigines, it highlighted another stereotype of Aborigines who needed protecting from themselves.

It is difficult to exaggerate the importance of Cathy Freeman's win. It was absolutely essential for Australia. I asked several people what would have happened if she lost. 'The country would have had a nervous breakdown,' said a teacher. 'Australia would have been totally deflated,' agreed a radio producer.

The country's luck held. The pride and patriotism heaped on her shoulders were repaid with victory, and grace under pressure, and the country felt unified as never before.

There is, nevertheless, a danger that conservative politicians will wrongly consider the race issue solved. Aboriginal author Ruby Lanford Ginibi suggested that Cathy Freeman run for political office to continue the elevation of her cause into a national cause.

And while the triumph of the Sydney Olympics has muted the self-doubt that has been a feature of public commentary in Australia, it has produced a euphoria which has verged towards xenophobia. The disqualification of Australian walker Jane Saville, for example, provoked media outbursts against the Olympic referees, despite photographic evidence that she broke the rules by lifting both feet off the ground.

The elevation of sport as the great national goal also worries many Australians. 'There is a strain of anti-intellectualism in Australia,' said a teacher. 'This means bright kids are often mocked for being studious, and kids from immigrant families devote all their energies to sport as a way of being accepted.'

There is much to debate as the Olympics come to a close on the implications for Australia of crowds indulging in the patriotic cry of 'Aussie! Aussie! Aussie! Oi! Oi! Oi!' while draping themselves in the official Australian flag, comprising a Union Jack on a blue background with six stars.

Pro-republican Australians would normally not be seen dead with the British ensign. There is little evidence, however, of the country turning away from the republic ideal. Indeed the idea of Australians subjecting themselves to a monarch in a faraway country has less validity than two weeks ago.

'A republic is the next event,' read a headline in the *Australian Financial Review* yesterday. After the Olympics, Australians could believe in themselves, wrote columnist John Hewson. 'We should fight for complete independence. We should now fight for a republic.'

Only time will tell whether the Olympics have changed Australia. But few would disagree with the government adviser quoted yesterday in the *Herald*: 'We've spent two weeks in another country,' he said, 'and we like what we've seen.'

(*Irish Times*, 30 September 2000)

Text 3 *Death be not proud by Robert Badinter*

Stage 1 Pre-Reading

Task: In pairs or small groups, discuss some or all of the questions below for ten minutes, and then report back to your class.

OR

Your teacher may choose to discuss the questions with the whole group. The most important thing is that you *take notes* of other students' points, for possible use later in one of the *composing* tasks in Section C.

Questions

1. Broadly speaking, what is your image of America and Americans? Is this image based on actual experience of having visited the States, or on television and film depictions of American society?
2. In America, statistics show that African-Americans and Hispanics are more likely to be sent to the death chamber than people of European descent; that poor defendants are condemned to death more often than rich ones; and that teenagers (minors) are treated as adults when it comes to the death penalty. How do you feel about this?
3. What are the three strongest arguments you can make *against* the death penalty?
4. Are there arguments that can be made *for* the death penalty in certain circumstances? For example, in the case of serial killing, mass murder, or the murder of members of the police force.

Stage 2 Reading

Death be not proud by Robert Badinter

Capital punishment is a blight on America's image in the world

1. I belong to a generation of Europeans for whom the United States embodies democracy, progress and liberty.

   That is why I am writing this article. I don't believe that Americans fully understand how their use of the death penalty has profoundly degraded the country's image in the eyes of other democratic nations. Today, all the Western democracies have abolished the death penalty. Almost all of Europe has banished it. Can one seriously believe that, if it constituted an effective instrument for fighting murderous crimes, the leaders of Europe's great states would not have reinstated it long ago? Every study done in the abolitionist countries has reached the same conclusion: the death penalty has never been a deterrent to crime. In the US itself, the murder rate is higher in Texas than it is in the twelve states that have dropped the death penalty.

2. Capital punishment is infected by racism. African-Americans and Hispanics are the most at risk. Are they condemned to death more often than whites because their crimes are more atrocious or because they are black or Hispanic? This question alone should suffice in a democratic society to rule out the death penalty, as it has in South Africa.

The death penalty is not only racist but inegalitarian. Most prisoners on death row come from the poorest classes, those excluded from American society. They're criminals, we are told. Without a doubt. But has the society that puts them to death really given them the same chance as those more fortunate? Moreover, capital punishment strikes mainly those who don't have the money to hire competent, motivated and well-paid lawyers. Financial inequality before the law can lead to the worst possible consequences.

3. Worse still, many innocent people have been condemned to death. Some have been saved in extremis, but how many others have been executed without anyone asking for a reconsideration of the trial? If a crime that goes unpunished is a challenge to society, the execution of an innocent person is the worst act that any community of free men can commit. It is the complete negation of justice. What kind of justice is it that, in order to avenge victims, becomes criminal itself by executing innocent people?

4. What about the barbaric practice, in the 21st century, of executing the feeble-minded and mentally defective, or the men and women whose crimes were committed when they

Studies show that execution is not a deterrent

from
Desiderata 1692
(found in St Paul's Parish Church
Baltimore dated 1692

With all its sham and
drudgery and broken dreams,
it is still a beautiful world.
Be careful. Strive to be happy.

Ivan

Tadpoles 1692
(from St. Paul Ranch Club
Bottom of dated 16.92)

But all it's Shan and
Brudders and bigger Shaun,
it is still a beauty, world
be caught. Glue the tapes?

were minors? What kind of society is it that treats adolescents as adults when it comes to sentencing them to death? Is this society ignorant of the fact that every adolescent is a human being in progress; that for every young murderer, part of the responsibility lies with the parents, the associates, the brief life he has lived so far – all of which means he cannot be considered guilty in the same way as an adult?

5. It is true that the suffering of the victims calls for both justice and punishment. But to make the execution of the criminal a bloody retribution for the victim's pain is a return to the darkest practices of the past. Other forms of punishment exist. The criminal's death does not bring the victim back. It merely adds one death to another, and adds society's injustices to the horror of the crime.

6. When France abolished the death penalty in 1981 and I gave the guillotine to a museum, there were 35 abolitionist nations in the world. Today, there are 108. Therefore, I ask my American friends: Where is your place in the world, you who aspire to assume its leadership, not just militarily and technologically, but also morally and culturally? Among the democrats who have banned the death penalty? Or alongside totalitarian China and fanatical Iran?

Robert Badinter, a French Senator and former Justice Minister, was the prime mover behind his country's decision to abolish the death penalty in 1981
Time, 21 May 2001

Question A

(i) Basing your answer on the whole text, how critical is Robert Badinter of the role and stance (position) of the USA in relation to the death penalty? (30)
*There is a sample answer to this question at the end of this section.

(ii) To what extent do you find yourself in agreement or disagreement with his viewpoint on this issue? Outline your response in 150–200 words, supporting your point of view by reference to at least *two* points from the text. (20)

Question B

Imagine that you have been corresponding with an African-American prisoner on death row in the USA. It is the week before his/her execution. Compose the *last letter* you would write to this person. You have been asked by the prison authorities to keep it short, 150–200 words. (50)

Text 4 *Images of Race and Racism*

1.

3.

2.

Race and Racism 45

4.

6.

46 Write Now!

Note: As in Unit 1, Text 4 requires a different approach. You are asked to 'read' a series of images with usually no written text. You should examine each of them closely before attempting to answer the questions. Be especially attentive to detail in the photographs – the setting, the personalities/characteristics of people and objects, their gestures, facial expressions and body language. Look too at colour, light and shade, and for the underlying message or intention inherent in each image, in terms of the overall theme of *Race and Racism*.

Question A
(i) Study pictures 1 and 2 closely. From the perspective of race, they portray two very different experiences of Irish life. Comment briefly on the *specific* differences you observe in each photo, and your personal response to them. (20)

(ii) (a) Imagine this series of images is to be used in a brochure whose objective it is to promote racial tolerance and inclusion among young people in Ireland. Which one of the images would you choose for its front cover? Justify your choice. (15)

(b) You are the editor of the brochure mentioned in part (a). Which one of the images would you judge to be *least representative* of racial tolerance and inclusion? Justify your choice. (15)

Question B
A Day in the Life
Choose *one* of the people pictured in Text 4 and write *four* short diary entries that your chosen person might write on *one important day* in his/her life. You should indicate clearly the person you have chosen and you should write the diary entries as though you were that person. (50)

Sample Answer to Question A (i) [page 43, text on pages 41–43]
- In your answer to Question A (i), focus on the language of *argument* as employed in the text.
- Read the text *twice* before answering either question.
- Highlight or underline the key point and/or the most impressive argument in the paragraph to which you are referring.
- *Quote* from the text to support your points. Examiners will reward evidence of engaging with the text. Use it therefore, to strengthen and reinforce your own points.

> The headline 'Death be not proud' appears to admonish America, to suggest that it has no cause to be proud of its policy on capital punishment. The subheading too is a direct criticism: 'Capital punishment is a blight on America's image in the world.'

In paragraph 1, Badinter focuses on the words 'image' and democracy. He clearly views America's stance on the death penalty as running contrary to such ideals: 'their use of the death penalty has profoundly degraded the country's image in the eyes of other democratic nations.' He argues for the abolition of the death penalty because 'Almost all Europe has banished it.' At this point, he asks the first of a series of rhetorical questions designed to contrast the experience of the European states with the US on this issue. 'Can one seriously believe that ... long ago?' He cites evidence from the abolitionist countries where they have reached the conclusion that the death penalty has never been a deterrent to crime. He quotes a statistic from the US itself, to prove his point. 'The murder rate is higher in Texas than it is in the twelve states that have dropped the death penalty.'

In paragraphs 2 and 3, Badinter criticises capital punishment as being 'infected by racism and ... inegalitarianism'. He quotes the example of African-Americans and Hispanics on Death Row, who come from the poorest classes; those excluded from American society. The writer criticises a system that 'strikes mainly those who don't have the money to hire competent, motivated and well-paid lawyers'.

In paragraph 3, also, Badinter reasons that 'many innocent people have been condemned to death'.

In paragraph 4, he questions the 'barbaric practice' of 'executing the feeble minded and the mentally defective', and asks: 'What kind of society is it that treats adolescents as adults when it comes to sentencing them to death?'

In paragraph 5, Badinter acknowledges that the suffering of the victims calls for 'both justice and punishment'. However, he also argues that 'the criminal's death does not bring the victim back. It merely adds one death to another.'

In the final paragraph, Badinter cites his own country's abolition of capital punishment in 1981. At that time, he says, 'there were 35 abolitionist nations in the world. Today there are 108.' He addresses his final rhetorical question directly to his 'American friends':

'Where is your place in the world, you who aspire to assume its leadership ... among the democrats who have banned the death penalty? Or alongside totalitarian China and fanatical Iran?'

SECTION B FOCUS ON ... THE LANGUAGE OF ARGUMENT

> 'The aim of argument ... should not be victory, but progress.' (Stefan Joubert)

To the student

You will undoubtedly be familiar with the word 'argument' in terms of a quarrel or a dispute, where you refuse to accept the other person's viewpoint, or to change your own. This type of argument is often irrational and subjective, based on opinion rather than fact, and devoid of logic or clear thinking. In terms of comprehending and composing the *language* of *argument* is quite the opposite. It requires you to be objective and to manage a range of abstract skills. For example, in order to make a rational argument you need to:

- Select your evidence for the argument.
- Structure your thoughts.
- Be coherent in your expression of those thoughts.

The language of *argument* is the language of debate, concerned with logic and the presenting of evidence to support an argument for or against a particular motion. Similarly, if you watch post-match panel discussions on TV, or current affairs programmes like *Questions & Answers*, you hear the panellists challenge each other's viewpoints on a wide variety of issues. They examine the **facts**, produce **evidence** and **quote statistics** to support their opinions. The language of argument is used to evaluate and refute their opponents' views.

The language of argument is also the language of the law. If you watch courtroom dramas on TV, you will note the importance of logic in arguments and summations, and how reason and strongly supported evidence are essential to a case. So, you already have some knowledge of the language of argument. The skills required to use it effectively in your comprehending and composing tasks can be built on and developed.

The Revised Syllabus

The Department guidelines tell us that 'students should encounter a range of texts with an *argumentative* function. The range of texts should encompass material ... used in journalistic, philosophical, scientific and legal contexts.'

Note: Written sources of the language of argument are found in quality journalism, current affairs' magazines, books on science and the law, and philosophical and literary essays. However, you can also look at your own textbooks for examples of how political, economic and social arguments have changed the course of history. Throughout the centuries, there have been debates on the universal issues of human rights, injustices and inequalities in society, the elimination of slavery and poverty, the safeguarding of our planet's resources; the list is endless. The language of argument, in the true sense, therefore, is at the centre of all our lives, essential for our progress as human beings.

Let's now look at some short text examples of this genre, with a brief commentary on the characteristics that shape the individual arguments.

Example 1 Letters to the Editor

Here are three letters from contributors to the 'Letters to the Editor' page of the *Irish Times*. They are a good source of the language of argument because the writers feel strongly about the issues involved, and are careful to argue their viewpoints clearly and succinctly.

> ### *Slavery in the Twenty-First Century*
>
> Sir, – We are writing on behalf of our CSPE class to express our strong opposition to modern-day slavery. *According to Trócaire there are 27 million slaves in the world today.* Anti-slavery laws are being ignored. Drastic measures are needed to stop this.
>
> *In Sierra Leone, children as young as seven are being captured by the army and trained as soldiers. In Brazil*, it is estimated that there are over 100,000 bonded slaves working on large rural estates. *In 1850 a slave could be bought for around $40,000. In India today, a child can be sold into bonded labour for as little as £30.*
>
> In the 21st century it is ridiculous to think we call ourselves civilised, when we stand idly by and allow such inhuman practices to continue. We urge people to support Trócaire's anti-slave campaign and to lobby our politicians to act on this issue.
>
> – Yours, etc
> MARK KEENAN,
> JEFFREY WHITE,
> BRIAN HENNELLY,
> JAMES HIGGINS,
> PAURIC MURPHY,
> On behalf of class 2B2,
> St Patrick's Community College,
> Naas
> Co Kildare

Comment

This letter is a good example of a group of students quoting some impressive *statistics* from a reliable source in order to express their opposition to 'modern day slavery'. One cannot easily refute arguments supported by factual evidence '... 27 million slaves ... 100,000 bonded slaves ... as little as £30'. Their appeal to our collective conscience in the last paragraph of the letter '... it is ridiculous to think ... continue'. is a strong point on which to conclude, in that undoubtedly no reader of this letter would wish to be perceived as either uncivilised or inhuman.

Stadium Ireland Controversy

Sir, – Tony Clyn's observations on the need for proper sporting facilities for the youth of our now modern and prosperous country (May 4th) would be laudable were it not for the fact that the priorities should be:

- *A properly funded health service* with well-paid staff and adequately equipped hospitals for all our areas, backed up with after-care for elderly and young alike.
- *Services* capable of providing *care to the disabled, geriatric and mentally infirm* (including adequate *financial help* and *respite aid* for all types of carers).
- *Funding* for educational special needs.
- *Decent pensions* for our senior citizens.

The list is endless, but it has been part of our national social agenda for years. If we are a modern, progressive country, the only way to show it is to cherish those who can best benefit by these priorities. *Sporting stadiums can wait till the next 'tiger' comes along.* In the meantime Fianna Fáil and other parties aspiring to power would do well to remember that the Roman Empire philosophy of giving the masses *'bread and circuses'* no longer washes with the people of Ireland.

– Yours etc.,
DEREK PEYTON,
Blackrock,
Co Dublin

Comment

This letter is a good example of **counter argument**. The writer *refutes* an argument made by a previous correspondent (Tony Clyne). He does so in a succinct manner, by presenting four strong counter arguments, clearly marked by bullet points. They are convincing as they are rational points, based on people's actual needs. Again, in the final paragraph of the letter, this writer appeals to our sense of pride in our 'modern, progressive country' by asking us to cherish 'those who can best benefit by these priorities'. Because of the strength of these arguments, it is difficult to disagree with his point that: 'Sporting stadiums can wait till the next "tiger" comes along.' He concludes with a parting shot at the politicians, warning them that 'bread and circuses' no longer wash with the people of Ireland.

The Trials of Rail Travel

Sir, – *I'm writing this letter from somewhere in Kildare – just beyond the Curragh, I imagine – but as we don't have windows in 'steerage', I couldn't be sure.* 'Steerage, for anyone unfamiliar with the trains from Cork to Dublin on a Friday, is the section between the carriages – the place for the luggage, the toilets, and the many people who don't get seats.

In saying this *I must not begrudge CIE anything, as today I've secured a lovely stainless steel bin to sit on.* However, not all of us are so happy. The three girls on the floor alongside me have just been awoken from their well earned sleep by the mumble over the intercom announcing: 'We're sorry, but the trolley service has been cancelled due to overcrowding'.

Between the 10 of us in steerage (six adults, four students), we've paid CIE over £280 for seats we never got! I can understand the demand for such a service, to escape the frenzy of Dublin for the peace and tranquillity of the real capital. What I do not understand is why, week in week out, I and so many others pay a lot of money for something we don't get.

– Yours, etc.,
CORMAC MURPHY
Mourneabbey,
Mallow,
Co Cork

Comment

This is a good example of the use of humour and a lighthearted tone in order to argue a particular point, i.e. the non-provision of adequate seating for those who have paid for them. The letter begins on a humorous note: 'I'm writing this letter from somewhere in Kildare … we don't have windows in "steerage", I couldn't be sure'. The long-suffering commuter goes on to explain what 'steerage' is to those 'unfamiliar with the trains from Cork to Dublin on a Friday'. Although the tone is humorous, as readers we are shocked at the idea of people having to travel in 'the place for the luggage' or the toilets.

The writer uses sarcasm to good effect in the second paragraph '... I must not begrudge CIE... anything, as today I've secured a lovely stainless steel bin to sit on'. There is a lovely 'tongue-in-cheek' reference to the 'mumble over the intercom announcing: "We're sorry but the trolley service has been cancelled due to overcrowding".' However, the writer's use of an exclamation mark, when referring to the cost of the seats (£280) strongly expresses his genuine frustration and annoyance at the inadequacy of the service. Citing the actual cost of the seats clearly strengthens his argument against CIE.... Despite the lighthearted tone of this letter overall, the writer concludes with a serious point: 'What I do not understand is why, week in week out, I and so many others pay a lot of money for something we don't get.' It is a strong concluding argument.

Example 2 Woman for Cairo Adds Insult to Inquiry

Here are five paragraphs (courtesy of the resource materials from the Dept. of Education) from a longer **opinion column article** by Nuala O'Faolain, writer and journalist with the *Irish Times*.

The writer herself has stated that this opinion column was 'prompted by the news that the Irish Government had arranged to send an all-male delegation to a UN conference in Cairo, the subject of which was the implications for the planet of women having babies, or alternatively not having babies.'

Woman for Cairo Adds Insult to Inquiry

1. It's like a Paddy joke. Question: Whom did the Irish Governments send to Cairo to a conference on reproduction with themes like 'Gender Equality, Equity, and Empowerment of Women'? Answer: a dozen men. They couldn't find a woman, not a single one, to empower. Equality and equity were too much for them. So they arranged an all-male delegation. Last Friday, just as they were leaving, and after furious protests, they added one woman to the dozen or so men. I don't know whether this is more pathetic than insulting or the other way round. All I know is, left to themselves, they saw nothing odd about sending only men....

2. The sheer weirdness of the Republic of Ireland in dispatching a group of men to discuss the status of women is one thing. But when it comes to the formal endorsement of objectives, weirdness comes very close to hypocrisy. The Irish delegation will be endorsing in Cairo the paragraph that enshrines the objective that 'governments, international organisations and non-governmental organisations should ensure that their personal policies and practices comply with the principle of equitable representation of both sexes, especially at the managerial

and policy-making levels...' Equitable representation. 12:1; ha, bloody ha....

3. What is the point, after all, of one Labour Minister, Niamh Bhreathnach, bravely trying to combat gross gender imbalance in college governing bodies, when other Labour Ministers – in this case Ministers Spring and Howlin – think nothing of letting their departments send only men to a powerful, official, conference, while throwing a few pounds to women to go, second class, to the accompanying non-official conference? Could condescension be more blatant?

4. And don't tell me that there are no women in the Department of Health and Foreign Affairs, or in the Dáil, or in the Seanad, who could contribute to a conference on reproductive issues. I don't at all criticise the male civil servants who are going. I'm sure they're experts at their jobs. But there's something wrong with the service if they have no female colleagues.

5. It makes you wonder what you can do, when you're persistently, year in year out, treated as second class. Can you hope ever to be treated with natural, not forced, respect? To have your experience accepted as fully authentic, and as being as valuable and weighty as male experience? The parallels with a minority are obvious. When you want equality that is what you want. Real equality, that doesn't even have to be thought about. That's the ideal, the thing yearned for.

Nuala O'Faolain

(From *Resource Materials of Teaching Language Leaving Cert.* English Syllabus)

Comment

Paragraph 1. The *mood* of this piece is one of bitter anger and outrage. She is addressing her remarks to the men – at the top of the Civil Service – who made the decision to send *only* men to the conference. She is *arguing against* the wisdom or sense of that decision. Although the column begins with a reference to a 'joke' it is clear from the content of the question which follows that the writer is certainly not amused by the situation.

'Whom did the Irish Government ... women?' She is scornful of the Government's decision and employs sarcasm as a powerful weapon here. 'They couldn't find a woman, not a single one, to empower. Equality and equity were too much for them. So they arranged an all-male delegation.'

The writer is unapologetic in her criticism of the behaviour of the Government in this instance.

Paragraph 2. She further accuses them of hypocrisy when it comes to the 'formal endorsement of objectives' in Cairo. She quotes from the paragraph that enshrines the objective that 'governments, international organisations ... comply with the principle of equitable representation of both sexes, especially at the managerial and policy-making levels ....'

She heaps scorn yet again on the Government, by repeating the words 'equitable representation', and immediately quoting the ratio of men to women in the Irish delegation – '12:1. Ha bloody ha....' The writer exploits quotation here for her own purpose. It is an effective weapon, and reinforces her argument. She employs rhetorical questions, inviting the reader into the debate, into the whole process of the argument.

Paragraph 3. In this paragraph, she argues against gender imbalance in college governing bodies. 'What (is) the point, after all ... conference? Could condescension be more blatant?' Nuala O'Faolain argues her case with passion and her tone is frequently dramatic, as in paragraph 4.

Paragraph 4. '... don't tell me there are no women in the Department of Health ... reproductive issues.' It is difficult to refute her arguments here, because she appeals to her reader's sense of justice and fair play, the desire for equality and equity in public life. 'There's something wrong with the Service if they have no female colleagues.'

Paragraph 5. The final paragraph conveys her frustration at the way in which women are 'year in year out, treated as second class'. The two questions which follow this point further reinforce the impression that unfortunately, according to Ms O'Faolain, true equality for women remains 'the ideal, the thing yearned for'.

N.B. The language of argument in this opinion article is more impassioned in tone than the Robert Badinter piece in Section A. However, it is equally valid. Argumentation need not always be confined to cold reasoning. A passionate argument, written well, can have much value. A striving for the truth on the part of the writer, a genuine concern for the issue, and a strong belief in one's own particular point of view can result in a powerful piece of writing, as in the above article.

Example 3 Living by the Word by Alice Walker

The last example of the language of argument has been chosen because of its relevance to the overall theme of this Unit – *Race and Racism*. It is an extract from an essay ('On Seeing Red') by Alice Walker, the black American author of the novel *The Color Purple*. It is from a collection of essays entitled *Living by the Word*. Alice Walker's writing is meditative, passionate and provocative. She explores feminist, environmental and political issues in her work and she sheds new light on racial debates, as is evident from this extract.

On Seeing Red by Alice Walker

One day, in the parallel America we are constantly constructing alongside the one that is beginning to topple over, from its own distortions and lies, we will routinely have films about our real ancestors, not about the sanitized, error-free, unrecognizable-as-human stereotypes we *endure*, for the most part, today. More and more the America that really exists and the Americans that really were and are will be acknowledged and studied. This is what so many of us, happy to count ourselves *alternative Americans* (to the ones in power or rampant on TV), work toward. For we know none of us can really feel good about our country or ourselves if we don't know who we are, where we've been or why, where we are going – and are afraid to guess.

Or, to quote Doris Lessing, 'If we were able to describe [or see] ourselves accurately, we might be able to change.'

One of the reasons our country seems so purposeless (except where making money is concerned) is that Americans, even (and perhaps especially) genetically, have been kept from acknowledging and being who they really are. There are few 'white' people in America, for instance, and even fewer 'black' ones. This reality is metaphor for countless other areas of delusion. In all our diversity we have been one people – just as the peoples of the world are one people – even when the most vicious laws of separation have forced us to believe we are not.

I, too, sing America.

Comment

Alice Walker's opening statement is aspirational. She is advocating a 'parallel America', different from the one 'that is beginning to topple over, from its own distortions and lies'. The author is unapologetically critical of the current political regime.

She argues for a time in the future when the film industry will reflect her 'real ancestors', and not the 'sanitised, error-free, unrecognisable-as-human stereotypes' that she must 'endure' today.

An acknowledgement of 'the America that really exists and the Americans that really were and are' is her primary concern. She is careful to distinguish what she terms the 'alternative Americans' from 'the ones in power or rampant on TV' because, she argues: 'None of us can really feel good about our country and ourselves ... afraid to guess.' She quotes Doris Lessing to support her viewpoint on the importance of national self-awareness, of self-knowledge. 'If we were able to describe [or see] ourselves accurately, we might be able to change.'

Alice Walker argues that the reason 'our country' seems so purposeless is that Americans have been prevented from 'acknowledging and being who they really are'. The issue of colour, i.e. 'white' or 'black' for instance, she argues, is just one delusion among 'countless other areas of delusion'. She argues that our diversity as human beings is the core issue. In diversity there is also oneness, a universal human bond between all the peoples of the world. 'In all our diversity we have been one people – just as the peoples of the world are one people – even when the most vicious laws of separation have forced us to believe we were not.'

The extract concludes with a final eloquent argument, in just four words, for her rightful place in American society. It is her country also. 'I, too, sing America.'

N.B. You will find more examples of the language of argument in other Units of this book. Refer back to the above notes for clarification when you need to.

SECTION C COMPOSING

Starting the Essay

To the student
Let's look at ways in which you might *start the essay*. Beginning any piece of writing is difficult. It demands time and thought, but there are a number of tactics you can use:

1. **Quotations**: Build up a fund of these on a range of topics and themes. You can buy a dictionary of quotations, which will list entries alphabetically, by author, with an index of key words at the back, for easy reference. (See Oxford, Webster, or Collins for Dictionaries of Quotations.)

Saturday's edition of the *Irish Times* also has a 'This week they said' section, with quotations on current affairs from politicians and public figures. Magazines, advertisements and your textbooks are also excellent sources of quotations as is the Internet. See too 'Last Words' at the end of this book (pages 242–244) for a range of quotations on universal themes.

Remember too, that you are actively encouraged to use the *texts on your exam paper* as a resource for your essay – so feel free to quote from *any or all of the texts*.

2. **Statistics**: Startling or shocking ones are especially good. They attract the notice of the examiner, and focus his/her attention on the topic. Facts are impressive and irrefutable. This kind of opening is particularly suitable to the languages of argument, information and/or persuasion.

For example, 'Dublin Rape Crisis Centre figures for the period 1996–97 show that, of the 242 clients who had been raped, there were only five convictions (two per cent), despite the fact that almost half had reported the rape to the Gardaí. (DRCC)' *Amnesty Ireland* magazine, February 2001.

3. **Anecdote**: The dictionary defines this as 'a short account of an entertaining or interesting incident.' In a *narrative* essay, the use of anecdote works very well as a starting point.

For example, see the opening paragraph of 'Australia experiences a surge of nationalism', Text 2, Section A (Comprehending), in this Unit. The writer of the article, Conor O'Clery, *recalls a story* told to him by Phillip Dye, an Australian musician, who came to Ireland some years ago …

4. **Questions**: Readers are excited by questions. Interesting and stimulating ones will arouse the examiner's attention immediately. In preparing your essay overall it is useful to try writing a series of questions provoked by the title. Then choose one that most directly addresses the concern of the title for your opening.

For example, Essay 3, in this Unit, might provoke the following questions:
(a) Has Ireland become a nation of racist thugs?
(b) Just how racist are we in this country?
(c) How can we not feel shamed as a nation when we read of such blatant racial abuse and prejudice?

This type of opening is most suited to the language of argument or persuasion.

5. **Direct dramatic statement**: A strong opening statement immediately tells the reader/examiner what to expect from this essay. It has the appeal of honesty and straight talking, but you must be able to sustain this stance throughout the essay. It is particularly suited to a subject you have researched or that you know well. The opening could be a direct dramatic statement of fact, an outrageous assertion or an alarming newspaper headline entirely concocted by you. (Study the main headlines in newspapers and magazines as examples of these.)

This kind of opening will have shock value, but be careful to establish a clear link to the essay itself. It must be relevant.

Caution: Don't attempt this kind of opening unless you are confident you can carry it off.

Here are some examples you might use for Essay 5 in this Unit.

1. *Direct dramatic statement*: 'In 12 states (of the US) prisoners are strapped to a chair and shocked with 500 to 2000 volts. Malfunctions are not unknown: in 1977 an inmate's head burst into flames.' (*Time*, 21 May 2001)
2. *Outrageous assertion*: 'Murderers are the scum of the earth. They should all be hung.'
3. *Alarming newspaper headline*: 'Bye Bye McVeigh! Mad Bomber Fries Today!'

Now that I've given you some 'starters', let's have a closer look at the seven essay titles for this Unit. You will find notes on genre, and possible **sample openings** for each one. As in Unit 1, the titles reflect the format of the exam.

The Titles – Theme: Race and Racism

Task: Write a composition on any one of the following. Each composition carries 100 marks. The composition assignments below are intended to reflect language study in the areas of information, argument, persuasion, narration and the aesthetic use of language.

Essay 1
Language of Narration/Information/Argument

'The African Refugee Network Survey of 1999 questioned 40 refugees about their experiences.
• 30 said they were denied service because of skin colour.
• 11 said they had been verbally abused.
• 4 claimed physical abuse.' (Text 1)

Race and Racism

Write a letter to the Minister for Justice in which you, as a refugee, outline your personal response to the findings in the survey.

Note on genre(s): The examiner will expect you to make use of the information contained in Text 1 as a whole. The language of narration is appropriate in terms of recounting your experiences as a refugee living in Ireland, as is the language of information, when relating the facts, figures and statistics in order to reinforce your points. Argue the case for a more just and equitable treatment of refugees, employing the language of argument. The tone and manner of your address to the Minister should be formal, reflecting the register of a serious, informed letter of protest.

Sample Opening

Direct dramatic statement
Dear Minister,
As a Nigerian refugee, currently living in Dublin, I wish to call your attention to the issues raised by the results of the enclosed survey carried out by the African Refugee Network in May 1999. My experience mirrors closely that of the 40 refugees surveyed. Allow me to expand further …

Essay 2
Language of Information/Argument

'The Olympic Games, he concluded, had given Australians a sense of personal and national pride to match that of the Irish and Americans.' (Text 2)

Write a personal essay in which you explore your sense of what 'national pride' is, or should be.

Note on genre(s): 'A personal essay' allows you the freedom to write in a genre of your choice, and even to mix genres within the one essay. However, you should perhaps decide from the outset which genre will dominate in your essay. For example, the language of argument might be employed to argue the notion of

what constitutes 'national pride', in your opinion. The language of information might also be used in attempting to establish the role history has to play in determining a nation's sense of pride in itself.

Sample Openings

Here are some **quotations** on the subject of nations and national pride:

(a) 'How much more are men than nations?' (Ralph Waldo Emerson)

This quotation allows for a broad sweep of this subject, i.e. what it is that defines a nation and nationhood.

(b) 'There is no such thing as a little country. The greatness of a people is no more determined by their number than the greatness of a man is determined by his height.' (Victor Hugo)

This quotation allows for a comparison perhaps between America and Ireland, or Australia and Ireland. What constitutes national pride in each? What are the differences in our perceptions of national pride?

(c) 'The political life of a nation is only the most superficial aspect of its being. In order to know its inner life, the source of its action, one must penetrate to its soul by literature, philosophy and the arts, where are reflected the ideas, the passions, the dreams of a whole people.' (Romain Rolland)

This quotation allows for a consideration of the part that the *arts* and *literature* have to play in the life of a nation and how they contribute to our sense of pride in our country.

(d) 'I still have a dream. It is a dream deeply rooted in the American dream that one day this nation will rise up and live out the true meaning of its creed – we hold these truths to be self-evident, that all men are created equal … I have a dream my four little children will one day live in a nation where they will not be judged by the colour of their skin but by the content of their character.' (Martin Luther King Jnr., 28 August 1963)

This quotation allows you to focus specifically on the theme of race and racism in your essay. What is national pride if it is not inclusive of all the inhabitants of a country? Should the content of one's character be central to a country's image of what constitutes national pride?

Essay 3
Language of Persuasion/Argument

Write an article for your school or local magazine in which you publicly condemn the appalling racial abuse and prejudice evident in the letter received by the black woman living in Dublin. Your aim is to persuade your readers that not all Irish people are racist. (Text 1)

Note on genre(s): Your *purpose* here is to persuade. Be mindful of your *audience*. You are writing for your peers – so this will determine the *register* and tone of the language you use, e.g. thoughtful, rational, or provocative and sensational. You may wish to shock your readers into a realisation of the seriousness of this issue. The letter from Text 1 itself is shocking. Make good use of it. Use the language of argument to quote figures and statistics, to support your points. Remember you can use all of the texts and the accompanying illustrations.

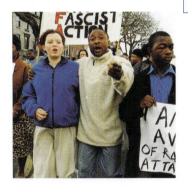

Sample Opening

Question: Has Ireland become a nation of racist thugs? Judging from the above letter, it would certainly appear so ...

Essay 4
Language of Narration/Aesthetic Use of Language

'This is my friend, Daniel ...'
Imagine you are the woman in picture two of Text 4, and Daniel is the young man beside you in the photo. Tell the story of your friendship with Daniel, culminating on the day of the occasion depicted in the picture. (Text 4)

Note on genre(s): The examiner will expect a sense of story, a beginning, middle and end. Focus on the two central characters, how they met, became friends, a

Sample Openings

defining moment in their relationship perhaps. Make use of the details in the photo, i.e. the setting, the atmosphere, the occasion suggested to you by these images. This essay may also lend itself to some aesthetic use of language, as this is an important characteristic in narrative writing. You may also quote from, or draw ideas from any or all of the texts and accompanying illustrations.

Anecdote

(a) 'I was in the launderette, doing my weekly wash, when he walked in. Everyone stared ...'

(b) 'Mrs. Green said she'd met "one of them" in the supermarket. I knew by the way she sniffed that she disapproved ...'

(c) 'Last Christmas, it was. I was carrying my bag of shopping home from the bus stop, when he asked if he could help ...'

Essay 5

Language of Argument/Information

'... the death penalty has never been a deterrent to crime.'

> Write the speech you would make in a school or public debate for or against the death penalty. (Text 3)

Note on genre(s): Use the questions and/or the notes you made from the *Pre-reading Exercise* for Text 3, as a stimulus. Read Text 3 itself, for information and arguments against the death penalty, including those which refer to racism.

Remember the three key points of *purpose*, *audience* and *register*. The *audience* here is the peer group (school) and/or a more general audience of peers and adults (public debate). You must decide on your audience, then adopt an appropriate *register*, i.e. a colloquial, familiar language register (peers) perhaps, or a more serious, formal one for a general audience. Either way, the *purpose* here is to argue your case clearly, with concrete references and strongly supported evidence.

You must adopt a particular stance here, either a supportive or oppositional one, in relation to the statement. Therefore, this essay would benefit from some research in advance of writing the essay, on the levels of support worldwide *for* the death penalty.

Sample Openings

Refer back to my notes on *direct dramatic statement*, and use them for the examples given here.
OR
Formulate a **challenging question**, e.g. Just how effective has the death penalty been in combating crime worldwide?
OR
Use a **quotation** from Text 3 itself, e.g. 'Today, all the Western democracies have abolished the death penalty. Almost all of Europe has banished it. Can one seriously believe that, if it constituted an effective instrument for fighting murderous crimes, the leaders of Europe's great states would not have reinstated it years ago?'

Essay 6
Language of Information/ Narration

'Aussie! Aussie! Aussie! Oi! Oi! Oi!'

> Write an account of your experience of a national sporting event you attended and/or participated in. The account is to appear in a popular sports magazine for older teenagers. (Text 2)

Note on genre(s): Your *purpose* here is both to inform and to narrate your experience, for an *audience* of your peers. You may shape your account within the very broad parameters of what constitutes a 'popular sports magazine'. Clearly, your account may be written in a serious or humorous *register*, or a combination of both, e.g. serious in terms of the importance of the event itself, humorous in terms of your own experience of it. This essay allows for a broad interpretation of the task outlined. Refer to Text 2 for the Australian experience of hosting the Olympic Games in 2000, and make use of

64 Write Now!

the language used to describe the atmosphere and excitement of the Games, and the sense of national pride exhibited at the time.

Sample Openings

Anecdote

'I never expected to be asked. One moment I was sitting at home, watching the game on the telly, the next I was being whisked off to Rome for the Ireland/Italy match! …'

'This is my life …'

Essay 7

Language of Narration/ Aesthetic Use of Language

Imagine you are in the world of one of the pictures in *Text 4*. Tell your story.

Note on genre(s): This is a good example of an essay that allows for an imaginative, personal response, with a broad parameter of possibilities of purpose, audience and register. The examiner will, however, expect a narrative, a telling – the sense of story, a beginning, middle and an end, a central character (you), a defining moment, action and a setting. The language registers you use can mix and mingle here, perhaps emphasising the aesthetic use of language, because it is an important feature of narrative writing.

Use the world of the picture you choose as a stimulus. Examine it carefully – the background, the individuals and their actions, their facial expressions and environment. Focus on these images while writing your story. Make a *link* between the picture chosen and your life as described in your essay.

Sample Openings

(a) Use **a quotation**: Is there a line from a song or poem that you know that might sum up your life, as depicted in the story you're about to tell?

(b) **Anecdote**: 'I'm nothing special. I live in a council estate. I have some good mates but some shun me because my family are Travellers. It normally doesn't bother me, but last week I was . . . '

SECTION D LANGUAGE SKILLS

Efficiency of Language Use 2

> 'Management and control of language to achieve clear communication, e.g. vocabulary, syntax, sentence patterns, paragraph structure, punctuation appropriate to the register, ... use of lively interesting phrasing, energy, style, fluency ... appropriate to the delivery of the task (30%).'
> ('Criteria for Assessment', Leaving Cert. English)

To the student
In Unit 1, we concentrated on the basics of punctuation and spelling. In this Unit, you will find more practice in these, but we are also going to look at language in terms of *syntax*, *sentence patterns*, *paragraph structure* and the use of '*lively, interesting phrasing*'.

Syntax
Simply defined, syntax is the grammatical arrangement of words in a sentence showing their connection and relation to each other. Good writing ensures that the words in your sentences are arranged in the *best* order. Making meaning in written English very much depends on this. The examiner will reward you for care in this area, under the heading 'Efficiency of Language Use', which accounts for thirty per cent of the marks overall. In addition to the ten per cent awarded for 'Accuracy of Mechanics', you can see that it's certainly worth working on language skills in order to maximise your marks.

Structure and Syntax
To make sense in written English, the order of the words in a sentence, i.e. the *syntax*, must follow a particular pattern, viz.,

	Noun (subject)	Verb (action)	Object
e.g.	Colm	loves	pizza.
	Mary	hates	broccoli.

- Every sentence must have a *subject* ... the doer or performer of the action. This is usually in the form of a named person (Colm, Mary) who is a *noun*, grammatically

speaking, or a *pronoun* (he, she).
- Every sentence must have an *action* word (loves, hates), a *verb*, in a specific tense, i.e. past, present or future.
- An *object* is not absolutely necessary to create a meaningful sentence, but in most instances, the action passes over to another person or object. The action is thus completed, e.g. 'pizza' is the object of the verb 'loves', and 'broccoli' is the object of the verb 'hates', in the above examples.

You could, of course, create nonsense sentences using this pattern. For example, 'Broccoli hates Mary'! The *order* of the words here is correct. The sentence has a noun (broccoli), a verb (hates) and an object (Mary) – but it is fundamentally unsound, in terms of possible *meaning*. The more likely arrangement required for meaning is the initial example – 'Mary hates broccoli'.

N.B. It is the *arrangement* of the words in the *best/right order* that makes meaning.

Kinds of Sentences

There are basically four types of sentences:
- Statements: David Beckham plays for Manchester United.
- Questions: Does Peter have a DVD player?
- Orders: Eat your vegetables.
- Exclamations: You can't have eaten the whole lot!

Exercise 1

Here are eight sentences, two of each kind. Can you correct the syntax, so that they make sense, and identify the type of sentence each is? The *punctuation* will help.

A. south-east in a coastal town is Wexford the.
B. now it do better time next the.
C. the tickets concert for book you did?
D. day what a! to school going no way I am!
E. nightmare constant maths my is.
F. out way the door shut your on.
G. eat you did rubbish all that?
H. serious be you cannot!

Lively Interesting Phrasing

Syntax becomes more complex, but also more interesting when we add colourful adjectives and lively verbs to our sentences.

For example: Pop music's *adored* entertainer, Mr Robbie Williams, *burst* onto the stage in Slane yesterday, *leaping* into the air, obviously delighted to be *strutting* his stuff in front of 50,000 *ecstatic* fans.

The use of adjectives 'adored' and 'ecstatic', and the verbs 'burst', 'leaping' and 'strutting' give life to this sentence. We can visualise the scene and the performer. Remember that the examiner will reward the use of language that has 'energy, style and fluency'. (Efficiency of Language Use)

Exercise 2

Rearrange the words in their correct order in the following sentences. They are more complex than in Exercise 1, so be prepared to spend some time on making the syntax work, in order to create meaning.

A. in defeated Wexford final hurling Limerick prowess a magnificent of display incredible point one an yesterday by the in Leinster.
Begin: In a ...

B. environmental glimpse the into bravery and protesters intent on documentary the offers fascinating a idealism the of area saving ancient woodland natural an of
Begin: The documentary ...

C. celebration of the detailed of movies 'Paradiso Cinema' nostalgic in a richly letter love enduring of power film the cinema is a
Begin: In a nostalgic ...

D. grumpy princess title computer the green entertaining with falls love in this character is a animated comedy a who 'Shrek' ogre in
Begin: The title ...

E. academic quirky Latin gained whose songs recording status in cult has Finnish been medal honorary Pope a Presley awarded of been from the Elvis have
Begin: A Finnish ...

Exercise 3

Highlight/underline the *verbs* and *adjectives* in each of the (rearranged) sentences in Exercise 2. <u>Write five sentences of your own, in which you use those verbs and adjectives.</u> Remember that your aim is to use 'lively interesting phrasing' in order to achieve 'energy, style and fluency'.

68 Write Now!

For example in sentence A:
Verb: defeated
Adjectives: magnificent, incredible
Sentence: No one could deny the *magnificent* effort made by the young O'Sullivan girl who *defeated* her nearest rival by an *incredible* 4.26 seconds.

Exercise 4

Let's take this a stage further.
Rearrange the *sentences* in the following recipe (in *two paragraphs*) from Jamie Oliver's book *The Return of the Naked Chef*, so that the syntax makes sense. The language is lively and funny and the 'bacon sarnie' is delicious!

- Squeeze the 2 bits of bread together and now its ready to be eaten, preferably with some HP sauce.

- Third, I buy a small, fresh sandwich loaf (gotta be white unless you need your roughage) which should be about 25cm/10ins long.

- So, you've got your bacon and your bread. Lovely.

- At this point, I shuffle all the bacon up one end of the pan to carry on cooking a little longer while I toast off my two long pieces of bread in the pan.

- There is a key to this recipe and in my view this is the way to do it.

- Second, I would suggest that you get hold of thicker-cut bacon; not the wafer-thin stuff that became fashionable a few years ago – you need something you can really get your teeth into.

- But if you fancy yourself as a bit of a fryer get yourself a ridged griddle pan, which I get as hot as possible (about 4 minutes on the highest heat) and then begin to grill 4 slices of bacon (per person if you're greedy like me).

- When it has toasted on both sides you could butter your toast – I don't bother – and lay your bacon across each slice.

- First, you need the best dry-cured bacon you can get hold of.

- After about 1 minute you can turn the bacon over and it will be golden with those funky charred marks across which I also think benefit the flavour slightly.

Race and Racism 69

Exercise 5

Let's take syntax a stage further again.

Rearrange the eight paragraphs in this newspaper article, (edited) entitled 'My Word! Homer's in the dictionary', so that the syntax makes sense. There is an obvious beginning, middle and end to the piece.

Simpsons' New Dictionary

- Subscribers are from around the world, including Scandinavia, South Africa, the US and New Zealand.
  The directory website is www.oup.co.uk

- 'Doh' is now an official word of the English language.
  Homer uses the word when things go wrong for him, which happens on a regular basis in the cartoon.

INSPIRATION

- Inspiration for new additions to the dictionary were taken from a wide variety of sources – from teenage chatter, the pop music charts and even Bridget Jones's Diary.

- **CARTOON** character Homer Simpson's catch-phrase has made it into the updated online edition of the Oxford English Dictionary published today.

- The Oxford English Dictionary launched its online service just over a year ago and the international fascination with the English language has proved lucrative.

- Originally, the term was used by the Christian Church in the 14th century for anyone spiritually renewed but now it refers to a man in touch with his feminine side.

- Although 'bad hair day' has been around for some years, it was Jones's use of this phrase in the best-selling novel by Helen Fielding that prompted the dictionary to include it to describe times when things aren't going quite right.

- **NAKED**
  The Full Monty now means to be naked.
  Among other new entries is 'new man'.

Punctuation
- Capital letters
- Full stops
- Commas
- Inverted commas
- Question marks
- Exclamation marks

Exercise 1
Rewrite the following amended extract from *Angela's Ashes*, by Frank McCourt. You will need to insert **capital letters**, **full stops**, **commas** and **three question marks**.
Note: There are no inverted commas (quotation marks) used in this novel, but the dialogue is clearly indented, as you can see from the extract.

if my pals see my mother dragging me through the street to an irish dancing class i'll be disgraced entirely they think it's all right to dance and pretend you're fred astaire because you can jump all over the screen with ginger rogers there is no ginger rogers in irish dancing and you can't jump all over you stand straight up and down and keep your arms against yourself and kick your legs up and around and never smile my uncle pa keating said irish dancers look like they have steel rods up their arses but i can't say that to mam she'd kill me

there's a gramophone in mrs o'connor's playing an irish jig or a reel and boys and girls are dancing around kicking their legs out and keeping their hands to their sides mrs o'connnor is a great fat woman and when she stops the record to show the steps all the fat from her chin to her ankles jiggles and i wonder how she can teach the dancing she comes over to my mother and says so this is little frankie i think we have the makings of a dancer here boys and girls do we have the makings of a dancer here we do mrs o'connor

mam says i have the sixpence mrs o'connor

ah yes mrs mccourt hold on a minute

she waddles to a table and brings back the head of a black boy with kinky hair big eyes huge red lips and an open mouth she tells me put the sixpence in the mouth and take my hand out before the black boy bites me all the boys and girls watch and they have little smiles i drop in the sixpence and pull my hand back before the mouth snaps shut everyone laughs and i know they wanted to see my hand caught in the mouth mrs o'connor gasps and laughs and says to my mother isn't that a howl now mam says it's a howl she tells me behave myself and come home dancing

(Extract from *Angela's Ashes* by Frank McCourt)

Exercise 2

Here is an amended extract from *Death and Nightingales*, by Eugene McCabe. Rewrite it carefully, inserting **capital letters**, **commas**, **full stops**, **inverted commas**, **three exclamation marks** and **one question mark**.

Note: You will see one example of the use of points of ellipsis (dots ...), in this extract. It suggests that a statement has been left unfinished, or a thought half formed, i.e. 'such frenzies broke as they seemed to so simply, so often ...'

what she remembered seemed mostly to be shouting from behind closed doors passionate screaming from window to yard things broken thumped thrown and torn the dread of being near while such frenzies broke as they seemed to so simply so often ... her mother talking in the dining-room about tirkennedy where she was born: an eighty-acre tenancy across the lough part of the corry estate old irish real gentry she insisted where her father red jack maguire was a horse-buyer-cum-horse-trainer; he was the best in ulster and maybe in ireland he had married her grandmother rosina quinn a parlour-maid in the corry house and they had three children – of which she catherine was the youngest she then decided how she had met billy winters at the rds in 1860 where her pacer pride of erne had not only eclipsed but outclassed (and she had accented the word outclassed) all other entries; how he had plagued her to marry him i was an old woman of twenty-nine he was a child of twenty-three the wedding arrangements in corry's private chapel; special dispensation from armagh and how a belfast or dublin journal had described billy as one of ulster's foremost young businessmen and her mother as having the white skin and flaming hair of an older more romantic ireland during the telling of this billy winters had kept silent when she had finished he said you left out the best part

(Extract from *Death and Nightingales* by Eugene McCabe)

Spelling
Bad Habits and Common Errors

1. Should of ... }   Should *have* ...
   Would of ... }   **Wrong!** Would *have* ...   **Right**!
   Could of ... }   Could *have* ...

This kind of error is a bad habit more than anything else. Here are a few more of them:

2. This *effected* her badly.   X
   This *affected* her badly.   ✓
   Effect = noun. The *effects* of the outbreak were felt throughout the region.
   Affect = verb. Your actions *affect* us all.

3. **There/Their/They're**
   (a) There you are! The box is over there, in the corner. There are 30 students in my class. There is a good description on page 24.
   (b) Their problem. Their school. Their day. Their parents. Their exam. (Possession)
   (c) *They're* not here. = *They are* not here. They're not coming. They're OK. (Contraction)

4. **Were/Where**
   'Where were you? Were you at Toni's?'
   'No. I was where I always am on Fridays – at the club.'
   'I saw where you went, young lady, and you weren't where you said you were!'

5. **To/Too/Two**
   'It's too late to buy two of them.'

Exercise 1

A. Highlight/underline the **spelling errors** in the following passage. You will find examples of all the above bad habits.

B. Re-write the passage inserting the *correct* spellings.

Alice knew that she should of told Tony that changing jobs would not effect there relationship, but she didn't. He would of reacted badly of he'd of realised that she was going to be promoted ahead of him. He'd always encouraged her to apply for new opportunities at work, but not were he was working! That would of been to close for comfort. If only they could of talked about there ambitions, things might of been different. Now, it was getting to complicated. At least too people on the staff knew about there situation, and there respective bosses to. No matter were she looked, their was no escape.

How Can I Correct These Bad Habits?

- **Read over everything you write** before you leave it. If you do, you will immediately spot ninety-five per cent of those spelling (and punctuation) errors.
- **Use your dictionary** to make sure you have spelled a word correctly, especially those key words you use all the time, like 'character' and 'scene'. Get into the good habit of doing this. Remember that you can win or lose ten per cent of your marks for accuracy of mechanics.
- **Make a list of those words that you personally misspell**, and keep it beside you when you write. Then make a conscious effort to spell them correctly. **Care** is the key word.
- **Do the spelling exercises** that follow at the end of each Unit, in Section D of this book.
- **Learn the list of frequently misspelled words**, and write a short sentence for each word. Learning and practising ten a week will see a marked improvement in your writing.

Exercise 2

The following sentences contain lots of common spelling errors! Re-write them with the correct spellings.

1. It was evedent that the charachter was extreamely unhappy at home.
2. The peot vividly discribes the scence, giveing the reader a keen sence of the joyfull nature of the bird and its eternel song.
3. The writter protrays the contrasting emotions of happyness and saddness equaly well in this peom.
4. Their is an extrodinary sceen at the begining of the film were the visiters loose all there posessions durning a freak storm.
5. The goverment excepted compleate responsability for the damage to the enviroment caused by the omision of toxic gases.
6. Colm thought it was extreamely unlikely that he would be sitting oppisite Mary durning the marraige ceremony.
7. Denise hopped their wouldn't be to many arguements over the speaches.
8. She allways studys alot befor exams.
9. He never would of known about it accept for Susan threathening to tell the principle.
10. I can appriciate her qualitys of leadership, but I'm not atal sure she won't exagerate the importance of the job, or how it will effect the whole team.

And finally ...

Here are ten words from Exercises 1 and 2 that you will use constantly in your writing, and a simple strategy for learning them, as in Unit 1.

A. Learn the spelling.
B. Cover it. Write the word in pencil in the 'Spell it' space.
C. Check to see if it's correct. If it isn't, rub it out and relearn it, before writing it again.
D. Write a *short* sentence containing the word, in the space provided. That part of the word which is usually misspelled is underlined.

Word	*Spell it*	*Short sentence*
evident	_____	_____
scene	_____	_____
beginning	_____	_____
environment	_____	_____
marriage	_____	_____
speech	_____	_____
thought (think)	_____	_____
taught (teach)	_____	_____
always	_____	_____
affect (verb)	_____	_____

Unit 3 Man and Nature

SECTION A **COMPREHENDING**

Introduction
This section contains four texts on the general theme of *Man and Nature*, including a set of pre-reading exercises on Texts 1–3.

Text 1
'They've got it sorted' is an article from the *Irish Times* magazine (17 March 2001). It is primarily an example of the **language of information**, but it also argues forcibly for the reduction of waste through recycling. The article raises questions about our attitude and responsibilities in terms of the environment. Bernie Walsh's ability to **persuade** people in authority to take the issue of recycling seriously is evident throughout the article. You will therefore find examples of the **languages of argument and persuasion** here.

Text 2
'Hitting the wall: first ascent of a Baffin Island peak' by Greg Child (mountaineer), with photographs by Gordon Wiltsie, is an extract (edited) from an article in the *National Geographic* magazine (January 1999). It is the account of a remarkable feat of climbing by a team of four mountaineers scaling the sheer blank wall of Great Sail Peak on Baffin Island off the coast of Canada, elevation 5,300 feet. It is primarily a **narrative account** of the last stages of the climb, with some exciting images, which are examples of the **aesthetic use of language**. We also learn about the actual details of the climbers' experiences, so the **language of information** is evident here too.

Text 3
'We may be brothers after all', is a speech made by the Native American Indian, Chief Seattle, in reply to an offer made by President Franklin Pierce of the USA in 1854 for a large area of Native American land. Chief Seattle was promised a 'reservation for the Indian people'. The full version of the reply was printed in the *Evening Press* on Friday 4 June 1976, to mark World Environment Day, on 5 June of the same year. It is primarily an example of

the aesthetic use of language in its eloquent and poetic description of the Native American way of life, and their respect for the richness and beauty of the Earth that we all inhabit.

Chief Seattle **argues** for his birthright, a continued respect for the environment, and a realisation of how precious Nature is. He believes we should preserve the Earth and pass that awareness on to our children. It is a **persuasive** speech, and has been described as the most beautiful and profound statement on the environment ever made. It is also an excellent example for you, as a student, of how language genres often mix and meld in good writing.

Text 4

Text 4 is a series of images, usually without a written text. They are intended to reflect the overall theme of *Man and Nature*. You are required to study the images and respond to them in a variety of ways and genres.

Text 1 *They've got it sorted*

Stage 1 Pre-Reading

Task: In pairs, or small groups, discuss some or all of the questions below for ten minutes, then report back to the class.
OR
Your teacher may choose to discuss the questions with the whole group. In either case, the most important thing is that *you take notes* of other students' points, for use later in one of the composing tasks in Section C.

Questions

1. What does the word 'environment' mean? Try to define it in as broad a context as possible. Feel free to consult a dictionary if you have one to hand.
2. Do you, your school or your family recycle cans, bottles, etc.? If you do, discuss why you think it is important. If you do not, discuss why you do not think so, or simply why you do not do it.
3. In the broader community of the area in which you live, how do people treat their own environment? Is there a conscious effort on everyone's part (or anyone's part!) to keep the neighbourhood clean and tidy? If so, why? If not, why not?
4. Whose responsibility is it, do you think, to safeguard the environment, and to manage and recycle waste products? Is it the Department of the Environment? The local authority? The Corporation? The County Council? Is it the community? Or *you*, as individuals?

Stage 2 **Reading**

THEY'VE GOT IT SORTED

1. Bernie Walsh explains how Sunflower Recycling takes the first step in encouraging their employees to look at the bigger picture. How reducing waste and recycling can have an impact on your standard of living:

'"What's the environment to you? It's not green trees in the countryside and it's not going to the zoo once a year. I want you to take this camera and come back and show me what your environment is." So, they come back and they might have pictures of the park, of their house or of their family. But in there you will also get a photo of a derelict site or of a bad street that's been vandalised or covered in litter. So all the pictures go up on the wall and we work out the one thing that's common with all of them; everybody keeps their house tidy and clean, but look what we do to the streets.'

2. Sunflower Recycling employs twenty-four people to collect, sort and grade recyclable goods from businesses and community centres in Dublin. Founder and manager of this five-year-old enterprise, Walsh came up with the idea after doing a Community Leadership course in Maynooth. Herself and Carol Bolger had worked at recycling in Holland and Denmark respectively and they drew up a plan for a project that would create jobs through recycling in their community, Dublin's north inner-city.

3. 'In our naivety we though at first we would get funding from the Department of the Environment, that they would be so delighted at somebody doing a bit of recycling,' says Walsh. But as far as they were concerned we were a non-entity. We could have been a crowd of headbangers, so they said no, we don't do community recycling. They got the same reaction from Dublin Corporation who didn't have any funds for this kind of project and had no idea how to deal with, let alone help, the far-thinking team.

4. In the end it was FÁS which gave them the support they needed, providing funding through Community Employment schemes for the long-term unemployed. The money was matched for two years by Integra, an EU funding programme which overall meant that they could cover some overheads, buy equipment ('we bought the forklift for a pound, but it's cost us plenty in repairs since!'), train and pay their employees.

5. 'Training can be anything from basic literacy to HGV driving and everything that goes on in-between. We do art through recycling – Christmas cards, stained glass – this year they're really into mosaics. A lot of training revolves around your work; the girl in the office would learn Excel and Sage, for example. But we also like to do things that people get a bit of creativity from, particularly people who come in at the other end of the scale with very bad literacy. A lot of the creative work gives them a feeling of self worth,' she says.

6. However, funding is a sporadic beast and she says it can give you a 'false perception'. For two years they received more EU funding from a programme called Youthstart. They had forty-two people working for them at that time, with ages ranging from fifteen to sixty-two, and they also have money to employ a management

team of four, including a financial controller and a development worker/co-ordinator. When the funding went, so did these two crucial jobs. With the FÁS money and the amount they bring in themselves (it costs £50 per annum plus £2 per bag after that for businesses to avail of the service) they currently have the funding to employ only twenty-six.

7. In the past six months the organisation moved from their original site in Lower Gardiner Street and into a site on the North Strand Road that has been specifically designed and equipped for them by Dublin Corporation: 'I have to say, since they came on board they've been very supportive but it just took that long to get there,' says Walsh.

8. The site they were in for five years was in an appalling state and, while North Strand Road is '100 per cent better,' the actual sorting sites are under the arches of the DART bridge and are damp and freezing.

9. 'We didn't want to move from the north inner-city – this project was designed to create jobs in a very marginalised community. We could have moved to Fingal but I wouldn't have been bringing the same catchment of workers with me and we would have been changing the whole ethos of the project. So really, getting a site of this size in the inner-city, only five minutes from O'Connell Street, is tantamount to a miracle.'

Sunflower Recycling, Shamrock Terrace, North Strand Road, Dublin 1.

Tel: 01-8560251

Question A

Read paragraphs 1–5 again.
(i) What problems did Bernie Walsh experience, in setting up Sunflower Recycling? (15)
(ii) Apart from recycling waste, how does Bernie Walsh feel that her employees benefit from the experience of working with Sunflower Recycling, in terms of their own creativity and self-worth? (15)
(iii) (a) Based on the information given in paragraphs 6 and 7, what do you think Bernie Walsh means by stating that 'funding is a sporadic beast', and that it can give you a 'false perception'? (10)
(b) Basing your answer on your reading of the whole text, write a short account of the kind of person you imagine Bernie Walsh to be. (10)

Question B

Read the supplementary text to this article, which is specifically related to the recycling issue. Then answer the following question:

Imagine that you are living in an area of the country where there is no 'Bring Centre'. Write a letter to the Dept of the Environment and Local Government, outlining your views on the issue (150–200 words). (50)

Supplementary text

There is no national scheme or national authority to implement the Department of the Environment's guidelines on waste, so it is left to the local authorities. Dublin is the only county to have a collection of recyclable goods, run by Oxygen. Using a wheelie-bin, they collect paper, light cardboard, steel and aluminium cans once a month from 70,000 houses in Dublin. Participation levels have been positive with alien goods making up only five per cent of what is collected. Discussions with Kepak, a packaging recycling company, may result in a collection service for plastics and tetra-paks too.

Areas serviced by **Oxygen**: Crumlin, Walkinstown, Clontarf, Ashtown/Cabra, Ballyroan, Belgrade, Clondalkin, Swords, Clonsilla/Blanchardstown, Churchtown, Clonskeagh, Ballinteer, Dundrum, Foxrock, Cabinteely.

Bring Centres: If you're not among the 70,000 in Dublin, hopefully you have a Bring Centre in your location. The deposit bins take glass, paper, steel cans, aluminium cans, batteries, textiles and plastics.

While the rest of the country is left wondering whether they will ever enjoy such a service, most of us are paying for waste collection. Most would agree that waste-related charges would go a long way towards tackling pollution. A pilot scheme is underway in Carrigaline, Co Cork, where bins are bar-coded with a microchip and weighed and scanned by the collection truck.

Regardless of what recycling facilities the Government and local authorities get around to putting in place, there is one sure, fast way of reducing the prospects of more landfill and an incinerator in your backyard – reducing the amount of waste we create. When you are doing your shopping, ask yourself:
- Can it be re-used?
- Does it have a long product life?
- Does it have minimum packaging?
- Does it have minimum toxicity?

To find out more about the recycling facilities in your area, contact you County Council.

Text 2 Hitting the wall: first ascent of a Baffin Island peak by Greg Child

Stage 1 Pre-Reading
Task: In pairs, or small groups, discuss some or all of the questions below for ten minutes, then report back to the class.
OR
Your teacher may choose to discuss the questions with the whole group. The important thing is that you *take notes* of other students' points, for use later in one of the composing tasks in Section C.

Questions
1. What is it in the human condition that drives man to constantly *challenge* Nature, to battle against it, or wish to conquer it?
2. Have you any ambitions to explore the far reaches of the planet or to *change* it, in any way?
3. Is man in tune with Nature? Think about our relationship with Nature. What is it, exactly?
4. Are we in danger of destroying Nature, as a result of pollution and the plundering of Nature's resources? Do we care?

Stage 2 Reading

Hitting The Wall: First Ascent of a Baffin Island Peak

Alone in a Canadian wilderness of ice-cut mountains, creeping glaciers, and frozen fjords, a team of climbers confronts the ultimate in technical climbing: scaling the sheer, blank wall of Great Sail Peak, elevation 5,300 feet.

None of us fully realised how much backbreaking work hauling our gear up Great Sail Peak would require. 'I'm so sick of schlepping these pigs.' Mark groaned, dumping an 80-pound haul bag onto a mound of loads at ledge camp. It was midnight on the fourth day of the climb, and we'd been on the move for 25 hours without sleep. The summer sun would not set again until August.

The lower cliff turned out to be an obstacle course of teetering rocks stacked as delicately as plates in a china cabinet.

'Whoa, that was close!' muttered Jared, after a chunk of granite whizzed by our heads and pounded the slope below.

The wall above the ledge camp was a 2,400-foot sheet of granite and gneiss – among the hardest, smoothest rocks found in nature. Free climbing it would be impossible, since there were too few natural edges to grip with our fingers and toes. Instead we used a technique called aid climbing, a tedious process in which a climber places a piece of hardware in a crack, then suspends a foot sling from the hardware to stand on to fix another sling. Given the steepness and cold, it could take 12 hours to climb a single pitch, typically a 200-foot rope length.

After 8 days of climbing we reached the Visor, where Alex drilled bolts to hang wall camp. We hoped the Visor would protect us from falling ice and stones. Before the climb we drew straws to decide who would lead each pitch.

Here, just above wall camp, I tackled the toughest pitch of my career. For nine exhausting hours in driving sleet I inched up a crack no wider that a strand of yarn. Teetering on my ladder-like slings, I tapped piton after piton into the fissure above my head. Each piton, a small blade of metal no thicker than the tip of a key, would not support an ounce more than my weight. Soon I lost sight of my companions, who hunkered a hundred feet below me in their porta-ledges. When I peered up the cliff, fusillades of snow pellets stung my eyes. Hugging cold rock, with nothing but a half mile of air beneath my feet, I took stock of the sublime craziness of my position.

If the piton I hung from ripped out, I would fall, and the flimsy bits of gear I'd rigged below it would rip from the crack like the teeth of a broken zipper. I'd survived risky moments on Everest, K2, and other climbs, but here I wondered if I was pushing my luck.

Just then the polar sun burst through the clouds. Dissolving fog unveiled acres of rocks dripping icicles. Warmth seeped into my numb, gloved fingers, and I was suddenly calm. My pulse slowed, and I knew, if I'd ever doubted it, that I belonged to steep places like this one.

I stretched up, slotted another piton into a crack, and tapped it in. Tinkering like a mechanic, I lost myself again in the ritual of climbing.

The final push to the summit began without much promise on 24 June. We had been waiting out a freezing rain squall at wall camp. Alex was nursing a knee he had twisted a week before carrying a heavy bag. Drips falling from the lip of the Visor had thumped a maddening drumbeat on our tents. We had finished reading our books, solved our crossword puzzles, exhausted our jokes. An edgy mood infected us.

'What's it like out?' I grumbled to Mark, who was peering out the flap of our tent through a spiderweb of string-tethered stoves, spoons, smelly boots, and ditty bags.

'More high cirrus clouds blowing in from the coast,' he said. 'Looks like the weather could spank us again, but right now we can climb.'

Mark and Jared took the lead, ascending our swaying highway of ropes to explore the way ahead. Twenty hours later Jared was sprinting up a gaping fissure, pounding his gloved fists into the crack like a boxer.

'The weather is clearing!' Mark radioed down to the rest of us. 'Jared has reached a big ledge we can all fit on, and the summit is close! Get up here!'

Alex, Gordon, John, and I raced up the ropes Mark and Jared had set in place, and at 10 a.m. on 25 June we surmounted the last shadowy cliff into the gentle sloping summit plateau. Having spent so long on the vertical, we wobbled as we walked to the apex of Great Sail Peak.

> We shook hands, stared across the Arctic vista, then kicked off our boots and shed our shirts to bask in the sun. Flopping into the lichen-covered granite, I felt the toll of our 23-day climb settle into my body. My muscles ached. Bloodied from constant scraping against rock, my hands stung. My unwashed body reeked. Living shoulder to shoulder in our porta-ledges and always connected by climbing ropes, my teammates and I were, frankly, fed up with each other and ready to head home.
>
> 'Are we in the middle of nowhere, or what?' Alex grinned broadly.
>
> Emerging from my fatigue I looked east, where iceberg-speckled waters shimmered like a mirage. To the west lay the wasteland of the Barnes Ice Cap. The granite walls of Sam Ford Fjord rose to the south, and a barrier of dark, sinister cliffs stood to our north.
>
> 'Gibbs Fjord,' Mark said, pointing to those mysterious walls. 'No one has climbed there yet.'
>
> My eyes locked onto those unexplored ramparts, and I knew that once we were safely home and the aches and pains faded, we'd feel that familiar itch to return to the harsh, beautiful world of Baffin Island.

Question A

(i) 'I took stock of the sublime craziness of my position.'
Based on your reading of the whole extract, comment on the 'sublime craziness' of this climbing expedition. (30)

(ii) Describe some of the mechanical elements of the actual 'ritual of climbing' in terms of the information supplied by the narrator. Quote from the text to support your points. (20)

OR

Question B

'Just then the polar sun burst through the clouds ... I knew ... that I belonged to steep places like this one.'

Imagine that you are Greg Child and on reaching base camp you are interviewed by a national TV station. You have been asked to summarise your feelings and those of your team at the very moment you reached the summit of Great Sail Peak. Write the text of the response you might make on this occasion (150–200 words). (50)

Text 3 *We May Be Brothers After All*

Stage 1 Pre-Reading

Task: In pairs, or small groups, discuss some or all of the questions below for ten minutes, then report back to the class.

OR

Your teacher may choose to discuss the questions with the whole group. The most important thing is that you *take notes* of other students' points, for use later in one of the composing tasks in Section C.

N.B. These questions are philosophical in the main, designed to make you ponder the larger questions of man's connection with (or struggle against) Nature in all its facets.

Questions

1. Who *owns* the Earth that we inhabit? Should we 'possess' land at all? Is the Earth ours to buy and sell?
2. When you observe Nature – sky, stars, rivers, trees, the animals and birds who share the planet with us, do you see yourself as part of it, or ruler of it?
3. 'To us the ashes of our ancestors are sacred and their resting place is hallowed ground.' Chief Seattle, chief of the Dwamish, upon surrendering his land to Governor Isaac Stevens in 1855. In the year 2002, is Nature sacred to man, or does he merely plunder its resources for his own gain?
4. How and why should we teach our children to respect Nature and our place in it?

Stage 2 Reading

We May Be Brothers After All

In 1854, the Great White Chief in Washington (President) made an offer for a large area of Indian land and promised a 'Reservation' for the Indian people. Chief Seattle's reply, published here (in full) to mark Word Environment Day tomorrow, has been described as the most beautiful and profound statement on the environment ever made.

(*The Evening Press* 4 June 1976)

How can you buy or sell the sky, the warmth of the land? The idea is strange to us.

If we do not own the freshness of the air and the sparkle of the water how can you buy them?

Every part of this earth is sacred to my people. Every shining pine needle, every sandy shore, every mist in the dark woods, every clearing and humming insect is holy in the memory and experience of my people. The sap which courses through the trees carries the memories of the red man.

The white man's dead forget the country of their birth when they go to walk among the stars. Our dead never forget this beautiful earth for it is the mother of the red man. We are part of the earth and it is part of us. The perfumed flowers are our sisters; the deer, the horse, the great eagle, these are our brothers. The rocky crests, the juices in the meadows, the body heat of the pony, and man – all belong to the same family.

So, when the Great Chief in Washington sends word that he wishes to buy our land, he asks much of us. The Great Chief sends word he will reserve us a place so that we can live comfortably to ourselves. He will be our father and we will be his children. So we will consider your offer to buy our land. But it will not be easy. For this land is sacred to us.

We know that the white man does not understand our ways. One portion of land is the same to him as the next, for he is a stranger who comes in the night and takes from the land whatever he needs. The earth is not his brother, but his enemy, and when he has conquered it, he moves on. He leaves his fathers' graves behind, and he does not care. He kidnaps the earth from his children, and he does not care. His fathers' graves, and his children's birthright are forgotten. He treats his mother, the earth, and his brother, the sky, as things to be bought, plundered, sold like sheep or bright beads. His appetite will devour the earth and leave behind only a desert. I do not know. Our ways are different from your ways. The sight of your cities pains the eyes of the red man. But perhaps it is because the red man is a savage and does not understand.

There is no quiet place in the white man's cities. No place to hear the unfurling of leaves in spring, or rustle of an insect's wings. But perhaps it is because I am a savage and do not understand. So we will consider your offer to buy our land. If we decided to accept, I will make one condition: The white man must treat the beasts of this land as his brothers.

I am a savage and I do not understand any other way. I have seen a thousand rotting buffalos on the prairie, left by the white man who shot them from a passing train. I am a savage and I do not understand how the smoking iron horse can be more important that the buffalo that we kill only to stay alive.

What is man without the beasts? If all the beasts were gone, man would die for whatever happens to the beasts, soon happens to man.

All things are connected.

RESPECT

You must teach your children that the ground beneath their feet is the ashes of our grandfathers. So that they will respect the land, tell your children that the earth is rich with the lives of our kin. Teach your children, that the earth is our mother. Whatever befalls the earth befalls the sons of the earth. If men spit upon the ground they spit upon themselves.

This we know: The earth does not belong to man; man belongs to the earth. This we know. All things are connected like the blood which unites one family. All things are connected.

Whatever befalls the earth befalls the sons of the earth. Man did not weave the web of life; he is merely a strand in it. Whatever he does to the web, he does to himself.

Even the white man, whose God walks and talks with him as friend to friend, cannot be exempt from the common destiny. We may be brothers after all. We shall see.

Footnote:

In 1855 (in the Port Elliott Treaty) Chief Seattle surrendered his land, on which the city of Seattle is now located and thereby doomed his people to reservation confinement.

Question A

(i) What aspects of the Native American way of life emerge most strongly for you from the above speech? (20)
(ii) In your opinion, how different is the perception and attitude of the 'white man' to the Native American way of life, as evidenced in this text? (15)
(iii) Write a paragraph (100–150 words) in which you comment on the appropriateness of the newspaper headline for this piece, 'We may be brothers after all'. (15)

Question B

Tatanga Mani, a Stoney Indian, in a passage from his autobiography, comments on the white man's education that he received.

Oh, yes, I went to the white man's schools. I learned to read from school books, newspapers, and the Bible. But in time I found that these were not enough. Civilised people depend too much on man-made printed pages. I turn to the Great Spirit's book which is the whole of his creation. You can read a big part of that book if you study nature. You know, if you take all your books, lay them out under the sun, and let the snow and rain and insects work on them for a while, there will be nothing left. But the Great Spirit has provided you and me with an opportunity for study in nature's university, the forests, the rivers, the mountains, and the animals which include us.

Write a personal response to the above passage. Comment on those phrases or images that appeal to you most, that you agree or disagree with in terms of your own experience of education (150–200 words). (50)

Text 4 Images of Man and Nature

Man and Nature 89

4.
5.

6.
7.

90 Write Now!

Note: As in previous Units, Text 4 requires a different response. You are asked to read a series of images, usually without a written text. You should examine each of them closely before attempting to answer the questions. Be especially attentive to the detail of the photographs – the setting, the personalities/characteristics of people and objects, their gestures, their facial expressions and body language. Look too at colour, light and shade, and for the underlying message or intention inherent in each image, in terms of the overall theme of *Man and Nature*.

Question A

(i) Taking all of the above images into account, in your opinion, what overall picture of *Man and Nature* is projected in this visual text? Outline your views in 150-200 words, supporting your points by reference to the images. (20)

(ii) (a) Imagine this series of images is to be used in a national brochure whose objective it is to promote World Environment Day. Which one of the images would you choose for its front cover? Justify your choice. (15)

(b) In your opinion, which of the above images is the most disturbing/beautiful. Justify your choice. (15)

Question B

Imagine that you are a reporter with a tabloid newspaper. You have been sent to report the story behind one of the images above. Write the headline you would use and a short exciting report (150–200 words). (50)

Sample Answer

Text 1: Question B

Imagine that you are living in an area of the country where there is no 'Bring Centre'. Write a letter of complaint to the Department of the Environment and Local Government, outlining your views on this issue (150–200 words).

To the student

Remember that your task here is to show that you understand the supplementary text and can use it in a specific way, as indicated in Question B. The letter you write here will be a formal one, so you should use the languages of information, argument, and possibly persuasion. However, the context here is functional and therefore you should not overuse persuasive language. Your aim is to inform, and to argue for the provision of a 'Bring Centre' for your area.

6 Crosshaven Avenue,
Ballylucas,
Wicklow,
Co. Wicklow
26 July 2001

The Minister,
Dept. of the Environment and Local Government,
Custom House,
Dublin 1

Dear Minister,
Our Residents' Association has been campaigning for three years now for a 'Bring Centre' for our area. The nearest facility is located in Wicklow Town – a good fifteen miles away. Ballylucas is a rapidly expanding area, which attracts hordes of visitors all year round.

Unfortunately, these visitors leave behind vast amounts of refuse, in addition to our own waste, which we have been attempting to manage and recycle.

In 1999 we took the initiative of setting up a small collection point, for the deposit of recyclable goods on the outskirts of Ballylucas. This centre is manned by a voluntary force of local people, without any funding whatsoever from the local authority or the government.

At present we are paying a considerable fee to Wicklow County Council to collect our waste monthly, for transfer to the 'Bring Centre' in Wicklow Town. This situation cannot be allowed to continue. Your Department must surely shoulder some responsibility for waste management in our area. We understand that a pilot scheme is underway in Carrigaline, Co. Cork at present, where bins are bar-coded with a microchip and weighed and scanned by the collection truck. Perhaps Ballylucas might be considered for a similar scheme? We certainly hope so. We await a speedy response from your office.

Yours faithfully,
Joseph Mullery
(Chairman, Ballylucas Residents' Association)

SECTION B FOCUS ON … THE LANGUAGE OF INFORMATION

> 'All men, by their very nature, feel the urge to know.' (Aristotle)

To the student
You will certainly be most familiar with this genre – the language of information. Information is central to all our lives; indeed we are bombarded by it at every turn in a variety of contexts – oral, visual, and in print.

Thanks to the contemporary revolution in computer technology, accessing and communicating information has never been easier. Via the Internet and a host of websites, we can immediately explore whole worlds of knowledge, unimaginable in the age of Aristotle. So you already have a keen knowledge of this genre, which can be built on and developed.

The Revised Syllabus
The Department guidelines tell us that 'students should encounter a range of texts composed for the *dominant purpose of communicating information*, e.g. reports, records, memos, bulletins, abstracts, media accounts, documentary films.' Listed below are some of the primary sources of the language of information.

1. **Newspapers/Magazines**
    - *Editorials* – politics, current affairs
    - *Reports* – politics, sports, business, finance, the arts
    - *Letters* – variety of topics of common interest
    - *Informative articles* – science, economics, current affairs, human interest
    - *Feature writing* – topic of the day
    - *Reviews* – books, films, the arts, TV & radio guides to programmes
    - *Commentaries* – politics, sport, property pages
    - *Surveys/polls* – political, social
    - *Advertisements* – public service announcements, Government information, national events
2. **Radio and TV**
    - *News* bulletins/programmes
    - *Documentaries* and reports – political, social, scientific, the arts, sports
    - *Reviews* – programmes, films, sport, music, the arts, etc.
    - *Surveys/polls*
    - *Science & money programmes*
    - *Advertisements*

3. Books – Non-Fiction
- *Encyclopaedias* – facts, facts, facts!
- *Text books* and sets of notes
- *Themed books* – on wildlife, art, music, cookery, crafts, science, business, economics, politics, sport, etc.
- *Instruction manuals* – DIY, cars, computers, machinery, equipment
- *Official documents* – Government publications, White papers, educational reports
- *Books of rules* – for entering competitions, for playing games, for codes of behaviour for specific occasions
- *Brochures/pamphlets* – tourism, travel guides, hotels, accommodation, amenities, geographical features, access routes, points of information
- *Autobiographies and biographies* – real lives, facts, events, dates, data, influences, contemporaries
- *Data gathering publications* – statistics, fact finding documents, surveys, polls, tables and their results, brochures for tourism, travel, accommodation, etc.

4. The Internet – The World at Your Fingertips!

The following are examples of the language of information from a variety of sources with a brief commentary on the characteristics that shape this genre.

Newspapers
The Front Page

Let's begin with an extract from the front page layout of the *Irish Independent,* 9 July 2001.

NEWS

Two bodies recovered from Bantry Bay
The bodies of two yacht club members were recovered from Bantry Bay, Co Cork, following a boating accident. **Page 3.**

Petrol prices fall but with big variations
Petrol prices have fallen by 3p a litre but an investigation is needed on huge price variations, the AA says. **Page 3.**

Gloomy tourist season as numbers drop
A gloomy tourist season has been forecast for the remainder of the year after business plummeted in the first five months. **Page 6**.

Surgeon saves boy's arm after shark attack
An Irish surgeon battled yesterday to save the arm of an eight-year-old boy after it was bitten off by a shark in Florida. **Back Page**.

BUSINESS

Preparing to extend territorial waters
The Government is preparing a UN submission to extend the territorial waters limit. **Page 15.**

Mean fiddler gets meagre response
Live entertainment group, Mean Fiddler, has raised just stg£7m from an institutional placing – down from the hoped-for stg£10m. **Page 15.**

SPORT

The Cats march on with ease
Kilkenny strolled to victory in the Guinness Leinster hurling final when they saw off the challenge of Wexford. **Sport 3.**

Tyrone the high kings of Ulster
Tyrone finally killed off Cavan's stubborn challenge and lifted their ninth Ulster football championship title by 1-13 to 1-11. **Sport 2.**

9877091 6950 14 28

Personal notices 2 World news 11 & 24 News Analysis 10 Racing Sport 14 Classified 17 Letters, Radio & Crosswords 21 Television 22 Family Announcements 23

WEATHER
Mainly dry and sunny with isolated showers
Max: 20c Min: 10c
Weather Maps: Page 23

Comment

You will note that the headline words are extremely clear – News – Business – Sport, all in bold type. They are immediately identifiable as the three main areas of interest to the reader. We are presented with four main News items, each with its own eye-catching headline ('Two bodies recovered from Bantry Bay', 'Surgeon saves boy's arm after shark attack'). This is followed by a brief summary of the News item in question and its page reference, for instant access.

The *presentation of the information* is all important here. It has to be interesting to arouse the reader's curiosity. It must give us a taste of what is to come in the longer feature article on the inside pages of the newspaper. The individual titbit of information accompanying each subheading must be well written. For example, note the following:

- 'An Irish surgeon battled yesterday to save the arm of an eight year old boy after it was bitten off by a shark in Florida.' – succinct and factual.

- The less formal register in the language of the Sports headlines – 'The Cats march on with ease', 'Tyrone the high kings of Ulster'. We learn the result of the matches, but we also look forward to the game being reviewed in more detail in the Sports section.
- The *regular features* of the newspaper are listed at the bottom of the page – again with their page references. (Personal Notices 2, World News 11 & 24, etc.)
- The weather is highlighted, as it is an important consideration in all our lives.

Short News Items

Brief snippets of local or world news are a common feature of the inside pages of our national and local newspapers. The headlines of these short news items can be very witty and are often based on a pun, for example see: 'Minister *nose* best', 'Poets are *all at sea*', or '"Thelma & Louise" jailed'. News snippets with a more serious or tragic content will have a factual headline: '6 electrocuted'.

Here is a selection of snippets I have read recently. I hope you find them both interesting and informative.

Minister nose best

The first month of the Special Savings Scheme has cost the Exchequer £1.5m on total deposits of £6m, Finance Minister Charlie McCreevy told the Dail.

He predicted the figures for June will be somewhat greater. 'My nose tells me there is a considerable amount of interest among all classes of people,' he said.
(*Irish Independent*, Thursday, 28 June 2001)

Poets are all at sea

SeaCat passengers will be treated to some of the country's poets reading their poems on sea crossings this summer.

As part of the SeaCat Irish National Poetry Competition, Dublin poet Enda Wyley, Moyra Donaldson from Newtonards, Co Down and Frank Galligan from Derry, will read on board from July 5.
(*Irish Independent*, 28 June 2001)

Thelma and Louise' jailed

Two women were jailed yesterday for acting out a Thelma and Louise-style fantasy. Cardiff Crown Court heard that Serina Gronow and Rebecca Wilson, both 22-year-old mothers of two, went on the rampage of theft and robbery in April this year after becoming fed up with their lives.

Sentencing them to two years and nine months each in prison, Judge Peter Jacobs described their offences as of 'considerable seriousness'. Wilson was also disqualified from driving for 18 months.
(*Irish Independent*, 28 June 2001)

Woman microwaved cat

LONDON – An English woman admitted in court yesterday that she had microwaved her pet cat after she was bitten by one of its fleas.

Ms Nadine Trewin (31), from Crawley, pleaded guilty to cruelty after she admitted microwaving ginger-haired Sasha, the Royal Society for the Prevention of Cruelty to Animals said. 'She claimed that the cat jumped into the microwave, she shut the door of the microwave and it switched itself on,' a spokeswoman said.

Ms Trewin, who the court heard had drunk a lot of beer and wine, took the cat out of the microwave and then threw it out of the window because it was hot. She was sentenced to two years' rehabilitation and banned from keeping animals for five years. – (Reuters)
(*Irish Times*, 24 July 2001)

Looking for a better world?

AMERICAN immigration officials were yesterday trying to determine how a group of 15 refugees, mostly Chinese nationals, reached the Kennedy Space Centre.

The eight women and seven men in their 20s were found on Friday sitting in shade on the edge of the Space Centre near the beach, said Calvin Burch, Kennedy Space Centre chief of security.
(*Sunday Independent*, 8 July 2001)

6 electrocuted

SIX teenage swimmers were electrocuted when they climbed out of a man-made lake in western Russia and unwittingly grasped a cable providing power to water pumps, officials in Moscow said yesterday.
(*Irish Independent*, 28 June 2001)

'First human clone 'likely soon'

The first human clone is likely to be produced 'very soon,' the American scientist leading the project said yesterday.

Brigitte Boisselier, the director of US company Clonaid, refused to be drawn on what stage the project was at. Two bills which would outlaw human cloning are being considered by the US House of Representatives, but Ms Boisselier said she believed cloning was a right.

(*Irish Independent*, 4 July 2001)

'Fattest' city loses weight

PHILADELPHIA was celebrating yesterday after its inhabitants lost an amazing 76 tons of fat.

Philadelphia had been named America's fattest city but after a 76-day diet and an exercise programme, it lost its crown yesterday to Houston, Texas, and slipped to third place, with Detroit, Michigan, second.
(*Irish Independent*, 4 July 2001)

Dennis the Menace is 50

LONDON – Britain's longest surviving comic villain, Dennis the Menace has celebrated his 50th birthday.

Dennis, who boasts a fan club of 1.5 million members, is famous for his spiky hair and striped jersey – the un-loveable horror who ultimately became the star of his own TV programme.

He first burst on to the pages of *Beano* in mid-March 1951 amid – according to editor Euan Kerr – fears among social workers that his atrocious behaviour might have a bad influence on children. – (PA)
(*Irish Times*, – 14 March 2001)

Sport

For the sports fans among you, here is a short informative piece from the *Sunday Independent* (8 July 2001) on Kilkenny hurling.

Nothing Compares to ...

Kilkenny hurling

The nickname. The Cats. Lithe, feline, cunning, sophisticated. As Michelle Pfeiffer so memorably put it in Batman Returns: 'Miaow.'
The jersey. Black and amber stripes. Instantly recongnisable. No other county has anything like it. ('Thank God for that.' Some may be inclined to retort.)
The stylists. Meagher, Langton, Keher, Fitzpatrick, Carey. A one-county culture club.
The All-Ireland senior titles. Twenty-six in all, two behind Cork and two ahead of Tipperary – both of which are much bigger counties with much bigger (in Cork's case, infinitely bigger) populations. Pound for pound, Kilkenny are hurling's leading county by a mile.
The rugby player. Ned Byrne won an All-Ireland in 1972 and was capped in the front row a few years later by Ireland. Okay, so he wasn't exactly Keith Wood, but who cares?
The school. St Kieran's College. Producers of great victories – they top the colleges' roll of honour. Producers of great players – Eddie Keher and Brian Cody and Nicky Rackard and new Tipperary starlet Eoin Kelly.
The pub. Eamon Langton's in John Street, the spiritual and spirituous home of Kilkenny hurling. Is there a better-known hostelry in the country? Good beer, better chat. Pity about the hordes of Dubliners it attracts on Saturday nights, though.
The man – can't remember his name just at the moment – who didn't make the Team of the Millennium when it was picked last year. He'd make it now.
The wonderful 1931 yarn. Many moons later, a Kilkenny forward who played in all three instalments of the epic All-Ireland encounter against Cork and distinguished himself by finishing with the combined total of one point spotted an acquaintance moving determinedly in the direction of a Kilkenny city pub. Are you off for a pint, the 1931 survivor enquired? 'I am,' the acquaintance replied. 'And it won't take me three hours to get it, either.'
The evangelists. Diarmuid Healy in Offaly, Ned Power in Wexford, Georgie Leahy in any number of counties. Spreading the hurling gospel.
The sheer good taste to avoid any truck with Gaelic football.
The Wexford joke. Well, there were lots of them, but we're particularly fond of the one dating from Wexford's dark night of the soul in the early 1990s. Near the bridge into New Ross, which separates the Model County from Kilkenny, there was a sign reading 'You are now entering a nuclear-free zone.' A bunch of local Kilkenny lads erected their own sign for the benefit of motorists crossing the Barrow into Wexford: 'You are now entering a trophy-free zone.'

Comment

- The headline 'Nothing Compares to …' acts as a prefix to each short, note, effectively separated by alternate light and bold typefaces.
- The black subheading 'Kilkenny hurling' leaves the reader in no doubt as to the subject matter of this article.
- The opening point, with its reference to Michelle Pfeiffer and the 'miaow' link to the Cats, sets the humorous tone for the rest of this piece.
- There are numerous facts on hurling in this article, but they are all varied, and therefore interesting even for the general reader or the non-hurling specialist, i.e. the reference to the school (St. Kieran's College) which produced 'great players', to the pub 'Eamon Langton's … the spiritual and spirituous home of Kilkenny hurling' and – to the final 'Wexford joke'.
- The mixture of humour and information works well. Bald statistics can be boring to read, but wit enlivens the writing. See the reference to 'The jersey' or 'the man – can't remember his name just at the moment … He'd make it now,' or the side swipe at Gaelic football in 'The sheer good taste to avoid any truck with Gaelic football.'

Feature Article [See page 99 opposite]

Comment

- This is a longer piece of informative writing, from the *Irish Times Magazine* supplement. Again, the presentation of the information is all important, but equally important is the image that accompanies it. The **text bubble** accompanying the illustration is the first thing to catch the reader's eye here. Even those with little French should get the joke of 'Où sont mes pantalons?', as the ladies are clearly not wearing any!
- **The layout of the text**, too, makes the information more appealing. The questions What? Why? How/Where? etc; in blue, focus our attention on the answers to these key questions, which provide the basic information required.
- **The question 'Body Language?'** at the end of the article, doesn't appear to have any immediate relevance in terms of learning French but it is humorous, and reminds us of how important gestures are to the French, especially in conversation. It also recalls the visual image at the top of the article, with its cartoon text insert: *Où sont mes pantalons?*
- **The register is informal** and the tone is light and humorous throughout, demonstrating how information, when conveyed humorously is more attractive to the reader, and encourages us to read on.

so you want to ...
SPEAK FRENCH

Où sont mes pantelons?

WHAT? Being able to converse *en français*, using more than that much-loved invitation to become bedfellows.

WHY? Spoken in over 25 countries, it is also seen as many as the language of love, guaranteed to make your intended beau's toes curl.

HOW/WHERE? The Alliance Française, the French Institute in Dublin, has classes from beginner to advanced levels, with the chance to obtain recognised certificates in specialised courses such as Business French and Legal French. Private tuition is also available. And for those who wish to add a little bit of culture to their education, the institute also provides themed workshops in French cinema, French literature and French media.

HOW MUCH? The beginner/intermediate/advanced courses start from £185 for an eight-week course at four hours a week, to £300 for a 16-week course also at four hours a week. Specialised courses run at £270 and private tuition starts from £30. For further information call 01-6761732 or check their website www.alliance-francaise.ie

BODY LANGUAGE? Like many cultures, the French use a variety of gestures in conversation.
Check out http://french.about.com/homework/french and click on French Gestures to discover how useful your limbs are in speaking French.

(Kusi Okamura, *Irish Times Magazine*, 14 July 2001)

Reviews

- Film
- TV (Documentary series)
- Book reviews
- TV (Sport)
- Dance
- Comment

The following is a selection of reviews taken from the *Irish Times* and *Hello* magazine. A *review* takes the language of information a step further by adding the element of *appraisal and/or criticism*. We are certainly given points of information – facts and detailed references – but the reviewer also gives his/her own opinion/judgement of the item under review. Reviews create an expectation of a particular event that makes it more interesting.

Read the following reviews carefully and the comments which follow. You may be asked to write a review in your exam, under Question A or B in the section on comprehending, or as a longer writing task in the composing section.

Film

NEW FILM RELEASES by Lórien Haynes

FILM OF THE WEEK

Jurassic Park 3
Released 20 July – Certificate PG

When a film franchise churns out its second sequel, it's usually time to avoid the cinema, yet *JP3* is really rather good. This is partly due to the top quality cast of Sam Neill, William H Macy, Tea Leoni and Alessandro Nivola. But the unusually meaty storyline, peppered with even more amazing-looking dinosaurs, also plays its part.

Sam Neill resumes his role as wry palaeontologist Dr Grant. Unsurprisingly, he has zero desire ever to see a velociraptor again. However, due to his floundering research budget, he's bribed by a couple (Leoni and Macy) to do a fly over the prehistoric-infested Isla Nublar to celebrate their wedding anniversary.

With his research assistant in tow (Nivola), Neill soon discovers this journey is a trick. When the plane crash lands, it emerges that the couple are actually

estranged and have hired Neill and crew to try to find their eight-year-old son, who's lost on the island after a parachuting accident.

Once all the dispensable mercenaries have been munched, *JP3* really kicks off, and it's action all the way home as we follow the team as they search for the boy and try to escape before they become hors d'oeuvres themselves.

As well as the great special effects, there's a host of funny lines throughout the film which help to make it a real winner.

This is one blockbuster that'll really get the adrenaline pumping.

(*Hello*, 24 July 2001)

Comment

This is a well paced, interesting review. The language register is informal, the language itself energetic ('churns out', 'meaty', 'peppered with') and suited to the general readership. There is a tone of wry humour throughout this piece, 'Unsurprisingly, he has zero desire ever to see a velociraptor again', 'Once all the dispensable mercenaries have been munched, *JP3* really kicks off.' The review, coupled with the action clip from the movie, certainly makes one want to see the film.

TV (Sport)

Raising Tennis Aces: The William's Story
(Channel 4, 9pm)

Filmed over two months at the family's home in Florida, this is a fascinating portrait of Venus and Serena Williams, who stunned the tennis world by slamming their way to Wimbledon wins last year. Decide for yourself if the sisters are really as arrogant, aloof and ambitious as legend suggests.

What are sisters Venus and Serena Williams really like?
Raising Tennis Aces: The Williams's Story. Channel 4, 9pm.

(*Hello*, 24 July 2001)

Comment

Any of you who are tennis fans, or just like watching Wimbledon, will recognise the phenomenal success of these two ladies. The programme note combined with the photo grabs our attention, and certainly entices us to watch it. The language of this short review is informative, but there is also an implied criticism in the final sentence, 'Decide for yourself if the sisters are really as arrogant ...', and in the question posed under the photo, as a footnote to the review, 'What are sisters Venus and Serena Williams really like?'

TV (Documentary Series)

Spaced out with Sam Neill: BBC 1, 8.30pm

Space
BBC1, 8.30pm

Movie star Sam Neill takes viewers on a journey round our galaxy in this new documentary series. Astonishing imagery is promised, and you won't be surprised to learn that state-of-the-art computer graphics are used. The series meets scientists and experts who are exploring some of the most profound questions about space, including a man who recreates exploding stars in his laboratory, and another who is developing biospheres to enable humans to live on Mars.

(*Irish Times Magazine*, 21 July 2001)

Comment

Sam Neill – movie star attracts our interest immediately. The illustration shows him apparently holding a star in his left hand. This provides a visual link to the one word title *Space*, and we are intrigued at the prospect of 'touching' the stars. 'Sam Neill takes viewers on a journey round our galaxy' in this new documentary series. 'Astonishing imagery is promised' and the reviewer's reference to 'state of the art computer graphics' is sure to grab the attention of a young audience of viewers, as well as the more serious adult science buffs. Note the clever use of a pun in 'Spaced out with Sam Neill' immediately below the photo.

The Arts – Dance

CANDOCO

Meeting House Square, Temple Bar, Dublin Thurs/Fri 10pm Adm free, but collect tickets in advance from 18 Eustace St (01-6772255)

Since they were founded in 1991, British dance company Can*do*Co has re-defined the nature of dance by combining able-bodied and disabled performers. When I last saw them in October 1994, I was astonished at what could be achieved partnering someone in, or from, a wheelchair. Now they bring to Dublin two contrasting pieces for two performances at Meeting House Square, Temple Bar as part of Diversions. The first, *I Hastened Through My Death Scene to Catch Your Last Act*, is choreographed by Javier de Frutos, who was inspired by the works of Tennessee Williams, so naturally it is an intense dance drama about loneliness, longing, sexuality and frustration. *Sunbyrne*, in contrast, consists of eight short pieces by US choreographer Doug Elkins, set to a series of upbeat tunes by the Beach Boys and Talking Heads, which blend humour, eroticism and physical dexterity.

(Carolyn Swift, *Irish Times*, 'The Ticket' supplement, 11 July 2001)

Comment

It is the photograph that draws us to the text here. It is a powerful and original image of dance, with the wheelchair central to the movement. We read the text in order to find out more about its role in the performance. We learn that the British dance company Can*do*Co has 'redefined the nature of dance by combining able-bodied and disabled performers'. The reviewer admits to having been 'astonished at what could be achieved partnering someone in, or from, a wheelchair'. Even if we never actually experience this dance drama for ourselves, the written review combined with the stunning photographic image is more than mere information. It enlarges our knowledge and our perception of the art of dance.

Book Reviews

Comment

Each of the following book reviews informs the potential reader of the basic plot and background to the book, and the context in which it was written. They were included in a whole page of book reviews in the *Irish Times* under the heading of 'Summertime Books', and are, of necessity, brief. The original review of the book is summarised and paraphrased in one statement, i.e. book 2 'Hourihane paints the big picture and, said Tom Humphries (reviewer), nobody has coralled that inchoate sense of loss into a more coherent picture than Ann Marie Hourihane.'

N.B. Look up 'inchoate' in your dictionary!

• Top: painter Sidney Nolan's image of Ned Kelly – brought to life in Peter Carey's new novel.

She Moves Through the Boom by Ann Marie Hourihane (Sitric, £7.99)
Are we losing as much as we're gaining in Boomtime Ireland?

From the Liffey Valley shopping centre to a wine café in Mullingar, across motorway mania and through the world of the elite creche, Hourihane paints the big picture and, said Tom Humphries, nobody has coralled that inchoate sense of loss into a more coherent picture than Ann Marie Hourihane.

True History of The Kelly Gang by Peter Carey (Faber, £10.99 in UK)
This was the dream ticket: the prodigal son of Australian fiction takes on his native country's ultimate folk hero Ned Kelly – and it worked. Dead at 26 but known far and wide for his careering around the scrub in his bizarre metal armour – with just a chink for the eyes – the myth of Kelly, the easy-going rebel, is undermined here. Mary Morrissy's verdict: not perhaps the most engaging of Carey's novels, but one of his most intriguing.

Sushi for Beginners by Marian Keyes (Poolbeg, £6.99)
Leap into the world of a Dublin woman's magazine, cleverly evoked by Keyes at her very best.

"Anyone who's inclined to thumb their noses snootily at this type of fiction should think again. This one's a page-turner," said Bernice Harrison.

(*Irish Times*, 30 June 2001)

The Internet

>site of the week

www.webbyawards.com

The fifth Annual Webby Awards are truly the Oscars of the internet and the winners of this year's prestigious contest will be announced on July 18. The website for the awards shows all the nominations, and profiles some of the best and most cutting-edge websites on the world wide web

'The Internet is like a library' (*ECDL3*, by Brendan Munnelly)

Comment

I have absolutely no doubt that you are more familiar with this source of information, than any other. However, did you know that sourcing information on the Web can be made more interesting if you check out the 'Web Watch' series in the *Irish Times*, or the 'Navigator' or 'NetWatch' page of the *Irish Independent*'? Here are some websites from the 'Navigator' page of the *Irish Independent* (9 July 2001) that are interesting and certainly informative.

www.bookcrossing.com

The concept for this website is brilliant, depending on how attached you are to your books. It proposes to make the world one big library. How? Well, you register a book with the site. You'll receive a BCID number, which you stick onto the inside cover along with the URL (Address) of Book Crossing. You then leave the book in a public place, for example on a park bench, in a café, or on a bus for someone else to find. Finding one could be like finding a piece of hidden treasure. The person that picks it up is encouraged to read it, pass it on and register his/her experience at Book Crossing. A great way to share a book that you love with somebody, or of sourcing books that you might be interested in reading but otherwise might not have heard about.

www.playlouder.com

Such is this website's commitment to the outdoor music festival that it held a virtual 2001 Glastonbury in place of this year's cancelled real event. Highlights are available for viewing on the site and you can sift through a map of the festival grounds and enter the backstage area, dance tents and so on. **Playlouder.com** is a pretty fantastic place to source music trivia. Under it's Latest News heading you can read some well-written snippets about how Radiohead, who the site describes as "Oxford's grimmest four", are to appear in an episode of *Southpark* and how Kate Winslet is aiming for a Christmas number one with a ballad she's recorded.

www.movie-mistakes.com

Summer is a time for the release of blockbuster movies. If you tend to avoid the latest round of over-hyped, studio-produced dross and need proof that the $135 million price tag of *Pearl Harbour* was not money well spent you should check out this site. It lists movie gaffes like continuity mistakes regarding wardrobe, set design, etc. made in popular films. An extensive list of mistakes follows its *Pearl Harbor* entry begging questions about the craft of filmmaking. If you're one of the many people who have seen *Lara Croft: Tomb Raider*, did you, like one user of this site, spot the make-up coming off her arm to partially reveal Angelina Jolie's Billy Bob tattoo during one scene?

Napster sings once again

Napster, the online song-swapping service, has struck a landmark deal that will enable users to legitimately access music from artists including Moby, Badly Drawn Boy, Tom Jones and Paul Oakenfold.

The agreement involves UK and European music industry associations giving the controversial website access to music from 150 labels. The music will be available on Napster's revamped fee-paying service.

Napster is currently trying to fight off a court challenge for copyright infringement from 'the big five' music companies, including EMI and Sony, and hopes the new membership service will help its case. Previously, visitors to the site were able to download MP3 versions of hit records free of charge.

www.napster.com

SECTION C COMPOSING

Engaging with the Text

To the student

The Department of Education and Science has issued a CD-ROM to all schools, on the revised Leaving Certificate English syllabus. It is intended as a resource for teachers and students. Included in the CD-ROM is a section entitled 'Assessment Advice for Students'. You might ask your teacher to download this document for you, or you can visit the Department website at <http://www.irlgov.ie/educ>.

The following is a key point on Paper 1 from this document. I have already referred to it, in Unit 1 Section C (Planning the Essay), but it bears reading again. (The italics are mine.)

> When you come to shaping your composition in Section II – Composing, **think of all of the texts on the paper as a resource for your information**. They may contain information that will be useful to you; they may give you some ideas to use in your own composition. They may help you to clarify your own ideas on the topic you have chosen. But remember that it is not *necessary* for you to refer to any one of the texts on the paper. You are free to base your composition on your own store of knowledge, ideas and experience.

You can see that although it is not a requirement that you refer to the texts on the exam paper, it is worth bearing in mind that, where it is appropriate, engagement with the texts can make a positive impact on the whole process of composition. The texts are a resource, which you can use to your advantage. For example, the CD-ROM mentioned above contains student essays from the sample paper issued by the Department. **When candidates made good use of the text to which the composition referred, the examiners rewarded them for doing so**. It makes sense. The revised syllabus encourages you to use the text in a creative remodelling sense, i.e. to *imitate the model* of the reading text in your composition.

Remember too, that the word 'text' includes the *rubrics*, i.e. the *task* outlined in bold print on the exam paper, as well as the *quotation* from the text itself, and the *visual* text, i.e. the illustration that accompanies the text. All of these, *in addition to* the written text, are intended as a resource for the student.

Example: Here is a short extract from a student composition entitled 'Write a narrative,

Man and Nature 109

real or imagined, based on one or more of the images in Text 3.' (Sample paper, Ordinary level) Included is the image (D) chosen by the student.

> 'We walked slowly behind the horse-drawn carriage with the remains of the late, great president inside. It was a cold, miserable November afternoon. The trees along the roadway were dead and limp. Very much like the large crowds that paved the way for the funeral. As I look around, a lot of faces seem familiar. Now with tears though instead of smiles. They all had paved the way, two days earlier. It was a surprisingly warm November day. The suns rays bounced off the back of my neck as we stood in the convertible waving at the numerous spectators. I don't know how the secret service men kept from sweating as they jogged at each corner of the car for at least two miles.
>
> The people's flags along the way dance in the warm breeze. They were overcome with pride for their country and their president. Shouts of enthusiasm echoed through the streets, bouncing of the dull lifeless buildings.'
>
>
> *Family members at the funeral of President John F. Kennedy*

Comment

You can see why the candidate here was rewarded for 'creative remodelling using material from Text 3', and also for 'clear focus maintained throughout the narrative'. There is a direct relation between the written description of the event and the photo image – although the description itself is the student's own.

Let's now look at the seven composition titles for Unit 3, in terms of possible ways of *engaging with the text* to which each refers. We will also consider the language genre(s) appropriate to the task in each one. As in previous Units, the essay titles reflect the format of the exam.

The Titles – Theme: Man and Nature

Exam Task: Write a composition on *any one* of the following. Each composition carries 100 marks. The composition assignments below are intended to reflect language study in the areas of information, argument, persuasion, narration, and the aesthetic use of language

Essay 1
Language of Persuasion/Information

'... everybody keeps their house tidy and clean, but look at what we do to the streets.' (Bernie Walsh, Text 1)

> Write an article for your school magazine or local newspaper in which you attempt to persuade your readers of the value of recycling and reducing waste.

Note on genre(s): Your main purpose here is to persuade, but also to inform, your readers. Shape your article in a manner that would be appropriate to the register of a school magazine or local newspaper. Remember that you are either writing for an audience of your peers (school magazine) or for a more general readership (local newspaper). If you are writing for your peers, the register can be more casual, and informal. Use the language of information to make concrete references to any facts or statistics in relation to the provision or non-provision of recycling facilities in your area.

Engaging with the Text

• Begin by engaging with the spirit of the task set, printed in bold type on the exam paper i.e.

'...everybody keeps their house tidy'. Think about the contrast being made between the way in which we look after our houses, and 'what we do to the streets'.

• Make use of the actual rubrics of Text 1, i.e. the headline in bold at the top of the article, 'They've got it sorted!' as a possible starting point. For example, you might ask your readers 'Have you got it sorted?' imitating the format of a magazine headline. You can then go on to persuade them of the need to tackle the problem of waste and waste management in your area.

• Read all of Text 1 again, highlighting those points of information regarding the overall involvement, or non-involvement, of the various government agencies in this task. *Quote* from Bernie Walsh's own experience in setting up Sunshine Recycling. Use the text's statistics and figures to support your own points.

• You could use the example of Bernie Walsh herself, in order to highlight/underline her commitment to getting the community involved in recycling, and as a shining example of one individual who has made a difference.

Essay 2
Language of Narration/ Aesthetic Use of Language/ Information

'I knew ... that I belonged to steep places like this one.' (Text 2)

> Write a series of diary entries depicting the experience of a climber, adventurer or explorer in those moments/days leading up to the end of an expedition.

Note on genre(s): Diary entries are private texts. You may address the diary in the third person singular, i.e. Dear Diary ... or you may simply put a date and time/location at the top of the entry. Diary entries can be descriptive/narrative, relating to actual events, moments of importance or crisis in a person's life. They can be reflective, confessional or expository (commenting on or explaining or accounting for a particular event). The entries may vary in length.

Clearly the language of narration and the aesthetic use of language are appropriate to this task, but so too is the language of information, in terms of presenting the facts, times, locations, equipment, etc., involved in the events being related.

Engaging with the Text

- Engage with the spirit of the task set, printed in bold type on the exam paper. Think about the *kind* of person who 'belongs' to 'steep places'. How and why do they belong there? Reflect on possible answers to those questions, in your first diary entry perhaps. Remember, however, that diary entries are immediate – the story narrated on the day. You could create some mystery by leaving out a few days in the sequence of entries, i.e. 6 Monday, 7 Tuesday … 11 Saturday … What *happened* during those missing days? Will you tell the reader, or leave it to them to imagine what may have occurred? Your last diary entry should have a sense of completion, of the adventure/expedition/climb being over, the challenge accomplished, but also a sense of the challenges to come. Read the final paragraph of Text 2 for inspiration here.
- Make use of the actual rubrics of Text 2, i.e. 'Just then the polar sun …' as a possible opening to your first diary entry. Concentrate on just how you might *feel* at a point of crisis. Describe those feelings honestly, employing some of the actual language of the text perhaps. For example, 'We'd been on the move 25 hours without sleep … I tackled the toughest pitch of my career … I took stock of the sublime craziness of my position.' The aesthetic use of language is very appropriate to this task. See Unit 5, Section B Focus on … the Aesthetic Use of Language for examples of this genre, but there are many of them in Text 2.
- Read the text again from the point of view of narrating events. Underline the series of steps taken by the mountaineering team in order to reach the summit. The

language of narration is appropriate here, as is the language of information in terms of recording the details of the climb/expedition/adventure you choose to write about. See the text as a springboard for your own creative writing.

- The visual images accompanying Text 2 are particularly spectacular. Make use of them in your diary entries. Try describing the sensations you experienced while clinging to a sheer cliff wall, or sleeping in a tent on the wall, as described in the text.

Essay 3
Language of Argument/ Information/ Narration/ Aesthetic Use of Language

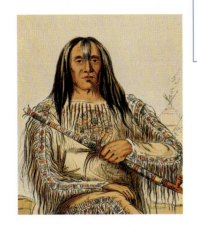

'This we know: the Earth does not belong to man; man belongs to the Earth ... All things are connected.'
(Text 3)

You have been elected Youth President of Greenpeace. Write the first speech you would make to its members. Your speech should begin with the above quotation from Text 3.

Note on genre(s): Your purpose here is to impress upon the members of Greenpeace your commitment to caring for the Earth and its resources, and to argue strongly for a continued respect for the planet we all inhabit. Be mindful of your audience. They are your peers. However, you should shape your points in a thoughtful register that reflects the seriousness and formality of the occasion. You will be presenting a personal viewpoint, as a young adult, but you should avoid inappropriate language, i.e. slang, or an off-hand, too casual delivery. The language of argument is most appropriate here, but there is also scope for the aesthetic use of language, and for elements of the languages of information and narration, in terms of recounting your own experience, and knowledge gained on your road to the presidency of this prestigious organisation.

Engaging with the Text

• Make use of the rubrics of the task set, in bold print. You are making a speech. Use a form of address suited to that occasion, i.e. Mr Chairman, Madame Chairperson, Fellow members, Honoured guests, Ladies and Gentlemen ... You have chosen me to represent you and I am humbled and grateful for your trust ...

• Locate the quotation 'this we know: The Earth ...' in Text 3, and read the section of the text to which it refers. Model your speech on some or all of the sentiments/philosophy inherent in the text.

• Read all the text again, noting the *connections* Chief Seattle makes all the time between *Man and Nature*. Underline or highlight these for possible inclusion in your own speech. Look too at how the Native Americans perceived the 'white man', and his early destruction and abuse of Nature's riches and her wildlife.

• Quote from the text to support your own points. Make use of the eloquence of the language, to enhance your own writing. The text is an excellent example of the aesthetic use of language. Imitate its lyrical, descriptive style in expressing your own aims and aspirations as the newly elected Youth President of Greenpeace.

Essay 4

Language of Narration/ Information/ Aesthetic Use of Language

'I tackled the toughest pitch of my career.' (Text 2)

Write an account of your experience of a difficult challenge you had to face in the last year. The account is to appear in a popular magazine for older teenagers.

Note on genre(s): Writing an account of your experience clearly lends itself to the language of narration. Maintain a clear focus on the task set, i.e. you are telling the story of this 'difficult challenge', and how you faced up to it. The narrative will be directed at an audience of older teenagers. Be aware of that. This will determine the language register, e.g. thoughtful/sensational/ humorous, etc. Address them directly – as your peers. Focus on the *informing task* also, in terms of relating the actual situation that gave rise to the challenge, and the people/events involved. You may shape your writing in the convention of a magazine – separate paragraphs, headings, subheadings, or adopt an alternative approach. In terms of describing how this challenge affected you personally and intellectually, you could also employ the aesthetic use of language.

Engaging with the Text

- Read the opening lines of Text 2, noting the use of *dialogue* to establish the background/origin of the challenge. Try beginning the account of your own experience in this way, with a short exchange between you and one or two other people.
- Alternatively, use the rubrics of the essay title itself – 'I tackled the toughest pitch of my career' as your opening sentence. The word 'pitch' has a number of meanings. You can 'pitch an argument', for example, or salespeople talk about 'making a pitch', in terms of advertising or selling their product. Its use in the composition title suggests a *challenge*, a very difficult task (the toughest pitch). However, you might consider writing about a challenge that involved you having to *persuade* another person or persons to your point of view.
- Study the visual text – the images for Text 2. How can you use them to inspire your own writing? The pictures depict the extraordinary nature of the challenge that faced these climbers, the difficulties and dangers they encountered, but also the excitement. Can you visualise a similar situation? Can you paint word pictures for the reader of your experience?
- Study the mood of the climbers in Text 2, in the paragraph beginning 'The final push to the summit

began ….' Could you use the edginess, the tension of these moments of drama and danger, in recounting the final moments of your own challenge? Look at the language of the text at this point, i.e. 'An edgy mood infected us.' 'What's it like out? I grumbled to Mark ….' Look at the last section of Text 2 for examples of the aesthetic use of language, 'I felt the toll of our 23-day climb settle into my body.' Can you re-create those sensations in your own writing? Study the last paragraph 'My eyes locked onto those unexplored ramparts …' and make use of it, to shape the conclusion of your essay – the sense of more challenges to come, ones that are perhaps even more difficult.

Essay 5
Language of Narration/Aesthetic Use of Language

Write a short story prompted by one or more of the images in Text 4.

Note on genre(s): This type of composition allows for an imaginative, personal response, with a broad parameter of possibilities in terms of purpose, audience and register. However, the examiner will expect some engagement with the visual image you have chosen and a sense of story, i.e. a beginning, middle and end. Your narrative should have a central character and a defining moment. Be careful to create a sense of atmosphere, a setting, time and place. The language registers can mix and mingle here, but the language of narration, and the aesthetic use of language, should dominate because they are important features of narrative writing.

Engaging with the Text

- Before choosing your image, study all of them carefully, making some short notes on the individual features of each. Look at the foreground and the background in the picture. Consider the location, time, season, and the angle at which the photo was taken. 'Read' the image closely.

Man and Nature 117

• Read again the extract from a student composition, (with the accompanying photo of the funeral of John F Kennedy) featured at the beginning of this Unit. It is a good example of a candidate engaging imaginatively with the *visual text* i.e. creative remodelling.

• If you choose *more* than one image, be conscious of the need to establish a *link* between them in your composition. Contrasts and comparisons between two or more images could prove interesting and compelling. Maintain focus on the visual images at all times, however, for consistency and clarity.

Essay 6
Language of Argument/ Persuasion/ Aesthetic Use of Language

'How can you buy or sell the sky, the warmth of the land?'

Write a personal essay inspired by the text of Chief Seattle's reply to President Pierce in Text 3.

Note on genre(s): A personal essay allows for a broad range of interpretation and language genres. There is scope for a mix of genres, but you should perhaps decide from the outset, which genre will predominate. For example, Text 3 itself is a wonderful example of the aesthetic use of language, and this essay provides you with the opportunity to explore the theme of Man's relationship with Nature in a similar way. For example, you might write about the beauty of Nature, and extend the image to the whole universe, and the place of our small planet in the larger scheme of things. The questioning tone of the composition title 'How can you …' may suggest some issues for *debate* (language of argument) in terms of the value we place on our Earth and the environment. In addition, you may wish to *persuade* your readers that the answer to the title question has to be 'No', that we can't 'buy' or 'sell' the Earth, which we have inherited from our ancestors. Your purpose here is a personal exploration of the essay title, for an audience of thoughtful intelligent beings of any age group. The *register* will be dictated by the tone you adopt from the outset, i.e. serious, philosophical, lyrical, persuasive, etc.

Engaging with the Text

- Make use of the introduction, the rubrics and the footnote to Text 3, in order to focus your mind on the theme of your essay. Refer to Chief Seattle's background, and to the history of his relationship with the US government at the time.
- Read the whole text again, underlining those sections that appeal to you most. Quote from them to support your own thoughts on this topic. You might refer to those parts dealing with 'Birthright' and 'Respect', and model your response on the philosophy they advocate.
- Text 3 reads as a series of lyrical, poetic images of the sacredness of the Earth, and the Native American's intimate relationship with it. The tone is respectful; therefore the *register* is formal and solemn, appropriate to the occasion. You might try to emulate this tone and language register in your own writing. Note how Chief Seattle repeats some phrases, which become a form of chant throughout this text. For example, '... this earth is sacred to my people.' '... this land is sacred to us.'

'This we know.' 'I am a savage and I do not understand.' 'All things are connected.' Normally you should avoid repetition – but the examples from this text are not needless repetition. They serve to remind the reader of the importance of the message. In this sense, the repetition has value and meaning.

- Consider the pride and dignity of the Native Americans, how they were debased and humiliated by the 'white man', and robbed of their lands and culture. Perhaps you could make a link between them and the film *Dances with Wolves* by Kevin Costner, which chronicles one white man's experience of the Native American way of life, and of his integration into their culture.

Man and Nature

Essay 7
Language of Narration/ Information/ Aesthetic Use of Language

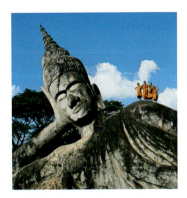

Engaging with the Text

This is my life ...'
Imagine that you are in the world of one of the pictures in Text 4. Tell your story.

Note on genre(s): The composition allows for an imaginative interpretation of any one of the images in Text 4. There is a broad range of possibilities of purpose, audience and register. The task here is similar to that posed by Essay 5.

You are expected to tell a *story* – so the predominant genre should be the language of narration, with elements of the aesthetic use of language – as it is frequently encountered in narrative writing.

• Choose your visual text carefully. As with Essay 5, jot down some notes that occur to you as you study each image. Remember that your task is to imagine that you are in the world of the photo, so you must picture yourself as part of it. In order to decide your place and role in this world, read the images carefully. Study the background and foreground of the picture, and any unusual features.

Read again the extract from a student composition, (with the accompanying photo of the funeral of John F. Kennedy) featured at the beginning of this Unit. It is a good example of a candidate engaging imaginatively with the visual text i.e. creative remodelling.

• Remain focussed on the particular direction and purpose of your story. Be mindful of audience and register. Are you writing for a local newspaper, or for a magazine for older teenagers, perhaps? The language register you use will be dictated by your choice. If your purpose is to interest a young audience, then the register may be informal, with scope for humour, a sensational story even, whose purppose is to amuse and/or shock the reader.

SECTION D LANGUAGE SKILLS

Efficiency of Language Use 3

> '... students' knowledge and level of control of the more formal aspects of language, e.g. register, paragraphs, syntax, punctuation and spelling, should be given particular attention in the new syllabus.'
>
> (From the preface to *The Leaving Certificate English Syllabus*, Dept. of Education and Science)

To the student

Units 1 and 2 stressed the importance of acquiring skills in the 'management and control of language to achieve clear communication'. In this Unit, we will be looking at the notion of **register** and also at **expanding your vocabulary base** with synonyms. In **punctuation** we will be concentrating on *apostrophes*, and in spelling on some combination vocabulary/spelling exercises.

Register

In Unit 2 we looked at the importance of *syntax* i.e. the organisation of words within sentences, and sentences within paragraphs. Equally important in your writing is the awareness of correct register, i.e. using the appropriate language for the task set. In very simple terms, register is concerned with the *kinds* of words we use when we write. The *Oxford Concise Dictionary* defines it as 'Each of several forms of a language (colloquial, formal, literary, etc.) usually used in particular circumstances.' By now, you should be very familiar with the words

- Purpose
- Audience
- Register

– PAR 3, you might call it!

   Being aware of purpose and audience will focus your attention on the written task, and help you to decide on the most appropriate *register*. For example, let's look at how the reporting of a single news event, like the imaginary visit of an Irish president to France, might be written in different registers in the print media.

Formal Register – Language of Information
For example: A diplomat reporting to the government.

> The President, Mrs. Grace McNamara met with President Dupont, and members of his cabinet at the Elysée Palace this morning. Following brief talks on the European Conference on Global Warming to be held later this year (which Ireland and France will co-host), the President was taken on a brief tour of the palace and grounds, before being escorted back to her car. A visit to the Irish Embassy is scheduled for this afternoon. Later today, at a reception to be held in her honour, President McNamara will meet members of the Irish business community living in Paris.'

Informal Register – Language of Narration/Information
For example: A journalist writing for a popular magazine or tabloid newspaper.

> President McNamara, resplendent in a lilac silk creation by Irish couturier Carlton, appeared relaxed and smiling on meeting the French President, Jean Dupont, at the Elysée Palace this morning. He too, looked 'très chic' in an expensively cut silk suit of pale grey. No prizes for guessing Armani there! They exchanged greetings on the steps of the palace, and obliged the many photographers and reporters looking for a photo op. President McNamara was then given the prerequisite tour of the palace before being whisked off for an engagement in the Irish Embassy - and a welcome cup of 'real' tea, no doubt! She'll greet the business heads this evening over a sumptuous feast of lobster, 'moules' and cartloads of vintage Dom Perignon at a reception in the opulent Ritz hotel. *Vive la Presidente!* As the French might say.

Formal register – Language of Argument/Persuasion
For example: A political commentator writing for a serious newspaper of magazine.

> The arrival of President Grace McNamara to Paris this morning coincides with a little publicised Conference on Women's Rights in Third World Countries taking place this weekend. Apart from attending the usual expensively dressed diplomatic functions one wonders if the concerns of the impoverished and largely powerless women of Africa and Asia will impact at all on the president's visit. Should Mrs. McNamara insist on making a brief appearance at the Conference, in order to boost the morale of these women and raise awareness of their plight? This is the important question which needs to be addressed.

Activity 1

Writing on the **same theme**, but in a variety of **genres** is excellent practice in using a 'register appropriate to the task'. Try writing the opening *paragraph* (50–70 words) of any one of the following topics in *two* or more genres. Here is an example of how you might approach Topic 1 – *Hair is Everything* – in each of the five genres.

1. Language of Information
The latest survey to emerge from the Students Union in U.C.D. has found that up to one third of male students now favour the Mohican cut as their preferred hairstyle.

2. Language of Narration
He wasn't sure about the Mohican now. It had looked fine in the hairdressers but that was before Deirdre had seen it....

3. The Language of Argument
Is it possible, one asks, that a seemingly highly intelligent and well-educated youth can be so easily influenced by fashion when it comes to deciding something as basic as a haircut?

4. The Language of Persuasion
Be yourself. Don't allow the fashion gurus to dictate your lifestyle or the manner in which you wear your hair – if you have hair, that is.

5. The Aesthetic Use of Language
Gone the cascading corn coloured locks, the silky tresses of eighteen years of washing, and crimping and brushing ....

Topics

1. Hair is everything
2. Violence in the twenty-first century
3. The drug culture
4. Love is …
5. Obsessions
6. The holiday from hell
7. Reality TV
8. Sexism
9. Ageism
10. Chat rooms

Vocabulary

By expanding your vocabulary base you gain 'management and control of language to achieve clear communication' (Assessment Criteria). More importantly, you gain power as a writer because you have more choice in terms of conveying meaning, which is not a problem if you have a range of expression. At Leaving Cert. level you are expected to have acquired a broad ranging vocabulary, so that you can discuss the often complex concepts and ideas inherent in the syllabus. Relying on the colloquial language of everyday conversation is not enough. For example, a student's description of events within a particular text as the 'goings on' is clearly inadequate to the task! As a student of English *language* - as well as literature - you need to take a real interest in increasing your word power. At the very least you must be businesslike in your pursuit of the *right* words for the particular context, by consulting a dictionary or thesaurus. **'Language appropriate to the task**' is a key phrase in the revised syllabus for Paper 1.

Activity 1 Better Words

Here are some sentences, based on students' work, which are vague and colloquial in expression. Replace the italicised words and phrases by choosing better ones from the box below, and rewrite the sentence. You may have to adjust the syntax slightly.

1. The *idea* that *runs through* the writing is 'Man and Nature.'
Rewrite as: _____

2. The *things said* by the *man* in Text 2 are *about* drugs abuse.
Rewrite as: _____

3. The writer in Text 1 is *writing about* a *huge amount* of ideas.
Rewrite as: _____

4. He disagrees *about* other poets *around the time*.
Rewrite as: _____

5. They *looked into* the problem of bringing the equipment to *the top of* the mountain.
Rewrite as: _____

6. She *jumped at the chance* to take *the job* at Thornfield, and so *off she went*.
Rewrite as: _____

7. He *kind of* wanted to *make the first move*, but he *wasn't able to*.
Rewrite as: _____

8. In the *part* of the play where Lear *gives away* his land, Goneril and Regan sweetalk him into giving them the biggest *bit*.
Rewrite as: _____

9. The poet *goes over the top* when he *talks about* how angry he was *about* the policeman.
Rewrite as: _____

10. Lear couldn't *stand the way in which* the daughters treated him, and for allowing himself to be such a *pushover*.
Rewrite as: _____

> capable of doing so, dividing up his kingdom, points made, with his contemporaries/other contemporary poets, seized the opportunity, the dominant theme throughout, the manner in which, the text/article, Act 1, Sc. 1, intended taking the initiative, exploring/describing/expressing, conveying/hoisting/carrying,

> take the position, flattered by, is exaggerating, toward (the policemen), the summit, related to/refer to/concerned with, various themes/a variety of concepts/ideas, left immediately, explored/researched, the largest portion, describes, couldn't tolerate, so easily fooled/duped/fooled so easily.

Activity 2 Synonyms – Words of Similar Meaning

Hardly any two words are exact synonyms. In English we have a wide-ranging vocabulary, which often gives us two or more words to choose from in any given circumstance. However, usually only one is correct, in terms of the **context** in which it is used.

Circle the correct word, in terms of its meaning according to the *context*, in each of the following sentences:

1. I like a newspaper which presents its news so that it's easy to ____
   (a) eat (b) drink (c) swallow (d) digest (e) chew
2. The television programme brought _____ to people the seriousness of the problem
   (a) near (b) home (c) thought (d) true (e) real
3. Many problems in Dublin _____ from the shortage of reasonably-priced accommodation
   (a) grow (b) blossom (c) harvest (d) raise (e) stem
4. The debate didn't come up to Denis's _____
   (a) promises (b) hopes (c) wishes (d) expectations (e) desires
5. Many monasteries in Ireland were _____ more than nine hundred years ago.
   (a) discovered (b) made (c) invented (d) founded (e) started
6. The _____ against the motorway plan caused the Council to think again.
   (a) shouting (b) noise (c) outcry (d) screaming (e) whistling
7. A system that allowed only buses and taxis in the centre of the city would solve the traffic problem at a _____
   (a) stroke (b) cut (c) swing (d) blow (e) flash
8. Ireland is a fisherman's _____
   (a) heaven (b) paradise (c) daydream (d) castle (e) joy
9. The interviewer asked the minister some very _____ questions.
   (a) examining (b) exploring (c) searching (d) exercising (e) hunting
10. Some people are against informality in class but personally I _____ the idea.
    (a) clap (b) cheer (c) shout (d) applaud (e) enthuse

Note: If you have the time you should try using the remaining synonyms also in sentences which demonstrate their correct usage. For example, from sentence 1:
1. The truth is hard to <u>swallow</u> sometimes.

2. He's still *chewing* over their latest proposal.
3. She may yet have to *eat* her words.
4. He's *drinking* in her every word at the moment.

Punctuation
Apostrophes
To the student
The problem with apostrophes is that we often put them in when they are not needed, and leave them out when they are. Not to worry. Shopkeepers, signwriters, restaurant owners, etc. often get them wrong too.
e.g. Hot dog's for sale.
    Tomato's, carrot's and potato's sold here.   Crisp's, Snack's, etc.,
    This sports centre and it's pool will be closed over Christmas.
So, what's the rule? It's quite simple, really. There are only two kinds of apostrophes. One indicates *possession* or ownership of something; the other indicates a *contraction* or abbreviation – i.e. a letter or letters left out of a word:
Possession
Tom's car is a write-off.
Patricia's book is a bestseller.
Contraction
Tom's thinking of buying a new car. = *Tom is* thinking …
Patricia's writing another book. = *Patricia is* writing …

Exercise 1
Rewrite the following sentences using apostrophes to indicate either possession *or* contraction. Place 'P' or 'C' in a bracket at the end of each sentence to indicate which one it is. Use sentence 1 as an example.
1. Hes not very co-operative.
   He's not very co-operative. (C)
2. Theyre off to America tomorrow.
3. Whos making the dinner?
4. Tracys friend stole her boyfriends car.
5. Johns a terrific golfer. Hes hoping to turn pro.
6. I hope Marias dad can cope.
7. Did you know the Dublins boardwalk opened yesterday?
8. Slanes in Co. Meath, isnt it?
9. Jack will be here tomorrow.
10. Michaels a really nice man.

Question: When should I *not* use an apostrophe?
Answers:
• With *plural nouns* – where no possession is indicated. For example:

My *friends* all love Robbie Williams.
His *ideas* are excellent.
Her *parents* disapproved.
But … 'My friend's parties are brilliant' is correct, when the parties 'belong to' just one friend.

- However, look at where you place the apostrophe if you are speaking about *more* than one friend i.e. *all* your friends, perhaps. 'My friends' parties are brilliant.'
- So, for *singular* possession we add 's, and for *plural* possession we add the apostrophe *after* the s – s'.
- With possessive *pronouns* i.e. his, hers, its, ours, yours, theirs. For example:

That's his problem   That's *his*   }
That's their pizza   That's *theirs*}   N.B. NO Apostrophe!

One of the most frequent mistakes occurs with '*it's*' used *incorrectly* to indicate the possessive form of 'it'. For example:

It's kennel is clean. WRONG
Its kennel is clean. RIGHT
It's a really nice day. RIGHT because here 'it's' is a contraction i.e. it is.
'It's' can also be used for 'it has', as in 'It's been a good day.'

Exercise 2 Contractions

This is a simple exercise in both punctuation and spelling. Practice is the key here. Contract or abbreviate the following, using apostrophes:

N.B. The apostrophe replaces the 'o' in 'not' e.g. 'does not' becomes 'does*n't*'

I have ------   You cannot ------
They are not ------   We should not ------
We are not ------   They are ------
They have ------   Who is …? ------
You have ------   There is ------
She was not -----   I will not ------
She does not ------   I could not ------
They have not ------

Exercise 3 Spot the Apostrophe Disasters!

This exercise requires concentration and care. Write the *correct* version of these sentences:

1. My dogs a Corgi. Whats your's?

Answer:_____

2. Samantha said the guitar was her's.

Answer:_____
3. Thats Tom's drink. Your's is over there.
Answer:_____
4. Seasons greeting's from Heatons.
Answer:_____
5. Countrie's like Ireland are popular tourist attraction's.
Answer:_____
6. Gary's trip to London with Bobs brother is off.
Answer:_____
7. Wexford welcome's you to it's Opera Festival.
Answer:_____
8. Students expectation's today are either too high or too low.
Answer:_____
9. Nelson Mandela is one of South Africas greatest leader's.
Answer:_____
10. The plan collapsed in it's final phase.
Answer:_____

Spelling

Students often misspell just one or two letters in a word. In this combination vocabulary /spelling exercise, write the word first, then check with your *dictionary* to see if you are correct:

Exercise 1

From the meaning given, fill in the gaps and identify the words:
1. A collection of literary works, excerpts or passages. ANTH _ _ _ GY
2. Something transient or short lived. EPH _ _ ERAL
3. To protest by refusing to deal with or buy from a person or organisation. _ OYCO _ _
4. Blatant and outrageous. FLA _ _ ANT
5. The quality of understanding and sympathising. _ MPATH _
6. Independent of others. AUTON _ _ OUS
7. Smug, aggressive belief in the superiority of one's country, sex, race or cause. CH _ _ _ INISM
8. Forcefully convincing, authoritative, to the point. COG _ _ T
9. Conversational, informal speech or vocabulary. COLLO _ _ IAL
10. Doubtful and uncertain. DUB _ _ _ S

A score of seven or over in this exercise would indicate that you already possess a good vocabulary, and have few problems with spellings, but don't be disappointed if your score was less than that. The really important point in vocabulary building and spelling is the follow up. **Double-check your words/spellings in a dictionary and memorise them**.

Exercise 2

Try writing each of the ten words from Exercise 1 in the four different types of sentences – Statement, Question, Order, Exclamation.

N.B. Keep them brief and simple. Your aim here is to *learn the spelling* and to memorise the meaning and use of the word.

For example: boycott

Statement: They're going to *boycott* the meeting.

Question: Is Tom going to *boycott* the meeting?

Order: *Boycott* that premises immediately.

Exclamation: Not a *boycott*, surely!

Note: Using these new words in your speech and writing is the best way to ensure that they will become part of your vocabulary. Remember that if you learn even *ten new* words a week, in one school year, you will have acquired 360. It's worth considering just what a difference that might make to the quality of the answers you write in your exam, not to mention the benefits of such an enlarged vocabulary in your life after Leaving Cert.

Exercise 3

Here are your ten most frequently misspelled words for this Unit. You will use these constantly in your writing so it is important to spell them correctly. Use the same strategy for learning them, as outlined in Units 1, and 2.

WORD	SPELL IT	SHORT SENTENCE
1. LITER<u>A</u>TURE	--------------	--------------------------------------
2. IMAG<u>E</u>RY	--------------	--------------------------------------
3. EXTREM<u>E</u>LY	--------------	--------------------------------------
4. TRULY (no 'e')	--------------	--------------------------------------
5. P<u>O</u>ETRY	--------------	--------------------------------------
6. DOM<u>I</u>NANT	--------------	--------------------------------------
7. QUALIT<u>IE</u>S	--------------	--------------------------------------
8. APP<u>R</u>ECIATE	--------------	--------------------------------------
9. RESPONS<u>I</u>BILITY	--------------	--------------------------------------
10. AP<u>P</u>AR<u>E</u>NT	--------------	--------------------------------------

Unit 4 Power and Powerlessness

SECTION A COMPREHENDING

Introduction
This section contains four texts on the general theme of *Power and Powerlessness*, including a set of pre-reading exercises on Texts 1–3.

Text 1
'Ain't I a Woman?' is the keynote question in a speech made in 1851 by a former slave, Sojourner Truth. The text is a mixture of the languages of **information**, **argument** and **persuasion**, but it is predominantly persuasive, in terms of its power and conviction in relation to women's rights.

Text 2
'Turning good people to evil acts' is an article from the *Irish Times* (2 June 2001) in which Derek Scally narrates the background to a new German film *Das Experiment* loosely based on the 1971 Stanford Prison Experiment. The text is **narrative**, but also **informative**. It raises questions about the ethics of the original experiment, which in turn will provoke **argument** and discussion on the nature of power, and the possible abuse of power.

Text 3
'The Power of Writing' is an edited version of an article from the *National Geographic* magazine (August 1999). It is a mix of the languages of **narration** (the story of Wei Jingsheng) and of **information**. It also contains elements of the **aesthetic use of language**.

Text 4
This is a series of photographs depicting the general theme of *Power and Powerlessness*. There is no written text. You are required to study the images and respond to them in a variety of ways and genres.

Text 1 Ain't I a Woman?

Stage 1 Pre-Reading

Task: In pairs, or small groups, discuss some or all of the questions below for ten minutes, then report back to the class.
OR
Your teacher may choose to discuss the questions with the whole group. The important thing is that you *take notes* of other students' points, for possible use later in one of the *composing* tasks in Section C.

Questions

1. Discuss the words 'power' and 'powerlessness' in as broad a context as possible. In which areas of life are they both evident? What does it mean to 'empower' oneself?
2. Try to define, in real terms, what it is to be a young woman and/or a young man at the beginning of the twenty-first century. What is your perception of your place and role in life? Are you powerful or powerless?
3. Are women's rights as much an issue today as they were in 1851? Or, indeed, in your mother's or grandmother's youth?
4. '... those men who value power above life, and control over love.' (Maya Angelou, 'Wouldn't take nothing for my journey now')

How true is this statement, do you think? What does the word 'power' mean in terms of politics and/or relationships between the sexes? How does it manifest itself?

Stage 2 Reading

Ain't I A Woman?

Sojourner Truth was born a slave in Ulster County, New York, her name simply Isabelle. After years of abuse from several different slaveowners, she gained her freedom on July 4, 1827. In 1843, Isabelle left her slave name behind and became Sojourner Truth. For the rest of her life, she worked tirelessly to end slavery and to help the many freed blacks who were suffering.

Sojourner travelled constantly, speaking and singing at meetings all over the Northeast and Midwest. In 1850, she published an account of her life, Narrative of Sojourner Truth. Sojourner continued to work until her death in 1883; in her last great campaign, she fought to secure land in Kansas and Missouri for freed slaves who were living in misery on the East Coast.

Sojourner Truth gave her famous 'Ain't I a Woman?' speech at the 1851 Woman's Rights Convention in Akron, Ohio. No formal record of the speech exists, but Frances Gage, a celebrated anti-slavery fighter and president of the Convention, recalled Sojourner's words. 'Ain't I a Woman?' made a great impact at the Convention and has endured as a classic expression of women's rights.

Several ministers attended the second day of the Woman's Rights Convention, and were not shy in voicing their opinion of man's superiority over women. One claimed 'superior intellect,' one spoke of the 'manhood of Christ,' and still another referred to the 'sin of our first mother.'

Suddenly, Sojourner Truth rose from her seat in the corner of the church.

'For God's sake, Mrs. Gage, *don't* let her speak!' half a dozen women whispered loudly, fearing that their cause would be mixed up with the abolition of slavery.

Sojourner walked to the podium and slowly took off her sunbonnet. Her six-foot frame towered over the audience. She began to speak in her deep, resonant voice:

'Well, children, where there is so much racket, there must be somethin' out of kilter. I think between the Negroes of the South and the women of the North – all talkin' about rights – the white men will be in a fix pretty soon. But what's all this talking about?'

Sojourner pointed to one of the ministers. 'That man over there says that women need to be helped into carriages, and lifted over ditches, and to have the best place everywhere. Nobody ever helps *me* into carriages, or over mud puddles, or gives *me* any best place. *And ain't I a woman?*'

Sojourner raised herself to her full height. 'Look at me! Look at my arm.' She bared her right arm and flexed her powerful muscles. 'I have plowed, I have planted, and I have gathered into barns. And no man could head me. And ain't I a woman?

'I could work as much, and eat as much as a man – when I could get it – and bear the lash as well! And ain't I a woman? I have borne children and seen most of them sold into slavery, and when I cried out with a mother's grief, none but Jesus heard me. And ain't I a woman?

The women in the audience began to cheer wildly.

She pointed to another minister. 'He talks about this thing in the head. What's that they call it?'

'Intellect,' whispered a woman nearby.

'That's it, honey. What's intellect got to do with women's rights or black folks' rights? If my cup won't hold but a pint, and yours hold a quart, wouldn't you be mean not to let me have my little half-measure full?'

'That little man in black there! He says women can't have as much rights as men, 'cause Christ wasn't a woman.' She stood with outstretched arms and eyes of fire. 'Where did your Christ come from?'

'*Where did your Christ come from?*' she thundered again. 'From God and a woman! Man had nothing to do with him!'

The entire church now roared with deafening applause.

'If the first woman God ever made was strong enough to turn the world upside down all alone, these women together ought to be able to turn it back and get it right-side up again. And now that they are asking to do it, the men better let 'em.'

'Obliged to you for hearin' me, and now old Sojourner ain't got nothing more to say.'

(Recommended for further reading: *Journey Towards Freedom*, by Jacqueline Bernard, an inspiring account of Sojourner Truth's life. Copyright © 1994 Historical Documents Co.)

Question A

(i) In your opinion, what are the most persuasive elements of the speech given by Sojourner Truth, in this text? Support your points by reference to the text. (30)

(ii) Write a paragraph (100–150 words) in which you comment on the appropriateness of the title 'Ain't I a woman?' (20)

Question B

'After years of abuse from several different slave owners, she gained her freedom on July 4, 1827.'

Sojourner Truth (Isabelle) was approximately thirty years old at this time. Imagine that you are this woman and write an account of your feelings on this momentous day in your life. You may write it in the form of a *journal* entry, or as an *interview* given perhaps much later in your life, in which you recount your memories of that day to the author of your biography. It is most important that you write as though you were Sojourner Truth.   (50)

Text 2   *Turning good people to evil acts*

Stage 1   Pre-Reading

Task: In pairs, or small groups, discuss some or all of the questions below for ten minutes, then report back to the class.

OR

Your teacher may choose to discuss the questions with the whole group. The important thing is that you *take notes* of other students' points, for possible use later in one of the *composing* tasks in Section C.

Questions

1. How do ordinary people change when they are given power over others?
2. Discuss instances of the *abuse* of power that you may have encountered in your own lives or in the lives of your friends, or in society as a whole.
3. Discuss ways in which power can be a force for good.
4. What circumstances in life cause people to feel powerless?

Stage 2   Reading

Turning good people to evil acts

A new film based on a psychology experiment which echoes the Nazi past is controversial in Germany, writes **Derek Scally**

There are certain questions Germans do not like to confront. But a German film has packed cinemas there by asking just such a question: how do ordinary people change when they are given power over others? *Das Experiment*, directed by Oliver Hirschbiegel, is loosely based on one of the most famous experiments in the history of psychology, the 1971 Stanford prison experiment. The study illustrated theories of obedience and aggression arising partly from the history of Germany under Nazi rule: that ordinary people could carry out antisocial acts if put in extreme situations.

'Power is an aphrodisiac,' says Prof. Philip Zimbardo, who led the 1971 experiment. 'When you give ordinary people a position of power, their behaviour changes dramatically. The study shows how easy it is to turn good people into devils.' His experiment began with a classified advertisement in a Californian newspaper: 'Male college students needed for psychological study of prison life' read the ad, promising participants $15 a day for up to two weeks.

From more than 70 applications, researchers used interviews and personality tests to eliminate candidates with a criminal record or any noted psychological problems. In the end, the number was whittled down to 24, and arbitrarily divided into two groups of nine, one of prisoners and one of prison wardens, with six stand-bys.

The experiment began without warning on the morning of August 17th, 1971, when police cars drew up in front of the houses of the nine applicants selected to be prisoners. Researchers had arranged with the local police to have them arrested, and as surprised neighbours looked on, the equally surprised prisoners were handcuffed and whisked away in police cars with wailing sirens.

At the police station, they were fin-

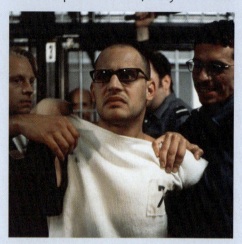

ger-printed and put in holding cells until they were brought, blindfolded, to 'Stanford county jail' – in reality, the basement of a University building. Researchers had redecorated the basement to resemble a prison, installing cell-doors, boarding up all windows and removing all clocks. Unknown to the prisoners and guards, they also installed hidden microphones and cameras.

The nine men selected to be guards were given no training, but told they were to maintain order in the prison in whatever way they felt necessary. Their first task was to strip-search the prisoners and issue them with the prison uniform, a numbered smock resembling a potato sack which each prisoner wore at all times, with no underwear. Prisoners also wore heavy chains on their right ankles to remind them at all times that they were captives.

The first day of the experiment began quietly, but trouble broke out on day two when prisoners used their beds to barricade themselves into their cells, taunting the guards – who retaliated by blasting the prisoners with ice-cold, carbon-dioxide fire extinguishers.

Then they broke into the cells, stripped the prisoners and threw the leaders of the disruption into solitary confinement.

The guards then began to devise psychological games to break prisoner solidarity and prevent a recurrence. For their part, researchers began to blur the line between role-playing and reality. They convinced a local priest to visit the prisoners and talk to them as if they were real criminals.

Researchers also set up a make-believe parole board to hear parole applications from prisoners. After only four days, the prisoners no longer believed that they were free to leave at any time. They no longer perceived their incarceration as an experiment.

After five days, the guards had won control of what had been a spirited group of middle-class college students and reduced them to blindly obedient prisoners.

The guards stepped up their harassment during the night, unaware of the researchers' surveillance. They forced prisoners to clean toilets with their bare hands, while one particularly sadistic guard made them participate in homosexual role-playing.

What began as an experiment had, in less than a week, descended to psychological warfare. Fearing for the safety and sanity of the prisoners, the psychologists ended the experiment, after just six days.

The researchers later organised a meeting between the former prisoners and guards. Emotional prisoners asked the guards why they had been so sadistic; the guards replied that anyone in their situation would have done the same.

Without realising it, they were echoing the words used to describe the Nazi colonel Adolf Eichmann: that 'normal people can take ghastly actions'.

'I began to feel that I was losing my identity,' one prisoner said afterwards. 'I don't regard it as an experiment or a simulation because it was a prison run by psychologists instead of run by the state. I began to feel that ... the person that had decided to go to prison was distant from me ... I was 416. I was really my number.'

Thirty years on, Zimbardo has mixed feelings about his experiment. It was ethical because there was no deception, he claims. However, it was also unethical 'because people suffered and others were allowed to inflict pain and humiliation on their fellows over an extended period of time'.

www.prisonexp.org

(*Irish Times*, 2 June 2001)

Question A

(i) 'Power is an aphrodisiac.' Based on your reading of the whole text, how true is this statement, in terms of the 1971 Stanford Prison Experiment? Support your points by reference to the article. (20)

(ii) In your opinion, why did those selected to be the guards behave with such cruelty? (15)

(iii) Write a brief commentary on the term 'psychological warfare' as you encountered it in this text (100–150 words). (15)

Question B

Imagine that you were one of those people who took part in the Stanford Experiment. You are being interviewed by a local TV station, immediately following the event. You have been asked to briefly describe the worst moment of the whole experience. Write the text of your reply (150–200 words). (50)

Text 3 *The power of writing*

Stage 1 Pre-Reading

Task: In pairs, or small groups, discuss some or all of the questions below for ten minutes, then report back to the class.

OR

Your teacher may choose to discuss the questions with the whole group. The important thing is that *you take notes* of other students' points, for possible use later in one of the *composing* tasks in Section C.

Questions

1. What do you think has been the *purpose* of writing, from the very beginning? Why did people feel the need to write things down?
2. What kinds of writing have the most effect on people's hearts and minds, and why?
3. How much *power* has the written word, in the twenty-first century? Try to concentrate on real examples.
4. Can you foresee a time when the written word will no longer have any power or influence? Discuss the circumstances/conditions that might bring this about.

Stage 2 Reading

THE POWER OF *Writing*

Handmaiden to history, chronicler of the mind and the heart, writing is humankind's most far-reaching creation, its forms and designs endless. During the U.S. Civil war, for example, a union soldier's letter home was written in two directions to save scarce paper. In India an artisan made such limitation a virtue by inking this article's bylines on grains of rice (above). And the words you are now reading were written on a computer equipped with some 800 styles of type. Yet the purpose of writing remains unchanged: to convey meaning, whether playful, mundane, or profound.

Chinese state security officers arrested Wei Jingsheng, an electrician, on March 29, 1979. Among his major crimes: writing essays arguing for democracy. Wei, who would spend 18 years in jail and become a prominent symbol of the power of the written word, was placed in the Beijing detention centre.

Chinese authorities feared Wei, recognising that writing has an almost magical power: Words on paper, created by ordinary citizens, have overthrown governments and changed the course of history. So powerful is writing that the beginnings of civilisation and history are most often defined as the moment cultures develop it. Anthropologists can only paint outlines of ancient societies that had no writing; a written record provides the human details – history, belief, names and dates, thought, and emotion.

No other invention – perhaps only the wheel comes close – has had a longer and greater impact.

From its beginning as recordkeeper to its transformation into one of humanity's most potent forms of artistic and political expression, writing reveals the power of innovation.

But the story of Wei proclaims writing's greatest power – its ability to move hearts and minds.

His cell measured four and a half feet by nine feet. Authorities kept the light on at all times. No one, not even his guards, was allowed to speak to Wei, and he was not permitted to read or write. His requests for paper and pencil were ignored.

Wei drew characters in his head, taking pride in his mental calligraphy. One morning, more that two years after he was placed in solitary confinement, his food tray included a ballpoint pen – another prisoner or a sympathetic guard had smuggled it to him.

Wei began to write letters to his family on the rough sheets he had for toilet paper. Guards found these letters and demanded to know where he have hidden the pen. Wei refused to say. After guards failed to find the ballpoint, which Wei had tied to a string and lowered inside the hollow metal rods of his bed, the warden ordered him to another cell. Wei sneaked the pen with him.

In the winter of 1981, after holding Wei in solitary confinement for more than two years, authorities realised they could not keep him from writing. They gave him a new ballpoint pen and better paper and authorised one monthly letter to his two sisters and brother.

In these letters Wei discussed art and offered advice on romance. He was forbidden to write about being beaten or deprived of sleep. He also could not mention his malnutrition, headaches, heart pain, diarrhoea, and rotting teeth.

Wei never knew if his letters were delivered. He told his fiancée to find someone else, not knowing that she had already married.

Many of his letters were to China's leaders, whom he criticised. As punishment, authorities sometimes took away the pen they had given him, but other prisoners took apart pens, often stolen from guards, and smuggled them to Wei.

'Why write?' the guards asked. 'No one will ever see your letters.'

In late 1993 authorities told Wei he would be released. They were trying to win international support for acting as host of the year 2000 Olympic Games. Wei, who had been in jail for nearly 14 years, refused to leave his cell without copies of his letters. 'They've been lost,' he was told.

'You can find them,' he replied. Twelve hours later, the warden returned with his letters.

Six months later, after the Olympic Committee rejected China, Wei was re-arrested. State security seized his papers but failed to find the computer disks onto which his letters had been transcribed.

After Wei's re-arrest in 1994 he was placed back in solitary confinement. Two walls of his new cell were glass, so constant monitoring could ensure he did not write. For more that six months not even his family knew whether he was dead or alive. In 1997 a book of Wei's letters, *The Courage to Stand Alone*, was published in the United States. Tong Yi, who transcribed his letters, had been sentenced to two and a half years in a labour camp. After serving this time, during which she was sometimes beaten, she was allowed to leave China.

In the summer of 1997 I read *The Courage to Stand Alone* and follow news accounts of Wei's treatment. He is frequently beaten and denied adequate health care. I fear he will die soon.

Then in November 1997 the Chinese government releases Wei. Largely in response to international pressure, and puts him on an airplane to the United States. A few weeks later I meet him at his office in the Centre for the Study of Human Rights at Columbia University.

I am startled by Wei's smile and how well he looks. He explains that he can eat only soft food until his teeth are fixed, and sips tea as we talk.

'Writing,' he says, 'kept me alive. I sometimes thought about a letter for a week before writing anything. It's something that you must do even if you do not have the leisure of being in prison. To write, you must work methodically, forming your thoughts and prompting other people to think as they read. Writing requires work at both ends. That's what makes it special.'

Wei plans to write a book about the experiences, feelings, and ideas he could not put in his letters, which he knew would be read by prison officials.

'I wish I could read it in Chinese,' I say.

Wei laughs. 'You can learn,' he says, writing 友谊.

'It means "friendship,"' Wei says.

(*National Geographic*, August 1999)

Question A

(i) What aspects of the power of writing emerge most strongly for you from the above article? Support your points by reference to the text. (30)

(ii) Based on your reading of the experiences of Wei Jingsheng, write a short account of the kind of person you imagine him to be (150–200 words). (20)

Question B

'In the winter of 1981 ... could not keep him from writing. ... authorised one monthly letter to his two sisters and brother.'

Imagine that you are Wei Jingsheng in prison. You are writing your monthly letter to your family. You have been instructed to keep it brief (150–200 words). Write out the text of the letter. (50)

Text 4 Images of Power and Powerlessness

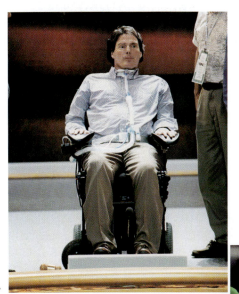

1.

2.

3.

4.

5.

142 Write Now!

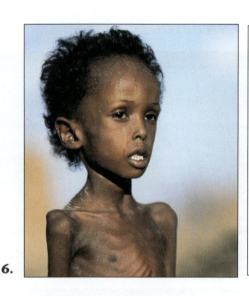

... and they can't wait for ever.

GOAL, PO Box 19,

Dun Laoghaire, Co. Dublin

Telephone: 01-2809779

6.

As in previous Units, Text 4 requires a different approach. You are asked to 'read' a series of images, with usually no written text. You should examine each of them closely before attempting to answer the questions. Be especially attentive to detail in the photographs – the setting, the personalities/characteristics of people and/or objects, their gestures, facial expressions, and body language. Look, too, at colour, light and shade, and for the underlying message inherent in each image, in terms of the overall theme of *Power and Powerlessness*.

Question A
(i) Study all of the images closely. In your opinion, which one represents power most strongly? Give reasons for your answer. (20)
(ii) (a) Choose an image that best captures a sense of powerlessness. Explain your choice. (15)
   (b) Write a description of the image you have chosen in (a) above. (15)

Question B
Write a letter to a national or local newspaper outlining your views on the plight of the powerless in our world today. Suggest some ways in which we might, as a nation, help to empower them. (50)

Sample Answer

Text 1: Question A (i)
In your opinion, what are the most persuasive elements of the speech given by Sojourner Truth in this text? Support your points by reference to the text. (30)
In your answer to Question A (i), focus on the following:
- Underline and number each point made by Sojourner Truth, in this speech.
- Count the number of times she asks the question 'Ain't I a woman?'
- Base your opinion on a close reading of the text.
- Support your points by specific references/quotations.
- Concentrate on the words 'persuasive elements'.
- Read the background information on Sojourner Truth, which introduces her speech.
- There is no specified word limit, but it would be wise to keep to 200–230 words.

The most persuasive element of this speech is the manner in which Sojourner Truth addresses her audience. She speaks without fear and with absolute passion and conviction. 'Ain't I a Woman?' becomes the keynote question in her address, and its repetition, her mantra. She persuades her audience of women's right to equality by quoting from the harsh reality of her own experience. 'Look at me! Look at my arm.' 'I have plowed, … planted, … gathered into barns. And no man could head me. And ain't I a woman?'
She bore the lash and the agony of seeing her children sold into slavery, but none of it diminished her sense of her own dignity and power as a woman. These hardships clearly persuade her audience of her absolute right of equality with men. 'The women in the audience began to cheer wildly.' She doesn't hesitate to challenge 'That little man in black there!' He says women can't have as much rights as men, 'cause Christ wasn't a woman.'

'"Where did your Christ come from?" she thundered (again). "From God and a woman! Man had nothing to do with him!"' Proof of the persuasiveness of this argument is evident in the reaction of the audience: 'The entire church now roared with deafening applause.'

Sojourner Truth's final appeal is to 'these women together' to bring about change, and her parting shot is a warning to the men! 'And now that they are asking to do it, the men better let 'em.'

SECTION B FOCUS ON ... THE LANGUAGE OF PERSUASION

> 'By persuading others, we convince ourselves.' (Junius, Letters 1769)
>
> 'Persuasive texts are dramatic forms in which feelings, images and words are so shaped that they manipulate the emotions and imaginations of the audience in a way that brings about agreement and consent.'
> (*Draft Guidelines for Teachers of English*, Dept. of Education & Science)

To the student
You may find it difficult to distinguish between the language of argument and the language of persuasion because they are quite similar. For example, they both have the purpose of convincing someone, of influencing another's opinion or belief. However, they each use very different techniques and approaches. The language of argument, in the main, will rely on logic and reason alone, while persuasion will use the **art of suggestion**, of **sensation** and **manipulation**. The language of persuasion can appeal to our emotions and our reason at the same time. It can urge, encourage, influence and convince a person to the stage where he or she is won over to a certain point of view or course of action. In our everyday lives, the language of persuasion, particularly in media, politics and advertising, has enormous influence and power. So you are already aware of the language of persuasion and its place in our lives. That knowledge can be built on and developed.

The Revised Syllabus
The Department guidelines tell us that 'students should encounter a range of texts which have a *persuasive function*, e.g. political speeches, advertising in all media, satiric texts, some forms of journalism.'

Note: The most immediate source of the language of persuasion is 'advertising in all media'. Look at the billboards on bus stops and walls on your way to school. Listen to ads on the radio, and take note of the catch-phrases that accompany TV, Internet and cinema adverts. What about the newspapers and magazines you buy? Study the way in which these use the language of persuasion to encourage you to read an article or an advertisement. For example, they are usually accompanied by a striking image, photo or cartoon. The ***visual*** is all-important in the print media, and on TV and radio; the music jingles, startling images and sound effects are the persuasive factors.

In terms of **speeches**, you need look no further than your nightly news or panel discussions on TV. Politicians make speeches all the time – especially during elections when their sole aim is to persuade the 'everyman' to vote for them. 'Here is a party political broadcast on behalf of the ... Party', is a familiar announcement. At the time of the referendum on the Nice Treaty (June 2001) the Commission took out full page ads in all the national newspapers, urging us to vote 'Yes'. (On this occasion, however, the persuasive tactics did not work, as the nation rejected that particular treaty!)

Satire is an important feature of the language of persuasion. Martyn Turner, political cartoonist for the *Irish Times*, is particularly clever in capturing the essential point of a current controversy and satirising it. You will find one of his cartoons in this section.

Here are some examples of the language of persuasion, with commentaries on their individual characteristics.

Advertising in the Media

Let's begin with some examples of advertisements from the print media. Their primary purpose is to persuade, of course, so they are an excellent source of the language of persuasion.

Irish Times Jobs (see page 146)

Comment

This advertisement for a website (ireland.com/jobs) is a good example of a combination of text and image that focuses on a particular target audience, i.e. young semi-professional or professional people, already employed who may be thinking of changing jobs. This focus determines the content and form of this advertisement. For example:
- The headline at the top 'We take the work out of building your career' draws the eye immediately to the image of two young people in the water, who are clearly relaxed, smiling, attractive and *not* working. The implication is that they have time/money to enjoy their leisure activities. So the connection between text and image is an immediate and persuasive one.
- The subhead located just above the picture 'Reach for the top ...' appeals to the ambitious young person, who intends to progress further up the professional ladder.
- The same target audience will obviously be persuaded by the 'dynamic website' indicated in the text note. The word 'dynamic' is carefully chosen, because the advertiser knows that his audience will identify with this word, and equate it with 'energy' and 'drive'. The young couple in the water reflect this image because they look active and energetic and therefore ready for the job opportunities that will come their way – if they log on to ireland.com/jobs, that is!
- Both the textual and visual elements of this ad are good examples of the language of persuasion, directly targeting a particular age and market.

John Rocha at Waterford Crystal

Comment
This is an excellent example of how the language of persuasion can employ the visual medium of a dramatic image, with virtually no text. For example:
• Look at how the contrast between black and white works so dramatically in this advertisement. The darkened profile of John Rocha – the designer, does not impinge upon the most important element of the photograph – the glass, but rather highlights it. We are drawn to its beauty and elegance, directed by the gaze of the designer himself.
• Note how he holds the glass lightly – almost on the tips of his fingers, so that we can observe all the delicacy of the glass. The man and the glass are the only objects in this picture and they are framed, appropriately, in black.
• The minimalist text is an excellent example of the language of persuasion used sparingly and well. There are just three bare but eloquent statements, linked by the three verbs: *designed* (by John Rocha); *crafted* (by Waterford); *made* (to be used).
• The collaboration between John Rocha and Waterford is clear, but it is interesting to note that Waterford Crystal previously had a reputation for producing very expensive and exclusive crystal. The inference in 'Made to be used', is that *this* range of glasses is being produced for a more main stream market, and is more affordable. This is an important message in terms of persuading the reader to buy the product.
• The Waterford Crystal logo at the bottom right hand corner of the picture fits neatly into the frame, and again reinforces the image of excellent design in combination with superb craftsmanship.
• Overall, this is a very persuasive and artistic advertisement, with the visual element being the predominantly persuasive factor.

Kerrygold Horse Show
Finally, here is an example of a witty, short advertisement for the Kerrygold Horse Show. It is a lovely example of the language of information combined with persuasion, and flavoured with humour.

Comment
The information element is immediately apparent, top and bottom of the ad with its distinctive green logo of horse and rider and the words 'Kerrygold Horse Show' clearly visible. These ensure that the all-important dates and booking details will be read either way. However, it is the cartoon and its caption that draws us initially to this ad, and persuades us to read on. For example:
• The gentleman in red is getting a well deserved slap from the enraged lady in pink, who's having none of his advances. The horse looks a little alarmed at the proceedings too and

WEDNESDAY AUGUST 8TH
~ SUNDAY AUGUST 12TH
Ticket Bookings:
Tel: 01 2407213 / www.rds.ie

Four faults

It's chic, it's cheek.

Passionately fashionable and

fashionably passionate.

It's thoroughly thoroughbred,

well heeled and well bred.

It's fabulous, it's fun,

it's sport at its best.

And it's definitely not cricket.

WEDNESDAY AUGUST 8TH
~ SUNDAY AUGUST 12TH
Ticket Bookings:
Tel: 01 2407213 / www.rds.ie

probably agrees with the rider being given a penalty of 'four faults' for his behaviour!

• 'It's chic, it's cheek' is a witty pun on the incident depicted in the cartoon.

• 'Passionately' is an appropriate word too, for the encounter between the rider and the lady. The inversion of 'passionately fashionable and fashionably passionate' is clever and does not take itself too seriously.

• 'It's thoroughly thoroughbred, well heeled and well bred' pokes fun at the possible snobbery associated with the event, but again, the indignity of the characters behaviour in the cartoon dilutes any possible seriousness.

• 'It's fabulous, it's fun, it's sport at its best' reads like a jingle and is entertaining and light-hearted.

• The last line 'And it's definitely not cricket' is very witty, and it plays on the well-known adage 'That's not cricket', meaning that certain behaviour is not sporting or appropriate – as depicted in the cartoon. At the same time it highlights the Horse Show, and implies that *it* may be much more fun. Persuasion through humour works very well here.

Political Speeches

Now let's look at three very famous speeches, each of which reflects two predominant features of the language of persuasion, i.e. eloquence and an ability to move one's audience. Note too that, although these extracts are primarily examples of the language of persuasion, different genres blend here – the aesthetic use of language, narration, and strongly worded argument.

I Have a Dream Today!

So I say to you, my friends, that even though we must face the difficulties of today and tomorrow, I still have a dream. It is a dream deeply rooted in the American dream that one day this nation will rise up and live out the true meaning of its creed – we hold these truths to be self-evident, that all men are created equal.

I have a dream that one day on the red hills of Georgia, sons of former slaves and sons of former slave-owners will be able to sit down together at the table of brotherhood.

I have a dream that one day, even the state of Mississippi, a state sweltering with the heat of injustice, sweltering with the heat of oppression, will be transformed into an oasis of freedom and justice.

I have a dream my four little children will one day live in a nation where they will not be judged by the color of their skin but by content of their character. I have a dream today!

I have a dream that one day, down in Alabama, with its vicious racists, with its governor having his lips dripping with the words of interposition and nullification, that one day, right there in Alabama, little black boys and black girls will be able to join hands with little white boys and white girls as sisters and brothers. I have a dream today!

I have a dream that one day every valley shall be exalted, every hill and mountain shall be made low, the rough places shall be made plain, and the crooked places shall be made straight and the glory of the Lord will be revealed and all flesh shall see it together.

This is our hope. This is the faith that I go back to the South with.

With this faith we will be able to hew out of the mountain of despair a stone of hope. With this faith we will be able to transform the jangling discords of our nation into a beautiful symphony of brotherhood.

With this faith we will be able to work together, to pray together, to struggle together, to go to jail together, to stand up for freedom together, knowing that we will be free one day. This will be the day when all of God's children will be able to sing the new meaning – 'my country 'tis of thee; sweet land of liberty; of thee I sing; land where my fathers died, land of the pilgrim's pride; from every mountain side, let freedom ring' – and if America is to be a great nation, this must become true.

(An extract from 'I have a dream today!' Martin Luther King Jnr, 1929–68)

Comment

This is perhaps the best known and most quoted address Dr King made. He delivered this speech before the Lincoln Memorial on 28 August 1963 as the keynote address of the march on Washington, D.C., for civil rights. The television cameras allowed the entire nation to hear and see him plead for justice and freedom. Mrs Coretta King once commented, 'At that moment it seemed as if the Kingdom of God appeared. But it only lasted for a moment.'

Let's consider some of the techniques of the language of persuasion that Dr King employed in his speech.

- **Rhythm and repetition of language**: frequently, this revolves around a memorable phrase, for example 'I have a dream'. Even if you have never read this speech, you will know the refrain. If you get a chance to see the televised address, you will hear the rhythm of Dr King's voice cadences – the way he leaned on the long 'e' vowel in 'dream', and the rising inflections of his eloquent, biblically inspired phrasing. You cannot but be moved by the sincerity of his plea, and the truth and justice of his aspirations for his people, and all people.
- **Images** are used as evidence, or to impress and leave a lasting emotional appeal e.g. '... a dream deeply rooted in the American dream ...'; '...one day on the red hills of Georgia ...'; '... the table of brotherhood'; '... the State of Mississippi ... sweltering with the heat of injustice ... oppression ... transformed into an oasis of freedom and justice.'
- **Tone**: the grand oratory of this speech reads as a powerful sermon on the subject of truth and justice. Martin Luther King Jnr was a preacher first and foremost, a deeply religious man. This speech is clearly inspirational in tone, with biblical influences and references evident throughout. His audience would have understood and empathised with the oratorical tone of this address. It reflected their own outlook and attitudes. Now read this last section of Dr King's speech, noting again the persuasive power of repetition in the phrase 'Let freedom ring'.

> So let freedom ring from the prodigious hilltops of New Hampshire.
> Let freedom ring from the mighty mountains of New York.
> Let freedom ring from the heightening Alleghenies of Pennsylvania.
> Let freedom ring from the snow-capped Rockies of Colorado.
> Let freedom ring from the curvaceous slopes of California.
> But not only that.
> Let freedom ring from Stone Mountain of Georgia.
> Let freedom ring from Lookout Mountain of Tennessee.
> Let freedom ring from every hill and molehill of Mississippi, from every

mountainside, let freedom ring.

And when we allow freedom to ring, when we let it ring from every village and hamlet, from every state and city, we will be able to speed up that day when all of God's children – black men and white men, Jews and Gentiles, Catholics and Protestants – will be able to join hands and to sing in the words of the old Negro spiritual, 'Free at last, free at last; thank God Almighty, we are free at last.'

(From *A Testament of Hope The Essential Writings and Speeches of Martin Luther King Jnr*)

Mark Anthony's Forum Speech

In Shakespeare's *Julius Caesar*, there is another very famous example of the language of persuasion in Mark Anthony's Forum speech to the Roman mob. You will almost certainly know the first line, even if you have never read the play! 'Friends, Romans, countrymen, lend me your ears ....'

Friends, Romans, countrymen, lend me your ears;
I come to bury Caesar, not to praise him.
The evil that men do lives after them,
The good is oft interred with their bones;

> So let it be with Caesar. The noble Brutus
> Hath told you Caesar was ambitious;
> If we were so, it was a grievous fault,
> And grievous hath Caesar answered it.
> Here, under leave of Brutus and the rest –
> For Brutus is an honourable man:
> So are they all, all honourable man –
> Come I to speak in Caesar's funeral.
> He was my friend, faithful and just to me:
> But Brutus says he was ambitious;
> And Brutus is an honourable man.
> He hath brought many captives home to Rome,
> Whose ransoms did the general coffers fill:
> Did this in Caesar seem ambitious?
> When that the poor have cried, Caesar hath wept;
> Ambition should be made of sterner stuff:
> Yet Brutus says he was ambitious;
> And Brutus is an honourable man.
> You all did see that on the Lupercal
> I thrice presented him a kingly crown,
> Which he did thrice refuse: was this ambition?
> Yet Brutus says he was ambitious;
> And, sure, he is an honourable man.
> I speak not to disprove what Brutus spoke,
> But here I am to speak what I do know.
> You all did love him once, not without cause:
> What cause withholds you then to mourn for him?
> O Judgement! Thou art fled to brutish beasts,
> And men have lost their reason. Bear with me;
> My heart is in the coffin there with Caesar,
> And I must pause till it come back to me ....
>
> (An extract from *Julius Caesar* by William Shakespeare.)

Comment

- The *context* of this speech is the challenge Mark Anthony faced, when addressing a hostile mob of Roman citizens, who had just learned of the death of Caesar, assassinated by his own Senators. Mark Anthony was supremely aware of his audience. He knew them to be, in the main, poor, ignorant, irrational and downtrodden. He sets out to win their sympathy, to persuade them of his earnestness, and of the sincerity of his own love for Caesar.

- He very cleverly includes the mob in this expression of love, 'He was my friend, faithful and just to me:' 'You all did love him once ....' Earlier, he had reminded them of Caesar's love for them, 'When that the poor have cried, Caesar hath wept;' and of the benefits that had accrued to them all from his successes in war. 'He hath brought many captives home to Rome, whose ransoms did the general coffers fill.'
- Mark Anthony uses sensational and emotive images, designed to rouse the mob to fury against Caesar's assassins. 'O judgement! Thou art fled to brutish beasts, ... my heart is in the coffin here with Caesar, and I must pause till it come back to me ....' The persuasive power of the emotional appeal is evident here.
- Note too the use of the phrase 'honourable men', and its repetition throughout this speech. Consider its impact on the mob, each time it is repeated, how the emphasis changes and the tone too, rising each time to instil hysteria in the mob. The last 'And, sure, he is an honourable man' is laden with sarcasm and irony. Mark Anthony succeeds in persuading his audience that he alone is the only 'honourable man' in their midst.
- The final 'And I must pause till it come back to me' is a wonderful oratorical trick, persuading his audience that emotion overwhelms him so completely at this point that he cannot continue.
- Examine other speeches in Shakespeare's plays for examples of the language of persuasion, i.e. Shylock's speech 'I am a Jew ...' in *The Merchant of Venice*, Act 3, Scene 1, lines 55–75, or Lady Macbeth's speech to Macbeth in *Macbeth*, Act 1, Scene 7, lines 36–72.

Note: See also Text 1 in Section A (Comprehending) of this Unit, for Sojourner Truth's speech 'Ain't I a Woman?', and Text 2 from the 2001 Leaving Cert. Higher paper, for President Mary Robinson's inauguration speech, delivered in 1990. Both of these speeches are very different, written in different times, but they are equally moving and persuasive, when you study them closely.

The Gettysburg Address

This last example of a political speech is 'The Gettysburg Address', by Abraham Lincoln. It was delivered at the ceremony of dedication of the National Cemetery at Gettysburg, Pennsylvania on 19 November 1863. Lincoln's presence at the ceremony was an afterthought. The featured speaker was Edward Everett, the former Secretary of State and President of Harvard, who was thought to be the finest orator in the country. The officials in charge of the National Cemeteries doubted that President Lincoln has sufficient skills as a speaker to do justice to the occasion. So they asked him to say a few words following

Everett's two hour (!) address. Lincoln said more in all of two minutes. It is persuasive oratory at its best, despite the fact that at the time Lincoln disclaimed it: 'I am distressed about it. I ought to have prepared it with more care.'

The Gettysburg Address by Abraham Lincoln

Four score and seven years ago our fathers brought forth on this continent, a new nation, conceived in Liberty, and dedicated to the proposition that all men are created equal.

Now we are engaged in a great civil war, testing whether that nation, or any nation so conceived and so dedicated, can long endure. We are met on a great battle-field of that war. We have come to dedicate a portion of that field, as a final resting place for those who here gave their lives that that nation might live. It is altogether fitting and proper that we should do this.

But, in a larger sense, we cannot dedicate – we cannot consecrate – we cannot hallow – this ground. The brave men, living and dead, who struggled here, have consecrated it, far above our poor power to add or detract. The world will little note, nor long remember what we say here, but it can never forget what they did here. It is for us the living, rather to be dedicated here to the unfinished work which they who fought here have thus far so nobly advanced. It is rather for us to be here dedicated to the great task remaining before us – that from these honoured dead we take increased devotion to that cause for which they gave the last full measure of devotion – that we here highly resolve that these dead shall not have died in vain – that this nation, under God, shall have a new birth of freedom – and that government of the people, by the people, for the people, shall not perish from the earth.

Comment

Note how this speech contains all the persuasive techniques present in political speeches.
- Awareness of audience – the respectful and inclusive 'we'.
- Images and anecdotes – 'Four score and seven years ....'
- Repetitions
- Tone
- Logical structure

Time permitting, when you have read this speech, it would be a useful exercise to compare it to the others in this section, under these headings.

Satiric Text

Finally, here is an example from our own time of a *political cartoon*, or *satiric text*. It is by Martyn Turner, from the *Irish Times* (24 July 2001).

At this time the Berlin summit was debating the Kyoto Treaty, and the issue of global warming. It sought agreement from all governments for a range of measures designed to reduce the effects of global warming worldwide. America was roundly condemned for rejecting the treaty being proposed by Europe and the rest of the world. Even Japan, who had expressed some concerns, had eventually agreed to accept the compromise treaty.

Comment

- When you first look at this cartoon, the dominant image is that of US President George W. Bush (see the hat! – a Texas Stetson) standing over a chair made from a barrel of oil. This symbolises his strong links to the oil industry, which supported him throughout his presidential election campaign. They are a powerful political lobby in his home state of Texas.
- Note the balcony or tower (an ivory tower, perhaps?) on which he is standing, the exaggeratedly large US flag, and his own disproportionate body size and stance. These clearly symbolise his position of power and dominance over the poor unfortunate 'serf' to his left, who addresses him as 'sire'. The satire is wonderful here, in that George W. Bush is a democratically elected president, and not a monarch as the 'sire' implies. However, Turner wishes to imply that Bush's behaviour smacks of the arrogance of a monarch whose

total disregard for the Kyoto Protocol, and the issue of global warming, is reflected in his reply 'Let them run air conditioning'. The phrasing here echoes Marie Antoinette's response to her starving subjects at the gates of Versailles – 'Let them eat cake'.

- The reference to air conditioning by George W. Bush is meant to remind the reader of another major industry in the US, which contributes a high proportion of the greenhouse gases which generate global warming. This is further endorsed by the small 'thumbs up' footnote in the bottom right-hand corner of the cartoon 'And let us *sell* it to you'. We are left in no doubt that President Bush's primary concern is not the environment and global warming, but America's own self interest.
- This clever cartoon is an example of how the language of persuasion operates on both a visual and written level. It illustrates how humour, in the form of satire, serves not only to amuse, but also to highlight the very genuine concerns readers may have on an issue of universal concern.

SECTION C **COMPOSING**

Concluding the Essay

> 'What we call the beginning is often the end
> And to make an end is to make a beginning.
> The end is where we start from.'
> (T.S. Eliot, 'Little Gidding' (*Four Quartets*))

To the student
In Units 1, 2, and 3, I have given you guidelines and examples of how to: **plan** your composition (Unit 1), **start** your composition (Unit 2), and **engage with the reading** texts, as a resource for your composition (Unit 3). In this Unit, let's look at ways of **concluding** your essay. Here are some useful tactics you might employ: quotation, statistics, anecdotes and direct dramatic statements. Read again the notes I gave you on these, in Unit 2, Section C, but this time consider them from the point of view of *concluding* your essay. Lets see how each might work as an ending.

1. Quotation
If you have used a quotation to *open* your essay, you might usefully return to it, or a similar one, for your ending. This gives a sense of cohesion and unity to your composition, and works particularly well with a debate style essay. Remember that your immediate source for quotations is the text itself, which inspired the composition title. So make use of your reading text for this purpose.

2. Statistics
These are particularly useful in an informative, argumentative or persuasive essay. Figures are factual and irrefutable. To conclude with a shocking statistic, for example, would be impressive and remain in the examiner's mind. Remember too, that if you use the reading text as a resource you could use one of the statistics quoted in the text itself. You could also invent a statistic of your own, but be careful to keep it within the bounds of credibility!

3. Anecdote
This works well in a narrative style essay, or in a personal essay inspired by one of the images from Text 4. Again, look for an example from the reading text itself, or recount one

from your own experience. You may, of course, create an anecdote that appears to fit well with the tone and register of your composition. Remember the definition of 'anecdote' from Unit 2 – 'a *short* account of an entertaining or interesting incident'. As a conclusion to your essay, therefore, be mindful of keeping your anecdote brief and to the point.

4. Questions
If the question with which you conclude is relevant and thought provoking, it will remain in the examiner's mind, and make an impression that could influence your marks. Look for questions in the actual reading text that inspired your choice of essay. Use one of these, if you can. If writing a composition based on one of the images in Text 4, for example, use your imagination to invent a question that appears to encapsulate some facet of the image or the message inherent in the image. It is also a good idea to try writing a series of questions provoked by the title, for your ending, as well as for your opening. Then choose one that most directly addresses the main theme/concern of your composition. This type of ending is most suited to the language of argument and persuasion, but could work well in a personal essay, with a philosophical theme. Questions are open-ended and, if good, are an excellent way to conclude an essay.

5. Direct Dramatic Statement
This is particularly suited to the languages of information, argument and persuasion. It has the appeal of honesty, directness and straight talking. Again, if you have opened your essay with a dramatic statement, you might usefully remind your reader of that same point in your conclusion. In this way, you are emphasising and reiterating the main premise of your essay. Be careful, however, as repeating a key point more than once dilutes its effect, and will appear weak to the examiner. Do not forget to 'engage with the text' also. You will surely find at least one good 'direct dramatic statement' there. So, use it!

Let's now look at the seven composition titles for Unit 4. You will find the usual notes on language genres appropriate to each one, plus a variety of suggestions for *concluding your essay*. As in previous Units, the essay titles reflect the format of the exam.

The Titles – Theme: Power and Powerlessness
Task: Write a composition on any one of the following. Each composition carries 100 marks. The composition assignments below are intended to reflect language study in the areas of information, argument, persuasion, narration, and the aesthetic use of language.

Essay 1
Language of Persuasion/ Information/ Argument

'I have plowed, I have planted and I have gathered into barns. And no man could head me'. (Text 1)

> Write an article for your school or local magazine in which you attempt to persuade your readers that women's rights are no longer an issue in the twenty-first century.

Note on genre(s): Your main purpose in this essay is to *persuade* your readers to your point of view, but in doing so, you may choose also to inform them of the history of the women's rights' movement perhaps, and how, where and why women have achieved equal rights with men. You may wish to *argue* against those who might have an opposing view i.e. that women's rights are *still* an issue. In that case, you will be employing counter arguments that need to be supported by strong evidence/statistics, as appropriate to the language of argument.

Concluding your Essay

Points to consider:
1. Quotation
(a) 'As a woman, I want women who have felt themselves outside history to be written back into history.'
(President Mary Robinson, Inauguration speech, 3 December 1990)
(b) 'I'm having a great time being Pres … being a senator from New York.'
Hilary Rodham Clinton, caught in a Freudian slip when asked if she planned to run for the US presidency. ('This Week They Said', *Irish Times*, 28 July 2001)

As possible concluding points for your essay, either of these quotations serve to remind the reader of the reality of women's increasing power in the twenty-first century, of how far women have progressed in terms of their rights. It reinforces the essential point of the essay, in that it demonstrates that the twenty-first-century woman can aspire to the highest political office in the land.

2. Statistics

Conclude with an impressive statistic that demonstrates just how far women have come in their quest for equal rights, since Sojourner Truth's era. Consider the extent of their involvement in the areas of career, education, politics, business, the arts, sport, etc. It's a little risky to invent statistics, but if they are reasonably accurate, they will appear credible to the examiner.

3. Anecdote

Engage with Text 1 itself by recounting the background of Sojourner Truth's own life, and her lifelong struggle for women's rights against the strongest odds. Refer to her experience as an example of what could be achieved by one extraordinary woman over 150 years ago. You might conclude by comparing her achievements with those of women in the twenty-first century.

Essay 2

Language of Narration/ Information/ Aesthetic Use of Language

'The experiment began with …'
Write a short story prompted by this title, and your reading of Text 2.

Note on genre(s): This type of composition allows for an imaginative, personal response, with a broad range of possibilities in terms of purpose, audience and register. However, the task is to write a short story, and the examiner will expect a sense of *narrative*, with a beginning, middle and end. You should create a central character, or group of interactive characters (as in the 1971 Stanford Experiment). There should be a defining moment, or point of crisis, a taut atmosphere, a sense of time, place and circumstance. The language of narration should dominate but the language of information, in terms of the background/origin of the 'experiment', will also form part of your composition. It might be interesting also, to explore the aesthetic use of language, in this composition, in terms of getting inside the minds of those who take part in the 'experiment', in exploring their emotions. This genre is an important feature of narrative writing.

Concluding the Essay

Points to consider:

1. Quotation

Text 2 is your most obvious and immediate source of quotation for this essay for example:

(a) 'Power is an aphrodisiac'

(b) 'When you give ordinary people a position of power, their behaviour changes dramatically.'

(c) '… how easy it is to turn good people into devils.'

(d) '… trouble broke out on day two when ….'

(e) ' … to devise psychological games ….'

(f) 'After only four days, they (prisoners) no longer believed that they were free to leave at any time.'

2. Question

Choose one question that most directly addresses the title of the essay, which brings the reader back to the beginning of the story, perhaps, or acts as a concluding comment on the entire experience. For example:

(a) 'How could I have become so completely obsessed with it all?'

(b) 'What have I become …?'

(c) 'When asked about that time now my standard reply is "Experiment? What experiment?"'

(d) 'When we found him he was mumbling the same question over and over "Where is man (woman) 46? Where is man 46 …?"'

3. Statistic

A chilling statistic would make a good conclusion to a grim story, a hopeful or humorous one for a more light-hearted tale of an experiment. Either way, you can be inventive and create your own statistics 'appropriate to the task'. Here are some suggestions:

(a) <u>Serious</u>

Of the twenty who took part in the experiment only two were willing to discuss it afterwards. Fifteen were treated for severe psychological trauma and three committed suicide as a direct consequent of the experience.

(b) <u>Humorous</u>

By the end of the week, Trina concluded that the 'reform Darren' experiment had been moderately successful. He no longer served up pasta with burnt bits, and the sick making purple shirt had found itself a new home in the dog basket. However, attempting to wean him off Bob Marley was proving a tad difficult. Ah well, 'two out of three ain't bad'.

Essay 3
Language of Narration/Information/Aesthetic Use of Language

'Writing has an almost magical power.' (Text 3)

> Write a personal essay in which you explore your feelings about the magical power of writing.

Note on genre(s): A personal essay allows you the freedom to write in a genre of your choice, and even to mix genres within the essay. However, you should decide from the outset which genre will predominate. For example, if you believe that writing has a magical power then the aesthetic use of language, in terms of your own creative and imaginative response to this title, may seem the most appropriate to the task. However, you may also choose to use the language of information as an introduction to this topic, perhaps, by giving the background history and origin of the written word. Engage with Text 3 as a resource here. You may decide to illustrate some points through *narration* i.e. recounting elements of the life of a favourite writer, poet, dramatist or historical figure, noted for the power of their writing. Use your knowledge of writers on your course here. Finally, you may wish to persuade your readers of the 'magical power' of writing in a universal sense – in which case, the language of persuasion might be used.

Concluding the Essay

Points to consider:

1. Quotation

Text 3 is your immediate source. For example:

(a) 'the purpose of writing remains unchanged: to convey meaning, whether playful, mundane or profound.'

(b) 'Writing has an almost magical power. Words on paper, created by ordinary citizens, have overthrown governments and changed the course of history.'

(c) 'No other invention – perhaps only the wheel comes close – has had a longer and greater impact.'

(d) 'Writing', he says, 'kept me alive'. (Wei Jingsheng)

N.B. There are many, many more in Text 3. Read it closely. Remember that 'engaging with the text' will make for a better essay, which will impress the examiner and ensure higher marks.

2. Anecdote

Recount a brief episode in the life of a writer of your choice, which serves to illustrate a point you wish to make about the power or writing. For example:

(a) Read the biographical notes on the poets on your course. These often give you insights into their lives and relationships. Think about John Keats dying at a very young age. Find out how he felt about the importance of writing poetry. Quote from one of his poems.

(b) Read the first chapter of Christy Brown's *My Left Foot*, for his description of writing the letter 'A' with his foot, in chalk, his first realisation of the magical power of writing.

(c) Use an anecdote from your *own* life to illustrate the moment you first realised the power and importance of writing. *Invent* one, if your need to!

The point is to conclude your essay with a

memorable image. A well-chosen anecdote could provide this.

3. Question

Go back to your Text 3, and try turning some of the most impressive statements into questions. For example:

(a) In conclusion, the real question the twenty-first century must ask is, 'Has the purpose of writing remained unchanged? Has it still that magical power to convey meaning, playful, mundane or profound?'

(b) The question remains: can words truly overthrow governments, and change the course of history?

(c) In conclusion, I am prompted to ask: will the power of the written work be diminished and lost in this high-tech world of the twenty-first century, and will we even mourn its passing?

'This is my life …'

> Imagine that you are in the world of one of the pictures in Text 4. Tell your story.

Essay 4

Language of Narration/ Information/ Aesthetic Use of Language

Note on genre(s): This type of composition allows for an imaginative personal response with a broad range of possibilities in terms of purpose, audience and register. However, the examiner will expect a sense of story, of narrative, so the language of narration should predominate in this essay. Your story should also have a beginning, middle and end. You are the central character in the 'world' of the picture you choose, so remember to write *your* story. You may include other characters/elements of the picture, of course, but remain focused on the direction and purpose of the story you are telling. The language of information may form part of the narrative, in terms of recounting of details, events, background, etc. An important feature of narrative writing is the aesthetic use of language – and this essay lends itself to that. Especially if you choose an image, such as number 5, which is shocking and charged with emotion, or number 6 in which the plight of the child cannot but move the person looking at it.

Concluding the Essay

Points to consider:

1. Direct Dramatic Statement

Study your chosen picture very closely. Focus on the outstanding emotion/image it evokes. Attempt to write a short, sharp statement that summarises the overall theme/intention of your essay. Here are some suggestions:

• Image 6: Quotation/Direct Dramatic Statement

Use the *text*, as a concluding message to the reader. It conveys the plight of this child most poignantly. 'The people of Ethiopia need help … and they can't wait forever.'

• Image 2: Quotation

Can you find a quotation from your history textbook that might fit the moment here? This is the actor Liam Neeson, playing the part of Michael Collins in the film of the same name. He might be saying, for example, 'They think if they arrest me, that will stop us. But who'll take my place? Will you? Or you? Or you?!' You will surely find a more accurate, factual quote from the era of the Civil War. Make use of your knowledge of history here.

• Image 5: Statistics

This is a stark image of the Holocaust. Look to your history books again, or to a good encyclopaedia for the facts surrounding this horrific event. The statistics are truly shocking. Six million Jews were slaughtered by the Nazis over the period 1939–45 of World War Two.

• Image 3: Direct Dramatic Statement

It's the dying moment of the game. What is the player in the centre thinking as he grimly holds on to the ball, fighting off the opposition? What are the other players thinking? Compose a dramatic headline style ending –

worthy of a tabloid newspaper, or an article from a serious sports journalist.

Power is central to this picture. Try to capture that in your concluding statement e.g. 'He's there! Yes! Morrison is there! The try of the match!' (N.B. Rugby fans among you will do much better than this!)

Essay 5
Language of Argument/ Information

> 'When you give ordinary people a position of power, their behaviour changes dramatically.' (Text 2)
> Write the speech you would make in a school or public debate for or against this motion.

Note on genre(s): Clearly, the most appropriate genre for this type of composition is the language of argument. (Look back to Unit 3, Section B, for points and examples of this genre.) Use the questions and/or notes you may have made from the pre-reading exercise in Section A of this Unit. They will act as a stimulus for your essay. Engage with Text 2 itself, by underlining and numbering the key points of argument outlined in the article. You may be able to use them, in terms of reference or quotation. Remember the key words of *audience, purpose* and *register.* Your audience, in particular, will dictate the register you use. It should be appropriate, i.e. a colloquial, familiar language register for an audience of your peers in school; a more serious, informed, formal tone for a more adult public audience. Your *purpose* is to argue your point of view clearly, with concrete references and strongly supported evidence. You will need to employ the language of information, in terms of concrete references, facts and statistics, relating to the debate topic.

Concluding the Essay

Points to consider:
1. Quotation
It is always good to conclude a debate with a quotation,

as it is to begin with one. Your aim is to redefine and restate your stance clearly. For example, you could conclude with the essay statement itself, and again categorically support or oppose it, appealing to your audience to agree with you. 'I strongly urge you to support this motion that ...' or 'I am absolutely opposed to this motion, and I urge you strongly to support my contention that when you give ordinary people a position of power, they do *not* change dramatically.' Engage with Text 2, as a source for quotation, as suggested for Essay 2. Research your own quotation(s) on the nature of power, from a dictionary of quotations i.e. The *Oxford Dictionary of 20th Century Quotations* or *Webster's Pocket Quotation Dictionary*.

For example, 'The essence of Government is power; and power, lodged as it must be in human hands, will ever be liable to abuse.' (James Madison, *Webster's Pocket Quotation Dictionary*)

2. Statistics

Statistics are clearly useful in a debate. Shocking or startling ones will persuade the audience to your point of view. Look at Text 2 again for examples. Do some research of your own from your history books, of figures that demonstrate the use and abuse of power by 'ordinary people'. *Invent* a good one with which to close the debate – but keep it credible!

Essay 6

Language of Persuasion/ Argument/Information

'Then in November 1997 the Chinese government releases Wei, largely in response to international pressure ....'

Write a letter to the Chinese authorities in which you outline your response to their imprisonment of Wei Jingsheng, with the intention of persuading them to release him.

Power and Powerlessness

Note on genre(s): This letter should have a formal *register*, appropriate to the task. Your primary *purpose* is to persuade the authorities of the injustice of continuing to detain Wei Jingsheng in prison, and of forbidding him to write. Be mindful of your *audience.* Your tone towards them must be formal, courteous and respectful – if you wish them to consider your point of view. You are not writing to your peers, so avoid the use of casual or colloquial language. Use the language of argument to cite examples of the behaviour of other countries concerning the detention of citizens, and the laws governing them. Read Text 3 again and use examples of the Chinese government's unjust treatment of Wei to further your case. See if you can acquire some statistics or figures from Amnesty International, which may support your case for Wei's release. Use the language of information to convey these points, to demonstrate your knowledge. Your composition must read as an informed, serious letter of protest.

Concluding the Essay

Points to consider:

1. Quotation

Use examples from Text 3, to support your case. Look outside the text for an appropriate quotation on freedom of speech, rights of the individual, just treatment of citizens, democracy, abuse of power, etc. Here are two you might use:

On *Democracy*:
'Man's capacity for justice makes democracy possible, but man's inclination to injustice make democracy necessary' (Reinhold Niebuhr, American theologian)
On *Power*:
'Power is not a means, it is an end. One does not establish a dictatorship in order to safeguard a revolution; one makes the revolution in order to establish the dictatorship.' (George Orwell, *1984*, 1949)

Note: Both of these quotations were taken from *The Oxford Dictionary of 20th Century Quotations*, published by Oxford University Press. I recommend you buy a good dictionary of quotations. It's an invaluable tool when you come to writing essays.

Essay 7
Language of Information/Argument/Aesthetic Use of Language

> Write an account of your experience of a rugby or football march you have seen. The account is to appear in the sports section of a popular magazine for older teenagers. You may use image 3 from Text 4, as inspiration for this composition.

Note on genre(s): This essay calls for a range of possibilities in terms of register and language genres, but keep your audience in mind at all times. You are writing for your peers, so the register may be narrative/colloquial and informal. The essay lends itself to the language of narration, and to humour. You may also wish to argue the merits of the game, both teams' performance on the day. Therefore, the language of argument may be appropriate, with elements of persuasion too. Audience registers will mix and mingle here, and if rugby and/or football inspire the poet in you, then the aesthetic use of language may be employed. Just remember to shape your account within the broad parameters of what constitutes a 'popular magazine'. Your personal experience of the game is what counts here.

Concluding the Essay

Points to consider:

1. Direct Dramatic Statement
You may have begun your essay with a strong headline statement. (Study the main headlines in the sports pages of newspapers for these). Refer back to that, perhaps, at the end. Have a complimentary, final parting image for the readers, which sums up you experience of this game.

2. Question

Conclude with a question that raises an important issue regarding the performance of the winning or losing team.

For example, 'Can Ireland beat Italy in the next round? That's the billion dollar question.'

3. Quotation

Footballers/rugby players usually like having the last word! Consult your friends, magazines, newspapers, etc., for quotable sports quotes.

Here are some I have found in *The Oxford Dictionary of 20th Century Quotations*.

Football

'Some people think football is a matter of life and death … I can assure them it's much more serious than that.'
(Bill Shankly, Scottish footballer and club manager, *Sunday Times*, 4 October 1981)

'Football. It's the beautiful game.'
(Attributed to Pele, Brazilian footballer. 1940–)

Rugby

'I wanted a play that would paint the full face of sensuality, rebellion and revivalism. In South Wales these three phenomena have played second fiddle only to Rugby Union which is a distillation of all three.'
(Gwyn Thomas 1913–81. Welsh novelist and dramatist, introduction to *Jackie the Jumper*, 1962)

N.B. See 'Last Words' at the end of this book for more quotations on a range of themes.

SECTION D LANGUAGE SKILLS

Efficiency of Language Use 4

> 'Use of lively interesting phrasing, energy, style, fluency ... grammatical patterns appropriate to the register'
> (*Assessment Criteria*, Leaving Cert. English)

To the student

By now, you should be familiar with the following terms: **syntax, sentence patterns, paragraph structure and register** (see Units 2, 3). In Unit 3, we also looked at **vocabulary** and how increasing your word power can help you to gain 'management and control of language to achieve clear communication' (*Assessment Criteria*). In this Unit, you will be doing some more work on **expanding your vocabulary base**, as well as looking at some grammatical patterns – **adjectives and nouns, adverbs and verbs**. In punctuation, we will be concentrating on quotation marks, and in spelling on some more of **those words that confuse i.e. homonyms** and **homophones**.

Expanding your Vocabulary Base

Exercise A

Choose the correct meaning from the three alternatives given below. Circle your choice. Then *check* your answer with the dictionary.

1. ACCRUE (verb)
(a) attack bitterly (b) increase by addition or growth (c) to turn sour
2. BOMBASTIC (adj.)
(a) using sarcastic, hurtful language (b) using pompous, boastful language (c) using flattering language
3. CONNOTATION (noun)
(a) the ability of human and animal tissue to heal naturally (b) the indication of a particular meaning (c) an idea or association suggested by a word or phrase
4. DEROGATORY (adj.)
(a) the part of a church tower which contains the bells (b) a church service for the sick (c) offensively disparaging
5. ETHOS (noun)
(a) the distinctive character or spirit of a culture or era (b) the difference between races of humans (c) a colourless volatile organic liquid

6. FALLACY (noun)
(a) a papal law (b) a deliberate lie (c) a false belief or argument
7. GRATUITOUS (adj.)
(a) given free for services (b) uncalled for; unwarranted (c) show appreciation for and to return kindness
8. HIERARCHY (noun)
(a) persons or things arranged in a graded order, ranked one above the other (b) the ruling group of a cult (c) the chiefs of Scottish clans
9. IDIOMATIC (adj.)
(a) writing that consists predominantly of slang (b) expressions common to a particular group and/or region (c) pertaining to ideas
10. JAUNDICED (adj.)
(a) an optimistic outlook (b) a process for making jam (c) a distorted, pessimistic point of view

Note: These are challenging words, intended for use at Leaving Cert. level. If after checking the answers in your dictionary, you find that you did not identify the correct meaning of all ten words, you should go back to those you got wrong and memorise them. In that way, you will be adding those words to your growing vocabulary. If you scored eight out of ten, you did really well.

Exercise B
Continuing with words from 'K' to 'T', let's shift the emphases from definition to **usage**. Select the *usage*, (a) or (b), which you think is appropriate or correct in the following sentences:
1. KUDOS (noun pl.)
(a) Sean's success in business brought him plenty of kudos.
(b) They spent days playing kudos.
2. LACKLUSTRE (adj.)
(a) There was a lacklustre taste to the soup.
(b) When it came to exams, Rita's lacklustre efforts spelt disaster.
3. MALIGN (verb)
(a) It was unfair of the Minister to malign his first secretary, as he had only been doing his job.
(b) The tumour was malign.
4. NONENTITY (noun)
(a) He managed to preserve his nonentity.
(b) According to the authorities, he was a total nonentity.

5. OPULENT (adj.)
(a) They lived an opulent lifestyle.
(b) Her manner was very opulent.
6. POIGNANT (adj.)
(a) That's a poignant outfit.
(b) 'Where youth grows pale, and spectre thin, and dies' is a poignant image. (Keats, 'Ode to a Nightingale')
7. QUALM (noun)
(a) He stole the money from the old lady without a qualm of conscience.
(b) The qualm before the storm was palpable.
8. RHETORICAL (adj.)
(a) Catherine was fascinated by his rhetorical past.
(b) Was that a rhetorical question? I think so.
9. SARDONIC (adj.)
(a) The critic made many sardonic references to the writer's style.
(b) Pam could be very hurtful and sardonic in her remarks.
10. TORTUOUS (adj.)
(a) The operation was tortuous.
(b) It was a tortuous route to the top of the canyon.

Note: More challenging words! If you scored over seven, you did well. If you misunderstood any word, do look it up in a good dictionary, the *Concise Oxford Dictionary*, for example.

There are two questions you can ask yourself to see if a word is truly part of your writing vocabulary.
1. If I hear a word, or come across it in my reading, do I know what it means immediately?
2. Can I use it spontaneously to express my thoughts and feelings?

This is what 'management and control of language' really means: instant recognition of the word, ease of usage.

Exercise C

This exercise affords you the opportunity to use the twenty 'new' words you have acquired in exercises A and B in a variety of ways. Time permitting, try to complete at least two of these tasks.

Task 1

As in Unit 3, try writing *five* words of your own choice from the exercises in a variety of sentence types. i.e. statement, question, order, exclamation

Task 2

Choose *five* more words and aim to write a short piece of *dialogue* (50–70 words), which uses each of the words once only.

Task 3
Choose a third group of five words and write a series of *headlines* for a newspaper, employing one of the words in each heading, e.g. 'Dowling's *jaundiced* views wreck talks' or 'Kudos to the King!'

Task 4
Write the *concluding paragraph* of an essay of your choice, from this Unit, or Units 1, 2, 3 or 5. Include as many of the twenty words as possible in your writing, but use each one once only. (75–100 words)

Grammatical Patterns
Adjectives and Nouns, Adverbs and Verbs
Exercise 1
Read the text of the advertisement for coffee on page 177 and then answer the following questions.

(a) Which *nouns* in the text do these adjectives describe?

(b) To which *verbs* do these adverbs refer?

evocative	deliciously
exotic	perfectly
adventurous	jealously
attractive	lovingly
soothing	highly
fragrant	wonderfully
notable	pleasingly
exquisite	admirably
light	
mysterious	

(c) Choose five *combinations* of *adjectives and nouns*, and five combinations of *adverbs and verbs* from A and B and write the text of a short advertisement for one of the following: tea, hot chocolate, fruit juice, beer, soup.

Note: Use the text of the coffee advertisement as your resource, for creative remodelling, in terms of appropriate register and genre. For example:

'There are few things as evocative as the aroma of home-made chicken ***soup*** …'

The language register is quite formal, aimed at a sophisticated audience/consumer. The appropriate genre is the language of persuasion, as is evident in the use of words like 'evocative' and 'aroma', both of which are designed to entice the reader to buy this product.

Punctuation
Quotation Marks
A. Writing dialogue
B. Including quotations

Writing Dialogue
Read this extract from the novel *How Many Miles to Babylon?* by Jennifer Johnston, as an example of how quotation marks are used in dialogue.

How Many Miles to Babylon?

'What does he know about anything?'

'I don't suppose he knows as much as you, but he knows a lot more than I do. About what happens.'

'You are never to see him again. Do you understand?'

'I understand what you're saying, but truly I don't understand why.'

'Then you must accept my judgement …'

She reached across me and pulled the bell, an ornate brass handle on the wall by the fireplace.

'But he's nice. We're … he's my friend.'

'Frederick.'

He sighed. The charred matchstick dropped from his fingers. 'In a way, my boy, your mother's right. It's an unsuitable relationship.'

'In every way.'

'I wouldn't quite say that. In many ways though. It is a sad fact, boy, that one has to accept young. Yes, young.' He paused and poked at the glowing tobacco with his little finger-nail. 'The responsibilities and limitations of the class into which you are born. They have to be accepted. But then after all, look at the advantages. Once you accept the advantages then the rest follows. Chaos can set in so easily.'

'Nothing. On and on about nothing. Always the same …'

The door opened and the parlour-maid came in.

'The curtains, please.'

She went back to the piano, smoothing her skirts under her as she sat down. The girl crossed the room and closed the windows. It was now quite dark outside.

> 'Pour me a glass of whiskey, young man,' ordered my father. The heavy glass decanters were on a silver tray. He liked his whiskey undiluted. I poured about an inch and a half into the tumbler. The Grande Valse Brillante swirled around us. The maid pulled and smoothed the curtains with long confident strokes of her hands. I put the glass on the table beside my father. He nodded.
>
> 'Will that be all, ma'am?'
>
> 'Thank you, yes.'
>
> Her voice, like the notes that came from under her fingers, was gay. I never had time to grasp her moods before they had changed.
>
> 'You never speak with authority,' she said as the door closed. 'You don't ever sound as if you know what you were talking about. You have always been an ineffective man.'
>
> His hand was trembling as he picked up his glass. He had temporarily laid down his pipe.
>
> 'I suppose that's as good a word for me as any.'
>
> 'Ineffective and old.'
>
> I put out a hand and touched his knee. It was a brief gesture, as ineffective as one he might have made himself.
>
> 'It's whatever you say. I'll do whatever ...'
>
> He laughed.
>
> 'You do what your mother tells you, my boy. That's the way ... Yes.'
>
> He picked up the pipe again and the process recommenced. I felt that they had finished with me. I got up to go. As I crossed the room, mother called after me, 'Promise then?'
>
> 'I suppose so.'
>
> 'Promise.'
>
> 'Very well.'
>
> I stood outside the door for a few moments after I had closed it, to hear what they would have to say to each other. They said nothing.
>
> (From *How Many Miles to Babylon?* by Jennifer Johnston)

Comment

Points to Note:

1. Single quotation marks are used here, but you may use double ones if you wish. It's a matter of personal choice. However, if you are writing a quote *within* a quote, it might be wise to do it as follows:

Susan said, 'I can't believe I have just spent six months completing this design and all my boss could ask was, "Does it come in red?"'

Note: *Single* quotation marks for Susan, *double* for the quote from her boss. This is purely for reasons of clarity.

2. All *other* punctuation marks must be placed *inside* the quotation marks i.e. full stops, question marks, commas, points of ellipsis (…) e.g.

'What does he know about anything?'

'I don't understand why.'

'Nothing. On and on about nothing. Always the same …'

3. If the dialogue is *interrupted* by description, as in the paragraph where the father paused to poke at the glowing tobacco with his fingernail, note how the quotation marks are *reinserted* when he begins speaking again. 'The responsibilities and limitations …'

4. Note how dialogue in a text is *indented* i.e. inserted in a little from the imagined margin line, and each individual's statement/question is placed on separate lines. This occurs with even quite short pieces, e.g.

'In every way.'

'The curtains, please.'

Note: Remember that handwriting is not as clear as print, so you must be especially careful in the exam when you insert dialogue into an answer. Write even one or two words on *separate lines*, in your exam booklet. This also helps to clarify for the examiner, which character is speaking at any one time e.g.

'Why.'	'What?'
'I don't know.'	''You heard.'
	'But…'

Exercise 1

'You are never to see him again. Do you understand?'

Write about twenty lines of an imaginary dialogue that took place between Frederick and his friend either *before* the scene in the extract you've just read, or *following* it.

Note: Remember those points on quotation marks and view this primarily as an example of the use of punctuation, for the purpose of making it clear and easy to read.

Exercise 2

Punctuate the following extract from *Cat's Eye*, by Margaret Atwood. Insert **quotation marks**, **capital letters**, **full stops**, **commas** and **question marks**.

did you have any female mentors she asks

female what

like teachers or other women painters you admired

shouldn't that be mentresses i say nastily there weren't any my teacher was a man

who was that she says

josef hrbik he was very kind to me i add quickly he'd fit the bill for her but she won't hear that from me he taught me to draw naked women

that startles her well what about you know feminism she says a lot of people call you a feminist painter

what indeed i say i hate party lines i hate ghettoes anyway i'm too old to have invented it and you're too young to understand it so what's the point of discussing it all

so it's not a meaningful classification for you she says

i like it that women like my work why shouldn't i

do men like your work she asks slyly she's been going through the back files she's seen some of those witch-and-succubus pieces

which men i say not everyone likes my work it's not because i'm a woman if they don't like a man's work it's not because he's a man they just don't like it i am on dubious ground and this enrages me my voice is calm; the coffee seethes within me

she frowns diddles with the tape-recorder why do you paint all these women then

what should i paint men i say i'm a painter painters paint women rubens painted women renoir painted women picasso painted women everyone paints women is there something wrong with painting women

but not like that she says

like what i say anyway why should my women be the same as everyone else's women i catch myself picking at my fingers and stop in a minute my teeth will be chattering like those of cornered mice her voice is getting farther and farther away i can hardly hear her but i see her very clearly: the ribbing on the neck of her sweater the fine hairs on her cheek the shine of a button what i hear is what she isn't saying *you're clothes are stupid your art is crap sit up straight and don't answer back*

why do you paint she says and i can hear again as clear as anything i hear her exasperation with me and my refusals

why does anyone do anything i say

Exercise 3

Write a short piece of **dialogue** on the theme of *Power and Powerlessness*. Create a situation in which two characters are arguing and sniping at one another, as in the Margaret Atwood piece.

Including Quotations

When you are quoting directly from a text, you must ensure that the words enclosed by your quotation marks are *exactly* those spoken. This is especially important when you are quoting from plays and poems. Here are some examples of *mis*quotes from my students' work.

(i) 'On first looking into Homer's Chapman' (should read: Chapman's Homer)
(ii) 'He (Keats) described his lover's chest as "a ripping brest."' (should read: 'ripening breast.')
(iii) 'The quality of mercy is not *sprained*' (should read: 'strained')
(iv) 'When he was told the queen was dead, Macbeth said: "She should have died *after* me."' (should read: 'hereafter')

Although these examples are funny, the examiner won't be amused! He/she will expect precision and care from you when it comes to quotations, especially if you are referring to an actual text on the paper itself.

Exercise 4

Read the following extract from a text entitled 'Om a Little Teapot …' from *Time* magazine (26 February 2001), and then answer the questions which follow, *quoting from the text*, in each answer, and using *quotation marks*.

Note: This is primarily a *punctuation* exercise. The answers will be immediately obvious. Note too that it is usual to introduce quotations with a *comma* or a colon (:). For example: 'The existential question facing Camille Faucheux is: "If you could be any butterfly, which butterfly would you be?"'

'OM A LITTLE TEAPOT …'
FOR STRESSED-OUT KIDS, YOGA OFFERS THE ROAD TO INNER PEACE. FOR THEIR PARENTS, ANY SORT OF PEACE IS NICE
By Nadya Labi

If you could be any butterfly, which butterfly would you be? That's the existential question facing Camille Faucheux, 3, as she sits on her purple exercise mat. She assumes the butterfly pose – knees splayed, the soles of her feet touching. 'Hold on to your butterfly wings.' Jodi Komitor instructs her Saturday morning class of mothers and toddlers in New York City. Camille clutches her toes and prepares for flight. Komitor continues: 'Lean back, open you butterfly wings and *whee*!' Her students flap their legs in the fantastical studio, where paper flowers seem to grow out of the bubblegum-pink ceiling. 'I'm flying to a flower,' reports Camille. 'A pink one.'

Komitor's students at Next Generation Yoga will become sleeping doggies, lions and snakes before the 45-minute session is over. They will walk on their hands and feet with their butts in the air, balance on one leg and sit chanting, 'Om'. Similar menageries are sprouting up across the country. With the zeal of the newly converted, baby boomers are introducing their children to yoga on the apparent theory that balanced lives begin with balanced children. And with their easy flexibility and willing imaginations, kids are proving natural yogis.

YogaKids, an organisation in Michigan City, Indiana, that certifies adults to teach yoga to children, expects to graduate 35 teachers this year, compared with only 25 in the past three years. *YogaKids*, a video tutorial created by that group's founder, Marsha Wenig, has sold 80,000 copies since 1996. And the shelves are filling with books touting the technique for kids of all ages, from *Yoga-baby* to *I Can't Believe It's Yoga for Kids*.

(*Time*, 26 February 2001)

Questions

1. According to the author, Nadya Labi, what is the existential question facing Camille Faucheux?
2. What is the name of the pose she assumes?
3. What is the first instruction Jodi Kamitor gives to her morning class of mothers and toddlers?
4. Describe the studio in which the yoga class is given.
5. What will the students at Next Generation Yoga become?
6. What will they chant?
7. What word does the writer use to describe these yoga classes, which she perceives as 'sprouting up across the country'?
8. Why are the parents (baby boomers) of these children introducing them to yoga at such a young age?
9. What is the name of the video tutorial created by the group's founder, Marsha Wenig?
10. Name two books on yoga for kids, mentioned in this article.

And finally …

Here are some other situations in which quotation marks are used:

1. Writing *titles*:
- Film: He said he'd seen the film 'Gladiator' ten times
  Books: Have you read 'The Butcher Boy'?
- Sayings: I always say 'Where there's a will, there's a way'.
- Songs: Robbie Williams' 'Let me entertain you' was a huge hit.
- Nicknames: Al Capone was known as Al 'Scarface' Capone.

2. To indicate *cynicism* or *doubt*:
- The building society stated that its lending terms were generous, even though most people would not consider twenty per cent interest repayments as 'generous'.
- The burgers were said to contain a blend of spices, chicken parts, liver and 'organic' sausage meat.

3. In *advertising*, to indicate that a word or phrase should not be taken literally:
- Ladies and Gentlemen, we are 'giving away' this terrific golf bag for just €30.

Spelling
Confusing Words: Homonyms and Homophones

To the student

You may well ask: 'What's the difference between these two?' It's a good question, but there is a real difference.

Homonym comes from two Greek words: 'homo' meaning 'same', and 'nym' meaning 'name'. It is a word with the same *sound* and the same *spelling* as another word but with a different *meaning* e.g.
- bank (of a river)
- bank (for borrowing money)

Homophone comes also from the Greek. It is a word with the same *sound* as another word, but with a *different spelling* and a different *meaning* e.g.
- meet: I'll *meet* you at six.
- meat: She doesn't eat *meat*.

Note: Homophones are the ones that are most often misspelt, and cause the most confusion.

Exercise 1 Homonyms

Write two short sentences for each of these homonyms which clearly show the difference in meaning and usage between them.

(a) Bow (noun) *clue*: of a ship
    Bow (verb) *clue*: to a person of importance
(b) air (noun) *clue*: on a 'G' string
    air (verb) *clue*: to do with freshening something *or* stating a grievance
(c) arms (noun) *clue*: body *or* artillery
    arms (verb) *clue*: getting ready for battle
(d) fine (adj.)
    fine (noun)
(e) bark (noun)
    bark (verb)
(f) club (noun)
    club (verb)
(g) fair (noun)
    fair (adj.)
(h) break (verb)
    break (noun)

Exercise 2 Homophones

'GRATE SAIL!
BYE NOW!
EVERYTHING GOING CHEEP!'

As you can see, the problem here is a confusion between similar sounding words, with completely different **spellings** and **meanings**. The correct version should, of course, read:

'GREAT SALE!
BUY NOW!
EVERYTHING GOING CHEAP!'

Correct the homophone error in each of the following sentences:

1. The principle called the cast of the musical together, to discuss arrangements for the knight's show.
2. She taught he new about the write way to change a plug.
3. I only want some piece and quite.
4. The children through stones at passing cyclists when they got board.
5. It was plane that Derek wouldn't here of Bairbre paying for the coarse.
6. Nothing could altar the fact that her ant and uncle were waisting there time looking for the thief.
7. Shirley past Ian bye on the street and went to meat Ciaran instead.
8. You never except my advise on cloths.

9. There having to many deserts with the meal when too would of bean enough.
10. He bought three pares of trainers in that shop on the key with the grate sail.

And finally …

Here is your list of most frequently misspelled words for Unit 4. You will use these often, so it is important to spell them correctly. Employ the same strategy for learning them, as suggested in Units 1, 2, and 3.

WORD	SPELL IT	SHORT SENTENCE
1. EXTR<u>A</u>ORDINARY	------------	---
2. OPP<u>O</u>SITE	------------	---
3. P<u>OR</u>TRAY	------------	---
4. INTE<u>RR</u>UPTION	------------	---
5. PERS<u>U</u>ADE	------------	---
6. ETERN<u>I</u>TY	------------	---
7. QUI<u>TE</u>	------------	---
8. NE<u>C</u>ESSARY	------------	---
9. O<u>CC</u>ASION	------------	---
10. SINCER<u>E</u>LY	------------	---

Unit 5 Journeys and Change

SECTION A COMPREHENDING

Introduction
This section contains four texts on the general theme of *Journeys and Change*, including a set of pre-reading exercises on Texts 1–3.

Text 1
'Four island students a class apart' is an article from the *Irish Times* (8 August 2001), which centres on the establishment of the first ever post-primary school on the island of Inis Meáin. It is primarily an example of the **language of information**, but the **language of narration** is evident in one islander's account of her own experience of boarding school.

The article also argues for the rights of parents to educate their children through the medium of Irish regardless of where he/she lives and might therefore contain elements of the *language of argument*.

Text 2
'Travels with an elephant' is the title of an article (edited) from the *RTÉ Guide* (12 January 2001), in which Teresa Nerney interviews Caroline Casey, a legally blind twenty-nine-year-old. Caroline undertook an expedition to India in January 2001, in order to raise a quarter of a million pounds for charity, and to change negative public perceptions of disability. The cover photo (by Frank Miller, in the *Irish Times*) is of Caroline, on her return from India in May 2001. The article in the *RTÉ Guide* contains elements of the **language of information**, in terms of background details of the Aisling Project Indian Challenge. It is predominantly **persuasive** in tone however, in its recording of the courage and determination of this exceptional young woman and her personal drive to persuade people to view disability in a positive light. The **language of argument** is clearly evident in the points she makes in relation to this issue.

Text 3
'Last Days' is the title of the final chapter in the first volume of Laurie Lee's autobiography

Cider with Rosie. The book is a wonderfully vivid memoir of the writer's childhood and youth in a remote Cotswold village. It is predominantly an example of the **aesthetic use of language**. 'It sings in the memory.' (*Sunday Times*).

Cider with Rosie also contains elements of the **language of narration**. The author achieves this by describing those characters who peopled his childhood; of the changes that have occurred in the life of the valley where he grew up; of his own personal journey from childhood to early manhood; and his first experience of writing poems.

Text 4

This is a series of photographs depicting the general theme of *Journeys and Change*. There is no written text. You are required to study the images and respond to them in a variety of ways and genres.

Text 1 *Four island students a class apart*

Stage 1 **Pre-Reading**

Task: In pairs or small groups, discuss some or all of the questions below for ten minutes, then report back to the class.
OR
Your teacher may choose to discuss the questions with the whole group. The important thing is that you take notes of other students' points, for possible use later in one of the *composing* tasks, in Section C.

Questions

1. Discuss the word 'journeys' in as broad a context as possible i.e. types of journeys – physical, intellectual, imaginary, educational, journeys of pilgrimage or encounter?
2. Explore the notion of 'change' and its connection to the idea of journeys. Why place the two *together* as a theme, for example? What do they have in common?
3. How would you feel about being one of just four students in a small island school with one-to-one tuition? What would be the advantages and disadvantages of this kind of school?
4. How would you feel about living on an island? Would it be a very isolated existence do you think? How different would it be from living on the mainland?

Stage 2 Reading

Four island students a class apart

**By Lorna Siggins,
On Inis Meáin**

FAINCHE ní Fhatharta, Seosaimhín nÍ Chonghaíle, Adrian Ó Coincheanainn and Seosamh Ó Fatharta aren't used to being the centre of attention. Barely teenagers, they certainly wouldn't regard themselves as making 'history'. Yet they will do just that next month when they enrol as pupils in Inis Meáin's first post-primary school.

Coláiste Naomh Eoin is its name and it was opened 'unofficially' on the island in Galway Bay yesterday morning. The island's parents are determined to make it work as most of them had to leave for boarding school when they finished primary level.

Ms Brid Ó Coincheanainn, mother of Adrian, remembers the trauma of being sent to the convent of Mercy in Galway. 'It wasn't Monday to Friday boarding. I remember the first time I got home after term started was at Christmas.'

She had considered keeping her son back for a year after finishing sixth class. 'Adrian would have been ready for secondary, yes, but he wouldn't have been ready for leaving home.'

Ms Mairín nÍ Chonghaile would have had to quit her native Inis Meáin if Seosaimhín her only child, had to attend school on the mainland. As a single parent, it wouldn't have been practical for her to stay. Coláiste Naomh Eoin gives her daughter an option she never had.

Inis Meáin is the only one of the three Aran islands to have been without secondary education until now, and there are many island residents who are still faced with tough decisions along the Atlantic seaboard. The support of Gaelschoileanna, the co-ordinating body for Irish-medium schools, and Údarás na Gaeltachta has been vital for the population of 192.

This was emphasised by Ms Jacqueline nÍ Fhearghusa, director of Gaelscoileanna, when she presented a cheque for £10,000 to the co-op manager yesterday to help with the running costs for the first year.

Gaelscoileanna believes in the right of every child to be educated through the medium of Irish, regardless of where he/she might live.

The Aran islands are regarded by the organisation as especially important in the campaign to foster and support the Irish language and the Gaeltacht. Ms Ní Fhearghusa said it was vitally important that parents could live on the island knowing that basic education rights would be available for their children.

Údarás na Gaeltachta is also committing £25,000, according to Ms Sorcha Nic Shonacha, the authority's manager of culture and language, who attended the opening in the community hall, Halla Naomh Eoin. A classroom built off the hall will be used and the principal will be Mr Niall Ó Murchadha, retired principal of Scoil Iognaid in Galway, and regarded as one of the finest educators in the west.

Mr Ó Murchadha will commute to the island from Spiddal until the Department of Education and Science makes a decision on official recognition. After that the post will be advertised, he said. A teacher is also about to be appointed and the pupils will have the benefit of one-to-one tuition.

The small size of the class and the need for socialisation is a concern among parents but plans are already afoot to address this. The school will travel to sporting events and debates on the neighbouring islands and a 'ceangail' or twinning arrangement is to be made with a north Dublin post-primary gaelschoil, Gaelcholáiste Dhomnach Míde in Donaghmede.

(From *Irish Times*, 8 August 2001)

Question A
(i) What aspects of island life emerge most strongly from the above text? (20)
(ii) To what extent do you find yourself in agreement or disagreement with the islanders' view of the right of every child to be educated through the medium of Irish, regardless of where he/she might live?
Support your point of view by reference to the text. (30)

Question B
Imagine a mainland radio station is broadcasting a programme from Inis Meáin, called 'Island Life'. You have been asked about your experience as a young person of your life and education on the island. Write out the text of a short talk you might make on this occasion (150–200 words). (50)

Text 2 Travels with an elephant

Stage 1 Pre-Reading
Task: In pairs or small groups, discuss some or all of the questions below for ten minutes, then report back to the class.
OR
Your teacher may choose to discuss the questions with the whole group. The important thing is that you take notes of other students' points, for possible use later in one of the *composing* tasks, in Section C.

Questions
1. What is it that makes people want to travel around the world? What is the attraction of travel? Can you explain why some people get the 'travel bug' after just one trip, and others never want to leave home?
2. If you were registered as legally blind, would *you* travel across India on an elephant? If so why? If not, why not?
3. As a society, how do we view disability? How do *you*, as a teenager, react when you encounter a person who is disabled – positively or negatively?
4. What changes in our thinking and attitudes should we make in order to accommodate the needs and aspirations of the disabled in our communities? What are the issues that must be faced?

Stage 2 Reading

TRAVELS WITH AN ELEPHANT

Caroline Casey, who is visually impaired, will spend the next three months trekking across India on an elephant. Teresa Nerney asked her why.

Ninety days spent travelling 1,000km on the back of an elephant across India, a lot of it through jungle. Two elephant keepers, a guide and a cook for company. Food at a campfire, sleep in a tent. Not an expedition for the faint-hearted, but for 29-year-old Dublin woman Caroline Casey it will be the fulfilment of a dream.

'I always wanted to travel in India,' she explains, 'and I thought the best way to do it was on an elephant.' But this journey is much more than a

Caroline Casey at Dublin Airport yesterday on her return from a 1,000 km trip by elephant across India. She raised £200,000 for charity. Photo: Frank Miller

travel adventure for Caroline. It is about her dream to change negative public perceptions of disability and raise a quarter of a million pounds for charity.

Caroline is visually impaired to the extent that she is registered as legally blind. Everyday tasks which people with perfect vision take for granted don't come easy to her – reading street signs, withdrawing cash from a bank machine, reading the paper. 'A few weeks ago a broadsheet wrote an article about me and I had to put my nose down to the paper to read it.'

But Caroline regards her disability as minor and has never let it prevent her from doing the things she wants. 'I am blessed in that I have an incredible amount of determination. I always wanted to make sure that I balanced things up because of my disability. I live my life as full as anybody else. I just have to work harder.'

From her own experience she is aware of the issues facing people with disabilities, and this spurred her last June to establish the Aisling Project Indian Challenge, appropriately choosing the Gaelic name which means 'dream' or 'vision'.

'I hope the Aisling Project will show that people with

disabilities are capable in different ways and independent in spirit ... I think it's really important that you're not stamping your feet and giving out about the fact that disability is often misunderstood. Nobody wants to hear someone moaning.'

The National Council for the Blind and Sight Savers International will each receive 40% of the money raised. The remainder will go to the Protection of the Asian Elephant, which is under threat. 'Every penny donated goes directly to the charities. That's something I feel strongly about,' comments Caroline.

This week she leaves Heathrow Airport for New Delhi and then on to Kerala where she will meet Bhadra, the 20-year-old elephant who will bring her on the 1,000km journey. 'I've seen photos of her and she is really pretty,' says Caroline. In February, after she gets to know Bhadra and learns how to ride, feed and bathe her, they will set off.

One of the most difficult things, she points out, will be that the people around her in Indian will not know her. Her family and friends in Dublin know how much she can and can't see, but in India she will have to explain it. The bond she forms with Bhadra will also depend on how much the elephant understands her disability.

She knows that there will be times when she will find the journey tough.

'I'm going to be lonely. The first month will certainly be difficult.' But if her Indian trek helps shift perceptions of disability and raise some much needed funds for the chosen charities, she's prepared to give it her very best shot. If people start to think and talk about disability in a different way because of the personal challenge she has set herself, it will be worthwhile.

'If you listen to people with a disability and you hear them, that's the first step. People who are different are spirited and independent. Disability has become a negative term. These are people who are capable in different ways. It's not easy living in a perfect world, I become scared when I have to play the part that I'm perfect. I don't want to be different and to say I can't. I want this project to say "I can" and to say "We all can". I'm not trying to save the world. I am just trying to make a positive point.'

A documentary will be made of her journey and a camera crew will accompany her in the initial stages, half way through, and at the end. Thanks to Esat Digifone she will be able to keep in touch with western media via satellite phone, and with the help of a laptop will be updating the Aisling Project website regularly with photos and video clips.

(*RTÉ Guide* 12 Jan 2001)

Journeys and Change

Question A
(i) Why was this trip so important to Caroline? Give reasons. (15)
(ii) According to the text, how is society's view of disability different from Caroline's? Give reasons for your answers. (15)
(iii) 'I am blessed in that I have an incredible amount of determination.' From what you have read of Caroline throughout the interview, how true is this statement, do you think? Give reasons for your answer. (20)

Question B
You are Caroline and you have been asked to appear on the Gerry Ryan Radio Show to give an account of your journey across India by elephant. Write out, in 150–200 words, the first *question* Gerry Ryan might ask you and the *answer* you would give. (50)

Text 3 'Last Days' from Cider with Rosie by Laurie Lee

Stage 1 Pre-Reading
Task: In pairs or small groups, discuss some or all of the questions below for ten minutes, then report back to the class.
OR
Your teacher may choose to discuss the questions with the whole group. The important thing is that you take notes of other students' points, for possible use later in one of the *composing* tasks, in Section C.

Questions
1. Discuss the most significant *changes* that have occurred in your town or district since you were a small child.
2. What are your most vivid memories of childhood? For example, the happiest moment(s), the most frightening or the most exciting.
3. Can you remember that point of change from childhood to adolescence? How did it affect, if at all, your life and relationships? How did your perception of things change?
4. Life is often described as a 'journey'. Discuss what you think this means. Are there stages in that journey? Which one are you experiencing at the moment? Is change inevitable? Do you welcome it, or find it frightening? Are you looking forward to the next stage of your 'journey' through life?

Stage 2 READING

Last Days by Laurie Lee

1. The girls were to marry; the Squire was dead; buses ran and the towns were nearer. We began to shrug off the valley and look more to the world, where pleasures were more anonymous and tasty. They were coming fast, and we were nearly ready for them. Each week Miss Bagnall held her penny dances where girls' shapes grew more familiar. For a penny one could swing them through Lancers and Two-Steps across the resinous floor of the Hut – but if one swung them entirely off their feet then Miss B locked the piano and went home....

2. Time squared itself, and the village shrank, and distances crept nearer. The sun and moon, which once rose from our hill, rose from London now in the east. One's body was no longer a punching ball, to be thrown against trees and banks, but a telescoping totem crying strange demands few of which we could yet supply. In the faces of the villagers one could see one's change, and in their habits their own change also. The horses had died; few people kept pigs any more but spent their spare time buried in engines. The flutes and cornets, the gramophones with horns, the wind harps were thrown away – now wireless aerials searched the electric sky for the music of the Savoy Orpheans. Old men in the pubs sang, 'As I Walked Out', then walked out and never came back. Our Mother was grey now, and a shade more light-headed, talking of mansions she would never build.

3. As for me – for me, the grass grew longer, and more sorrowful, and the trees were surfaced like flesh, and girls were no longer to be treated lightly but were creatures of commanding sadness, and all journeys through the valley were now made alone, with passion in every bush, and the motions of wind and cloud and stars were suddenly for myself alone, and voices elected for me of all men living and called to me to deliver the world, and I groaned from solitude, blushed when I stumbled, loved strangers and bread and butter, and made long trips through the rain on my bicycle, stared wretchedly through lighted windows,

grinned wryly to think how little I was known, and lived in a state of raging excitement.

4. The sisters, as I said, were about to get married. Harold was working at a factory lathe. Brother Jack was at Grammar School, and his grammar was excellent; and Tony still had a fine treble voice. My Mother half-knew me, but could not help. I felt doomed, and of all things wonderful.

5. It was then that I began to sit on my bed and stare out at the nibbling squirrels, and to make up poems from intense abstraction, hour after unmarked hour, imagination scarcely faltering once, rhythm hardly skipping a beat, while sisters called me, suns rose and fell, and the poems I made, which I never remembered, were the first and last of that time....

('Last Days' from *Cider with Rosie* by Laurie Lee, text and illustrations from *The Illustrated Cider with Rosie* published by Century Publishing Company, London 1984.)

Question A

(i) What are your impressions of the world of the author as described in this passage? (15)

(ii) 'As for me – for me …' From your reading of paragraphs 3, 4 and 5 how does the narrator feel about this time of change in his life? Give examples. (15)

(iii) Write a paragraph (150–200 words) in which you comment on the appropriateness of the title 'Last Days'. (20)

Question B

Imagine a TV station is producing a series of programmes entitled 'Last Days' in which people of all ages are being asked to submit their memories of a specific era in their lives.

Write the text of a submission you would like to make, *either* as a young adult *or* as an older member of the community (150–200 words). (50)

Text 4   Images of Journeys and Change

1.
2..
3.
4.

Journeys and Change

5. **6.**

As in previous units, Text 4 requires a different approach. You are asked to 'read' a series of images, with usually no written text. You should study each of them closely before attempting to answer the questions. Be especially attentive to detail in the photographs – the setting, the personalities/characteristics of people and/or objects, their gestures, facial expressions and body language. Look too at colour, light and shade, and for the underlying message or intention inherent in each image in terms of the overall theme of *Journeys and Change*.

Question A
(i) Taking all of the above images into account, in your opinion, what overall impression of the concept of *Journeys and Change* is projected in this visual text? Outline your views in 150–200 words, supporting your points by reference to the images. (20)

(ii) (a) Imagine one of these images is to be used as the accompanying illustration for a newspaper or magazine article whose headline reads: 'Time for change'. Which one would you choose? Justify your choice. (15)

(b) Write a description of the image you have *chosen* in (a) above. (15)

Question B
Choose one of the people pictured in Text 4 and write *four* short diary entries that he/she might write on *one important day* in their life. You should indicate clearly the person you have chosen and you should write the diary entries as though you were that person. (50)

Sample Answer

Text 3: Last Days Question B

Imagine a TV station is producing a series of programmes entitled *Last Days* in which people of all ages are being asked to submit their memories of a specific era in their lives. Write the text of a submission you would like to make, *either* as a young adult *or* as an older member of the community (150–200 words). (50)

> I remember looking out my bedroom window one morning when I was nine years old and seeing Miss Quirke's cottage being bulldozed by the Corporation. She'd lived in that house all her life. My brother Andy and I used to bang the shiny brass knocker on her door, then belt off down the lane into the 'Nun's field'. Poor Miss Quirke. She never caught us. But one day she caught sight of Andy's blond head as he ran past the window, and she complained to our mother. The shame of that. My father was furious and we weren't allowed out for three days. Then we had to go over to Miss Quirke with a naggin of whiskey and apologise. We got no pocket money either, which meant no 'pictures' on Saturday. We used to go every week with the gang from the 'Villas'. There was a ritual of calling round the houses first. Mrs Boland gave us apples, Mrs Foley, two Lemon's sweets each, and Mrs Roche sprinkled us with holy water! John Wayne was the 'chap' on the crackly screen and we roared at him all the long, lovely afternoon....

Comment

It is very difficult to keep within a limit of 150–200 words, but it is a good discipline for a writer. 'Less is more' ia a good adage. The first draft of this answer was 258 words. I think I did quite well in reducing it to 201!

SECTION B   FOCUS ON … THE AESTHETIC USE OF LANGUAGE

> 'In a world full of audiovisual marvels, may words matter to you and be full of magic.'
> (Godfrey Smith, letter to a new grandchild, *Sunday Times*, 5 July 1987)
>
> '… language can be an artistic medium. Words, like colour and shape in art and sound in music, can be used to create artefacts whose primary purpose is to give aesthetic pleasure, enrich imaginative perception and feeling and reveal insights.'
> ('The Aesthetic Use of Language', *Draft Guidelines for Teachers of English*, Dept. of Education and Science)

To the student

You encounter the aesthetic use of language every time you read the novels, plays and poems on your course. The word 'aesthetic' comes from the Greek, meaning 'concerned with beauty or the appreciation of beauty'. However, language used in this way does not mean creating merely pleasurable images. Some of the aesthetic use of language has to do with depicting dark, sometimes ugly or even frightening aspects of life and experience. For example, if you read Keats' 'Ode to a Nightingale', you will find beautiful but deeply sad and poignant imagery, i.e.

> 'Now more than ever seems it rich to die
> To cease upon the midnight with no pain …'

Similarly, the language of a thought provoking film or TV programme, with their complex amalgam of images and words, can be aesthetically powerful. When you hear a spirited and eloquent debate on an issue of universal importance, or when you are moved by the words of a famous speech, or the lyrics of a song, you become aware of the power and beauty of the aesthetic use of language.

Although you may find it difficult to write in this genre, you shouldn't recoil from it out of fear of 'not getting it right'. There is no 'right'. The impulse to create images as a means of portraying your thoughts and experiences, to 'paint' your own pictures in words is enough to begin with.

> 'One takes a deep breath and makes a leap.' (Hugh Leonard)

The revised syllabus gives you the opportunity to explore this genre in your reading and writing. It encourages the student to 'experience it as a creative, pleasurable and expressive mode of experience … (with) its potential to excite, surprise and reveal …' (*Draft*

Guidelines) So, your already growing knowledge of the aesthetic use of language can be built on and developed.

The Revised Syllabus

The Department guidelines tell us that 'students should encounter a wide range of texts in a variety of literary genres for *personal recreation and aesthetic pleasure*. This would include engaging with fiction, drama, essay, poetry and film in an imaginative, responsive and critical manner.'

Note: Your most immediate source of the aesthetic use of language is the literature on your Leaving Cert. course. You are required to engage with novels, plays, poetry and film for Paper 2. However, you will also encounter this aesthetic use of language in Paper 1 in the sections on comprehending and composing. At least one reading text will contain elements of the aesthetic use of language and you may choose to write your essay in this genre.

However, in order to experience literature as creative and pleasurable, and the text as art, requires you to look at how language works in terms of enriching your 'imaginative perception and feeling' and revealing insights. Here are some examples of the aesthetic use of language, in the areas of fiction, poetry and drama, with a commentary on the individual characteristics that shape this genre.

Fiction

The following three short extracts are from novels of my own choice. The range of fiction available is clearly immense, but the imagery in the books I have chosen is powerful and moving and these extracts are excellent examples of the aesthetic use of language.

I Know Why the Caged Bird Sings by Maya Angelou

'What you looking at me for …?'

The children's section of the Colored Methodist Episcopal Church was wiggling and giggling over my well-known forgetfulness.

The dress I wore was lavender taffeta, and each time I breathed it rustled, and now that I was sucking in air to breathe out shame it sounded like crepe paper on the back of hearses.

As I'd watched Momma put ruffles on the hem and cute little tucks around the waist, I knew that once I put it on I'd look like a movie star. (It was silk and that made up for the awful color.) I was going to look like one of the sweet little white girls who were everybody's dream of what was right with the world. Hanging softly over the black Singer sewing machine, it looked like magic, and when people saw me wearing it they were going to run up to me and say, 'Marguerite [sometimes it was "dear Marguerite"], forgive us, please, we didn't know who you were,' and I would answer generously, 'No, you couldn't have known. Of course I forgive you.'

Just thinking about it made me go around with angel's dust sprinkled over my face for days. But Easter's early morning sun had shown the dress to be a plain ugly cut-down from a white woman's once-was-purple throwaway....

'What you looking ...' The minister's wife leaned toward me, her long yellow face full of sorry. She whispered, 'I just come to tell you, it's Easter Day.' I repeated, jamming the words together, 'IjustcometotellyouitsEasterDay,' as low as possible. The giggles hung in the air like melting clouds that were waiting to rain on me....

If growing up is painful for the Southern Black girl, being aware of her displacement is the rust on the razor that threatens the throat.

It is an unnecessary insult.

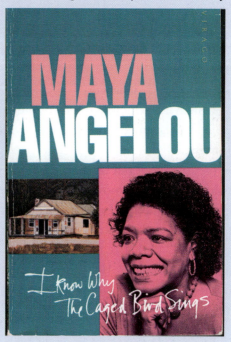

Comment

This extract is from the opening pages of the first volume of Maya Angelou's autobiography *I Know Why The Caged Bird Sings*. The book beautifully evokes her troubled childhood when she lived with her grandmother in the American South of the 1930s.

Look closely at the **imagery** in this extract for examples of the aesthetic use of language:
- '... now that I was sucking in air to breathe out shame it sounded like crepe paper on the back of hearses.'
- 'Hanging softly over the black Singer sewing machine, it [the dress] looked like magic.'
- 'Just thinking about it made me go around with angel's dust sprinkled over my face for days.'

- 'The giggles hung in the air like melting clouds that were waiting to rain on me.'
- '... being aware of her displacement is the rust on the razor that threatens the throat.'

Note the use of **simile:**
- '... like crepe paper on the back of hearses.'
- '... looked like magic, [the dress] ....'
- '... giggles ... like melting clouds ....'

Metaphor:
- '... angel's dust ....'
- '... the rust on the razor that threatens the throat.'

Alliteration:
- 'sucking in air ... shame ....'
- '... rust on the razor that threatens the throat.'
- '... plain ugly cut down ... purple throwaway.'

Contrast:

The reader cannot but be moved by her initial delight in the dress, in her belief that she would '... look like a movie star ... like one of those sweet little white girls'. Contrast this with her realisation on Easter morning that this magical dress, in which she has invested all her dreams of self-worth, is just a '... plain ugly cut down from a white woman's purple throwaway'. All that remained for her were the 'giggles' of derision in the church, '... waiting to rain on me'. Her awareness of her 'displacement', of the pain of growing up as a 'Southern Black girl' is summed up in the final metaphor of '... the rust on the razor that threatens the throat'.

The Prince of Tides by Pat Conroy

I have always loved my sister's voice. It is clear and light, a voice without seasons, like bells over a green city or snowfall on the roots of orchids. Her voice is a greening thing, an enemy of storm and dark and winter. She pronounced each word carefully, as though she was tasting fruit. The words of her poems were a most private and fragrant orchard.

But, at first, I could not hear her and I could tell she was aware of her audience, intimidated by it. But slowly, the language seized her; her language, her poems, and her voice lifted, steadied, and grew confident. And when it did, Savannah Wingo took that audience, that West Village audience, that cultured, jaded, city-hardened New York audience, by storm. I knew all the poems by heart and my mouth moved in congruence with hers and I told the stories of our life as she told them and I felt the supernatural power of poetry subjugate the crowd as Savannah's voice lifted up toward the choir loft, lifted up toward the shining battlements of the Empire State Building, toward the stars above the Hudson, and took us all back to the lowcountry of South Carolina where this beautiful sister was born to grief and sadness, and where all these poems, collected in fragments and images, grew in darkness like sharp pieces of coral, and awaited the annunciation of the poet, awaited this night, the collective breath of this audience, as she shared the poems of the heart by making the language sing and bleed at the same time.

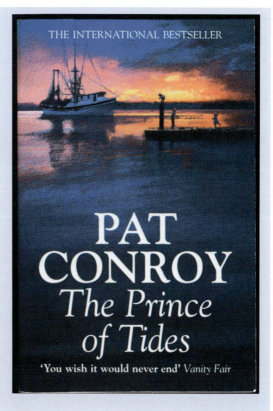

Comment

This extract is from Chapter 2 in the novel *Prince of Tides* by the American writer, Pat Conroy. The plot unravels the bitter history of the childhood of its narrator, Tom, and that of his sister, Savannah. They both share the searing memory of a single terrifying event in that childhood, which becomes the source of Tom's self-hatred and of his sister's suicidal despair. There are episodes of poignant lyricism in this novel. The first time I read it, I was moved by the power of its imagery and the poetic rhythms of its language. For example:

- Read the opening lines again, and concentrate on the language he uses to describe his sister's voice, '… clear and light, a voice without seasons, like bells … Her voice is a greening thing ….' I love that comparison between her voice and 'bells', and the sound of the word 'greening'. It suggests a growing towards, a ripening, perhaps of her work, her life.
- 'She pronounced each word carefully, as though she was tasting fruit. The words of her poems were a most private and fragrant orchard.' Note how the writer links the image of her voice to the sensuousness of 'tasting fruit' and the 'fragrant orchard'.
- Read the extract a second time out loud, and hear the rhythms of the prose from '… my mouth moved in congruence with hers … these poems … fragments and images … sharp

pieces of coral ... awaited the annunciation of the poet ... making the language sing and bleed at the same time.'

• This final image is aesthetically very beautiful, I think, linking as it does the twin realities of life's experience – pleasure and pain. I am reminded of a phrase from *Howard's End* by E. M. Forster – 'Only connect'.

City of the Mind by Penelope Lively

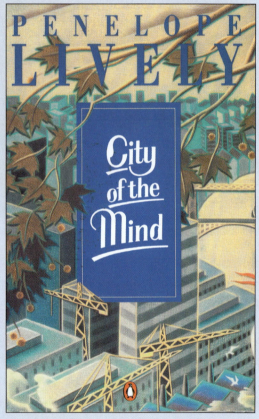

He was the only child: their pride, their worry. Fresh vegetables, cod liver oil, clean shirts. Sedate people, cautious, alarmed by excess. Matthew excelled; he did well at school, was noticed, began to stray. He loved them, and fumed to be off. Nowadays, when he went back to that house, to his mother, he saw his childhood as though through the wrong end of a telescope: brilliant and diminished. The same people, the same place; his mother's lopsided smile, the oak settle in the hall, that vase. He saw himself: minute, unreachable. He saw his father: distinct, continuous, gone. His widowed mother sat in the same chair in which she had once knitted him school jerseys and pulled him towards her to measure the sleeve; he could feel her hands and his own irritation. He took Jane to visit her and she drank from the Mickey Mouse mug that had been his. You travelled through time and space to find that the world had caught up with you. 'Where is Grandpa?' asks Jane. Grandpa is behind the glass of the photo on the mantelpiece, in his Royal Ordnance Corps uniform, in 1944, alongside the clock that they gave him when he retired from thirty years with Cooper Brothers of Enfield (clerical division). You cannot step twice into the

> same river, and yet you do. It has carried you away, and yet you stand on the bank, looking at the point of your own departure.

Comment

This is an extract from Chapter 2 of *City of the Mind* by Penelope Lively. The main character is Matthew Holland— the 'only child' referred to above. His parents wanted him to become a doctor, but he became an architect instead. In this extract he reflects on his childhood. Throughout the novel, he is occupied with building a new future for London in Docklands. The city becomes a metaphor to forge new beginnings in his own life too.

When you read this extract the pace of the writing is the first thing you notice. It's fast, as life tends to be. He is recalling memories of his childhood, in telescopic, camera like 'clicks'. Indeed, he refers to his childhood, as looking through '… the wrong end of a telescope: brilliant and diminished'. The same people, the same place, his mother's lopsided smile, the oak settle in the hall, that vase. He saw himself: minute, unreachable. He saw his father: distinct, continuous, gone.' There is a sense of time standing still in his parent's house, the measuring of his sleeve, his childhood Mickey Mouse mug being offered to his daughter, Jane.

'You travelled through time and space to find that the world caught up with you.'

'Where is Grandpa?' asks Jane 'Grandpa is behind the glass of the photo on the mantlepiece ….'

Humour here, too, in a gentle reminiscence. The *Sunday Telegraph* described this fragmented style of prose as a 'kaleidoscope of images', and *Time Out* said, 'Ms. Lively slots scenes from (the past) into the fabric of her narrative like mortar between bricks …'

That's an excellent description of the author's style of writing, I think. The associations, the links again, between objects, memory and time all interconnect in this novel. Note his use of the word 'river' as a metaphor: 'You cannot step twice into the same river, and yet you do. It has carried you away, and yet you stand on the bank, looking at the point of your own departure.'

Poetry

The following are three poems of my own choice, from the work of Thomas McCarthy, Eavan Boland and Brendan Kennelly, with commentaries (courtesy of Resource Material of Teaching Language, Dept. of Education and Science), from the poets themselves on the role and significance of poetry in their lives, along with some of my own observations.

Her Blindness
by Thomas McCarthy

In her blindness
the house became
a tapestry of touch
The jagged end of a dresser
became a signpost
to the back-door,
bread crumbles crunching
under her feet told
her when to sweep
the kitchen floor;
the powdery touch
of dry leaves in
the flower-trough
said that geraniums needed water.
I remember her beside
the huge December fire,
holding a heavy mug,
changing its position
on her lap; filling
the dark space
between her fingers
with the light
of bright memory.

Comment

'A poet begins with a private feeling and a private set of words that seem to fit the feeling perfectly ... one can hear the feeling as completely as you hear the voice of a beloved ... I am sure that poetry is one of the filters by which we can hear clearly the noises broadcast from other lives.'

Thomas McCarthy says 'Her Blindness' was one of the earliest of his poems to be published. It was originally called 'Dark Spaces', and then 'Grandmother'.

'... now I am happy with its published title because it focuses on the one truly important aspect of my grandmother, her blindness. She had become blind at the age of twenty so she knew the world as a sighted person. Whenever I brought her tea she clasped the warn

> mug in her hands and turned it round and round. I used to stand beside her for a few minutes in case she spilt the hot liquid onto her lap. She was always aware of my standing beside her, and sometimes reached out to squeeze my hand as if I was one of her huge collection of geraniums.'

- Already, in this description of his grandmother, you can see the poet at work, shaping images – the reference to the tea, for example, is echoed in verse 5 of the poem, and the geraniums in verse 4.
- The final choice of title, too, now seems the most apt one – since the core of the poem, its theme, is her blindness. However, note that his poem does not portray blindness as a handicap, and his grandmother, as Thomas McCarthy tells us, was '… a very dominant person, controlling her entire family from the wing-backed chair by her fireside. Nothing was ever done, no door was painted, no pig sold, no hurling match attended, until it was 'cleared' with 'Nan-Nan' as we called her.'
- Look at the lovely alliteration of 'a tapestry of touch', in the poet's description of the house. 'Tapestry' suggests a richness of experience, a variety of objects and images becoming familiar through touch. Look too at the detail of 'the jagged end of a dresser', with its implied danger and hurt, yet serving as 'a signpost to the back-door'.
- As readers, we gain an insight into the grandmother's *world of touch*, and how vital that sense was to her:

'bread crumbles crunching
under her feet …'
'…the powdery touch
of dry leaves in
the flower-trough'

- Note the *alliteration* in 'crumbles crunching' and 'touch' and 'trough'.
- Read again the final image of her 'holding a heavy mug' and note the contrast between that 'dark space between her fingers' and the 'light of bright memory'. It is a poem full of love and fond reminiscence.

The Black Lace Fan My Mother Gave Me
by Eavan Boland

It was the first gift he ever gave her,
buying it for five francs in the Galeries
in pre-war Paris. It was stifling.
A starless drought made the nights stormy.
They stayed in the city for the summer.   5
They met in cafés. She was always early.
He was late. That evening he was later.
They wrapped the fan. He looked at his watch.
She looked down the Boulevard des Capucines.
She ordered more coffee. She stood up.   10
The streets were emptying.
The heat was killing.
She thought the distance smelled of rain and lightning.

These are wild roses, appliquéd on silk by hand,
darkly picked, stitched boldly, quickly.
The rest is tortoiseshell and has the reticent,   15
clear patience of its element. It is

a worn-out, underwater bullion and it keeps,
even now, an inference of its violation.
The lace is overcast as if the weather
it opened for and offset had entered it.   20

The past is an empty café terrace.
An airless dusk before thunder. A man running.
And no way now to know what happened then –
none at all – unless, of course, you improvise:

The blackbird on this first sultry morning,   25
in summer, finding buds, worms, fruit,
feels the heat. Suddenly she puts out her wing –
the whole, full, flirtatious span of it.

Comment

> '… then why do I write it? [poetry] I write it, not to express the experience but to experience it further. Poetry … is a superb and powerful and effective way to experience an experience. … that power within poetry to offer its resources of language and music so that the experience can still be experienced, so that the feeling is still as fresh as the first moment it was felt….'

- Eavan Boland says quite simply that 'This poem is about a black lace fan' and that the fan actually exists. She tells us that it was the first gift her father gave to her mother. 'They were in a heat wave in Paris in the 'thirties and, as she once told me, he went to the Galeries Lafayettes, a big cluster of shops – and bought the fan just before he went on to keep his appointment with her.'
- According to the poet, the object itself – the fan, was 'entirely silent'. It would never be able to tell her the answers to her questions. 'But it would never be able to tell me whether my father rushed down the Boulevard des Capucines to be there on time. Did he rush? It would never be able to tell me what they said, or when the storm broke. What did they say? What did the storm look like?' However, these same questions made the poet want to 'recreate the event: the storm, the man and the woman, the drama and poignance of the first steps of courtship.' That impulse to 'recreate the event' centres round the fan.
- Study the way in which Eavan Boland tells the story, in short fragmented lines, and images. In the first verse she describes making the 'pronouns shimmer and disappear'. The pronoun 'it', for example, used three times in the first verse, the first and second one being the fan, and the third, the weather –

    'It was stifling.
    A starless drought made the nights stormy.'

The fan and the weather, the heat and the mystery of the occasion are 'deliberately confused and merged by those pronouns.' Note too, the alliteration in 'stifling', 'starless' and 'stormy'.

- In the second and third verses, the pronoun changes to 'they', 'he' and 'she' with the emphasis shifting to the couple. The relationship appears to have been a tense one, as is evident from the broken line images, the staccato rhythms of the verse:

    'They met in cafes. She was always early.
    He was late ….
    She ordered more coffee. She stood up.'

But the tension is also romantic. We know why he is late. She does not.

    'They wrapped the fan. He looked at his watch.'

Eavan Boland believes this practice of breaking the line gave a 'jerky, grainy feel to the stanza: a little like the frames of an old film. And that's what I wanted.'

- Look also for examples of *metaphor* in this poem – the fan itself, described as 'underwater bullion', the image of the past in verse 6:

    'The past is an empty café terrace.'

All the nostalgia of a time long gone, a romance once new and fresh is encapsulated in this metaphor.

- The final image of the poem:

    '…. Suddenly she puts out her wing –
    the whole, full, flirtatious span of it.'

Note the powerful visual imagery of the wing span of the bird compared to that of the fan.

In her own commentary on the poem the poet speaks about watching a female black bird in front of her apple tree.

> 'Suddenly, as I watched, she put out one brown wing: a wonderfully constructed fan-like movement. Now open, now shut. There and then the existence of the poem was guaranteed. I had wanted to write about the fan, the past, the lost moment. I lacked the meaning. Now here, in this evocation in nature, of the man-made object of courtship I found the meaning I needed and the final image for the poem.'

Poem from a Three-Year-Old
by Brendan Kennelly

And will the flowers die?

And will the people die?

And every day do you grow old, do I
Grow old, no I'm not old, do
Flowers grow old?

Old things – do you throw them out?

Do you throw old people out?

And how you know a flower that's old?

The petals fall, the petals fall from flowers.
And do the petals fall from people too?
Every day more petals fall until the

Floor where I would like to play I
Want to play is covered with old
Flowers and people all the same
Together lying there with the petals fallen
On the dirty floor I want to play
The floor you come and sweep
With the huge broom.

The dirt you sweep, what happens that,
What happens all the dirt you sweep
From flowers and people, what
Happens all the dirt? Is all the
Dirt what's left of flowers and
People, all the dirt there in a
Heap under the huge broom that
Sweeps everything away?

Why you work so hard, why brush
And sweep to make a heap of dirt?
And who will bring new flowers?
And who will bring new people? Who will
Bring new petals to put in the water
Where no petals fall on to the
Floor where I would like to
Play? Who will bring new flowers
That will not hang their heads
The tired old people wanting sleep?
Who will bring new flowers that
Do not split and shrivel every
Day? And if we have new flowers,
Will we have new people too to
Keep the flowers alive and give
Them water?
And will the new young flowers die?

And will the new young people die?

And why?

Comment

> 'Poetry discovers, protects and celebrates the deepest values of the heart, ... Makes articulate the sand, the shell and the stone ... Poetry makes a kind of singing sense out of confusing experience.'

Brendan Kennelly describes the circumstance which gave rise to this poem, which he saw as one example of the 'different voices [which] had entered my heart and mind over the years and had become the valid voice of poetry.'

> 'One night, my three-year-old daughter was noisily refusing to sleep, screaming her little head off, in fact. I brought her downstairs to the living-room and tried to have a chat with her. A vase of flowers stood on the table. Petals were falling from the flowers. She said, "What are these?" "Petals," I replied. "Why are they falling?" she asked. "Because the flowers are dying," I answered. She was quiet for a while and then the questions began to pour out of her. Needless to say, I wasn't in much of a mood to listen to a child's torrent of questions; but suddenly I was interested. Why? Because of the child's persistent, intense inquiry, her desire to know. Also, I was struck that in the middle of the torrential questioning, she said, time and time again, "I want to play." I tried to answer her as well as any sluggish-minded adult could hope to do so at that late hour and, I recall, she went back to sleep soon afterwards. So did I. Next day, her questions and her, "I want to play" kept coming into my head so I sat down and wrote 'Poem from a Three-Year-Old'. I could hear her voice clearly. I still can.'

- When you read this poem, the first thing you notice is that 'child's torrent of questions':
  'And will the flowers die?
  And will the people die?
  And every day do you grow old, do I
  grow old, no I'm not old, do
  Flowers grow old?'
- The child is 'playing' with questions, but there are deeper implications here, in terms of growth, ageing and death:
  'The petals fall, the petals fall from flowers,
  And do the petals fall from people too?'

Even though the three year old child does not understand or seek to understand these connections, we, as readers, are compelled to. The petals, flowers, old people, dirt and the sweeping broom are a continuous metaphor in the poem for the universal reality of youth yielding to age.

- The child however is merely concerned with a place to play

'... Who will
Bring new petals to put in the water
Where no petals fall on to the
Floor where I would like to
Play?'

- Note too, the connection between the image of the flowers hanging their heads and 'The tired old people wanting sleep'.

There is sadness in the realisation that even the 'new flowers' will 'split and shrivel'. There is poignancy too, in the final two thought provoking questions:

'And will the new young flowers die?

And will the new young people die?

And why?'

The rhythm of the child' voice is our last memory/impression of this poem.

> 'Rhythm', Kennelly says, 'is a magical thing. It is, if you wish, the unique sound of the music of the soul of the poem … The poem wants to share its meaning and its magic with you. Now read it again, but aloud.'

Drama

The following extracts are from three plays:
- *Shirley Valentine* by Willy Russell
- *Death of a Salesman* by Arthur Miller
- *Under Milk Wood* by Dylan Thomas

Shirley Valentine by Willy Russell

Background: There is only one character in this play – Shirley. This extract is from towards the end of the play when Shirley (real name – Mrs. Joe Bradley) has left England for Greece. She has met a Greek waiter there, called Costas. Although she knows it's just a short-term romance, Costas treats her with consideration and concern, and makes her feel that she is an individual with a sense of her own worth. In England, she had been the 42-year-old mother of two grown-up children, whose self-confidence had been broken by school, marriage and life. At this point in the play, she has decided to stay in Greece, and to work there.

Well I'm sittin' there an' he came out to serve me. 'Erm, excuse me,' I said to him, 'I know this sounds a bit soft but would you mind ... I mean would you object if I moved this table an' chair over there, by the edge of the sea?' Well, he looked at me for a minute. 'You want,' he said, 'you want move table and chair to the sea? What for? You don't like here at my bar?' 'Oh yeh,' I said, 'yeh, it's a lovely bar but – but I've just got this soft little dream about sittin' at a table by the sea.' 'Ah,' he said, an' he smiled. 'A dream, a dream. We move this table to the edge of the sea, it make your dream come true?' 'Erm, yeh,' I said. 'I think so.' 'Then, is no problem. I move the table for you. And tonight when I serve in my bar, I say to customer – "tonight, tonight I make someone's dream come true".' Well, I thought for a second he was bein' sarcastic – 'cos in England it would have been. But no, he carries the table an' chair over here an' he brings me out this glass of wine I've ordered. Well, I paid him an' thanked him but he said to me, 'No, I thank you. Enjoy your dream', then he gave a little bow an' he was gone, back to the taverna, leavin' me alone with the sea an' the sky an' me soft little dream. Well, it's funny, isn't it, but y' know if you've pictured somethin', y' know, if you've imagined how somethin's gonna be, made a picture of it in your mind, well it never works out, does it? I mean for weeks I'd had this picture of meself, sittin' here, sittin' here drinkin' wine by the sea; I even knew exactly how I was gonna feel. But when it got to it, it wasn't a bit like that. Because when it got to it, I didn't feel at all lovely an' serene. I felt pretty daft actually. A bit stupid an' – an' awfully, awfully old. What I kept thinkin' about was how I'd lived such a little life. An' one way or another even that would be over pretty soon. I thought to meself, my life has been a crime really – a crime against God, because … I didn't live it fully. I'd allowed myself to live this little life when inside me there was so much. So much more that I could have lived a bigger life with – but it had all gone unused, an' now it never would be. Why – why do y' get … all this life, when it can't be used? Why – why do y' get … all these … feelins an' dreams an' hopes if they can't ever be used? That's where Shirley Valentine disappeared to. She got lost in all this unused life. An' that's what I was thinkin', sittin' there on me own, starin' out at the sea, me eyes open wide an' big tears splashin' down from them. I must've sat there for ages because the noise from the hotel bar had died away an' even the feller from the taverna was lockin' up for the night. He came to collect me glass. It was still full. I hadn't even taken a sip. He saw that I was cryin' but he didn't say anythin'. He just sat down, on the sand an' stared out at the sea. An' when I'd got over it, when it was all right to talk, he said. 'Dreams are never in the places we expect them to be.' I just smiled at him. 'Come,' he said, 'I escort you back to your hotel.' An' he did. An; he told me his name was Costas an' I told him my name was Shirley …

Comment

'… I've got this soft little dream about sittin' at a table by the sea.'

- In many ways, this play is about being allowed to have dreams, and making these dreams come true, but, it is also about coping with life when the dreams are shattered. Read the extract again, and note the number of times the word dream(s) is referred to.

'… Enjoy your dream.'

'… me soft little dream.'

'… all these … feelins an' dreams an' hopes …'

'… Dreams are never in the places we expect them to be.'

- In the first part of the extract, Shirley is living the dream, enjoying it, but then her awareness of her own inadequacy, and the reality of her life, overwhelm her, and her 'dream' of sipping wine beside the sea suddenly seems 'daft'.

'… I felt pretty daft actually. A bit stupid an' – an' awfully awfully old. What I kept thinking about was how I'd lived such a little life.'

- The phrase 'I'd lived such a little life' is immensely sad and we are moved by this woman who feels that her life '... has been a crime really – a crime against God, because ... I didn't live it fully.' That she felt she could have lived a 'bigger life', and 'now it never would be'. We are moved by Shirley's tears and her admission that she has '... got lost in all this unused life'. Yet, the extract ends on a note of optimism and humour, and a hint of romance, with Costas, who reassures her and the audience that: 'Dreams are never in the place we expect them to be.'

- Shirley Valentine, who breaks out of the mould society cast for her, is shown with humour, sympathy and human insight. Remember that definition of the 'aesthetic use of language' from the introduction?

'... primary purpose is to give aesthetic pleasure, enrich imaginative perception and feeling and reveal insights.'

Death of a Salesman by Arthur Miller

Background: This play is on the list for Leaving Cert., as a Single Text option for the years 2001, 2002 and 2003. It can be studied for both Higher and Ordinary level.

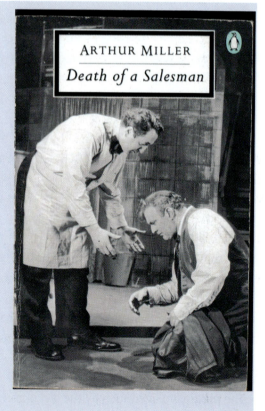

BIFF: No, you're going to hear the truth – what you are and what I am!
LINDA: Stop it!
WILLY: Spite!
HAPPY [*coming down toward* BIFF]: You cut it now!
BIFF [*To* HAPPY]: The man don't know who we are! The man is gonna know! [*To* WILLY] We never told the truth for ten minutes in this house!
HAPPY: We always told the truth!
BIFF [*turning on him*]: You big blow, are you the assistant buyer? You're one of the two assistants to the assistant, aren't you?
HAPPY: Well, I'm practically –
BIFF: You're practically full of it! We all are! And I'm through with it. [*To* WILLY] Now hear this, Willy, this is me.

WILLY: I know you!
BIFF: You know why I had no address for three months? I stole a suit in Kansas City and I was in jail. [*To* LINDA, *who is sobbing*] Stop crying. I'm through with it.
[LINDA *turns away from them, her hands covering her face.*]
WILLY: I suppose that's my fault!
BIFF: I stole myself out of every good job since high school!
WILLY: And whose fault is that?
BIFF: And I never got anywhere because you blew me so full of hot air I could never stand taking orders from anybody! That's whose fault it is!
WILLY: I hear that!
LINDA: Don't, Biff!
BIFF: It's goddam time you heard that! I had to be boss big shot in two weeks, and I'm through with it!
WILLY: Then hang yourself! For spite, hang yourself!
BIFF: No! Nobody's hanging himself, Willy! I ran down eleven flights with a pen in my hand today. And suddenly I stopped, you hear me? And in the middle of that office building, do you hear this? I stopped in the middle of that building and I saw – the sky. I saw the things that I love in this world. The work and the food and time to sit and smoke. And I looked at the pen and said to myself, what the hell am I grabbing this for? Why am I trying to become what I don't want to be? What am I doing in an office, making a contemptuous, begging fool of myself, when all I want is out there, waiting for me the minute I say I know who I am! Why can't I say that, Willy? [*He tries to make* WILLY *face him, but* WILLY *pulls away and moves to the left.*]
WILLY: [*with hatred, threateningly*]: The door of your life is wide open!
BIFF: Pop! I'm a dime a dozen, and so are you!
WILLY [*turning on him now in an uncontrolled outburst*]: I am not a dime a dozen! I am Willy Loman, and you are Biff Lonman!
[BIFF *starts for* WILLY, *but is blocked by* HAPPY. *In his fury,* BIFF *seems on the verge of attacking his father.*]
BIFF: I am not a leader of men, Willy, and neither are you. You were never anything but a hard-working drummer who landed in the ash-can like all the rest of them! I'm one dollar an hour, Willy! I tried seven states and couldn't raise it. A buck an hour! Do you gather my meaning? I'm not bringing home any prizes any more, and you're going to stop waiting for me to bring them home!
WILLY [*directly to* BIFF]: You vengeful, spiteful mut!
[BIFF *breaks from* HAPPY. WILLY, *in fright, starts up the stairs.* BIFF *grabs him*].

BIFF [*at the peak of his fury*]: Pop, I'm nothing! I'm nothing, Pop. Can't you understand that? There's no spite in it any more. I'm just what I am, that's all.
[BIFF'S *fury has spent itself, and he breaks down, sobbing, holding on to* WILLY, *who dumbly fumbles for* BIFF's *face.*]
WILLY [*astonished*]: What're you doing? What're you doing? [To LINDA] Why is he crying?
BIFF [*crying, broken*]: Will you let me go, for Christ's sake? Will you take that pony dream and burn it before something happens? [*Struggling to contain himself, he pulls away and moves to the stairs.*] I'll go in the morning. Put him – put him to bed.

Comment

- This play is also concerned with dreams – the American dream of happiness and success contrasted with the American reality of Willy Loman's failure to achieve that dream or to see that dream realised in his son Biff. In this scene in Act Two, Willy's son, Biff, forces Willy and Happy to face the truth:

'No, you're going to hear the truth – what you are and what I am!'

- Although his mother (Linda) tries to stop him, Biff is determined that Willy should see him for who he really is:

'Now hear this, Willy, this is me ... I stole a suit in Kansas City and I was in jail ....'

This is a scene of heightened tensions and stark, raw emotion, long suppressed. Biff's language wounds his mother and Willy, but the confrontation has to take place. The painful truth will out. For all of his life, Willy has refused to acknowledge that his son is not the epitome of the American dream, and that he, Willy, is not a 'leader of men'.

'Pop! I'm a dime a dozen, and so are you! ... I am not a leader of men, Willy, and neither are you ... I'm one dollar an hour, Willy! ... I'm not bringing home any prizes any more, and you're going to stop waiting for me to bring them home!'

- At the end of this extract, Biff is overcome by the enormity of his anger, and his love for Willy.

'Will you let me go, for Christ's sake? Will you take that phoney dream and burn it before something happens?'

'That phoney dream' is at the core of this play.

Note: In the introduction to this section, I stated that 'some of the aesthetic use of language has to do with depicting dark, sometimes ugly or even frightening aspects of life.' This scene is an example of that. The language is profoundly moving, although the images are not pleasurable. The beauty of it lies in the truth and passion of the language.

Under Milk Wood by Dylan Thomas

Background: *Under Milk Wood* was described by the playwright, Dylan Thomas, as an 'impression for voices, an entertainment out of the darkness, of the town I live in, and to write it simply and warmly and comically with lots of movement and varieties of moods, so that, at many levels ... you come to know the town as an inhabitant of it.'

It was originally conceived as a radio play, accompanied by music by Daniel Jones. There are sixty-nine characters in this play plus extras. *Under Milk Wood* portrays the writer's vision of the imagined small Welsh seaside village of Llareggub. In it, Thomas conjures up the dreams and waking hours of the village within the cycle of just one day.

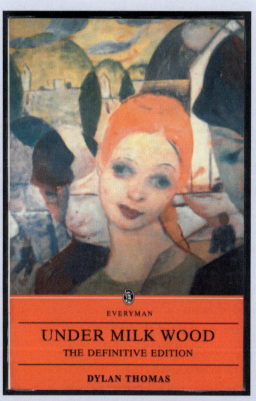

Hush, the babies are sleeping, the farmers, the fishers, the tradesman and pensioners, cobbler, schoolteacher, postman and publican, the undertaker and the fancy woman, drunkard, dressmaker, preacher, policeman, the webfoot cocklewomen and the tidy wives. Young girls lie bedded soft or glide in their dreams, with rings and trousseaux, bridesmaided by glow-worms down the aisles of the organ playing wood. The boys are dreaming wicked or of the bucking ranches of the night and the jollyrodgered sea. And the anthracite statues of the horses sleep in the fields, and the cows in the byres, and the dogs in the wetnosed yards; and the cats nap in the slant corners or lope sly, streaking and needling, on the one cloud of the roofs.

You can hear the dew falling, and the hushed town breathing. Only *your* eyes are unclosed to see the black and folded town fast, and slow, asleep. And you alone can hear the invisible starfall, the darkest-before-dawn minutely dewgrazed stir of the black, dab-filled sea where the Arethusa, the Curlew and the Skylark, Zanzibar, Rhiannon, the Rover, the Cormorant, and the Star of Wales tilt and ride.

> Listen. It is night moving in the streets, the processional salt slow musical wind in Coronation Street and Cockle Row, it is the grass growing on Llaregyb Hill, dewfall, starfall, the sleep of birds in Milk Wood.
>
> Listen. It is night in the chill, squat chapel, hymning in bonnet and brooch and bombazine black, butterfly choker and bootlace bow, coughing like nannygoats, sucking mintoes, fortywinking hallelujah; night in the four-ale, quiet as a domino; in Ocky Milkman's lofts like a mouse with gloves; in Dai Bread's bakery flying like black flour. It is to-night in Donkey Street, trotting silent, with seaweed on its hooves, along the cockled cobbles, past curtained fernpot, text and trinket, harmonium, holy dresser, watercolours done by hand, china dog and rosy tin teacaddy. It is night neddying among the snuggeries of babies.
>
> Look. It is night, dumbly, royally winding through the Coronation cherry trees; going through the graveyard of Bethesda with winds gloved and folded, and dew doffed; tumbling by the Sailor Arms.
>
> Time passes. Listen. Time passes.
>
> Come closer now.
>
> Only you can hear the houses sleeping in the streets in the slow deep salt and silent black, bandaged night. Only you can see, in the blinded bedrooms, the combs and petticoats over the chairs, the jugs and basins, the glasses of teeth. Thou Shalt Not on the wall, and the yellowing dickybird-watching pictures of the dead.

Comment

- This particular extract, occurs at the beginning of the play. I have chosen it because of the richness and originality of the writing. It is a night scene, a dream sequence and we are invited to 'Hush', and observe:

    '... the webfoot cocklewomen

    ... the bucking ranches of the night

    ... the jollyrodgered sea

    ... the wetnosed yards

    ... the sleep of birds in Milk Wood.'

- Inanimate objects assume life, movement and character:

    '...the hushed town breathing

    ... the invisible starfall

    ... the houses sleeping in the streets

    ... the blinded bedrooms

    ... the yellowing dickybird - watching pictures of the dead.'

Journeys and Change 221

- Read this extract more than once, and it will yield up more wonders each time. Study the slumbering, sleeping imagery, of babies:

    'It is night neddying among the snuggeries of babies.'

    'Neddying' and 'snuggeries' are unusual but wonderfully composed words, suggestive of warmth, baby softness and safe sleeping.

- What do you make of the listing of the various townspeople at the beginning. Of the 'webfoot cocklewomen and the tidy wives?' Have the cocklewomen webfeet because they wade in water to collect the cockles? Are the wives respectable because they are tidy? Examine the sensuous verbs Dylan Thomas uses to describe the sleek movement of the cats:

    '... lope sly, streaking and needling ...'

    Does 'streaking' suggest speed? What about 'needling'?

- Look too at the playwright's use of imaginative *adjectives*:

    '*wetnosed* yards'

    '*slant* corners'

    '*invisible* starfall'

    '*dewgrazed* ... dab-filled sea'

- And the alliteration in:

    'Slow deep salt and silent black-bandaged night ... bonnet and brooch and bombazine black, butterfly choker and bootlace bow ....'

    You can see how the rhythms here lend themselves to music.

- We are exhorted to 'Listen'. The repetition of the word is hypnotic, urging us to follow the writer in his 'tour' of the sleeping town. We visit Ocky Milkman's lofts, 'like a mouse with gloves', the simile suggesting stealth and a need for quiet.

- The 'Listen' changes to 'Look' and now we see night 'dumbly, royally winding through the Coronation cheery trees; ... winds gloved and folded ... tumbling by the Sailor Arms.'

- The 'Hush' of the opening line is echoed, at the end, with a reminder of time passing:

    'Time passes. Listen. Time passes.

    Come closer now.'

We are drawn into the intimacy of the interior of peoples' homes. We are told that 'Only you can see, in the blinded bedroom the combs and petticoats over the chairs, the jugs and basins, the glasses of teeth.'

- This play is a wonderful example of how words can be 'full of magic', as expressed in the opening quotation to this section:

    'In a world full of audio-visual marvels, may words matter to you and be full of magic.'

SECTION C COMPOSING

Bringing It All Together – The Exam Essay

To the student

On the day of the actual exam, you need to keep a cool head and follow some logical steps to ensure that you write your best composition. If you have done some practice in comprehending and essay writing beforehand, the task will not seem so daunting. However, the exam situation will test your ability to write well under pressure. This isn't easy, but you will handle it better if you take some time before writing, to plan and structure your essay.

Remember too, that all of the **comprehending** texts are intended as a resource for the **composing** task, and the essay titles will reflect this. Each title will indicate the text to which it refers. For example, 'Citizens of Ireland … you have chosen me to represent you … (Text 2)'. (Essay 1, 2001 Higher English paper)

Unlike the traditional paper, there is an **intrinsic link** between the two sections of Paper 1, in the revised syllabus. This is to your advantage in the exam because you will already have some material on which to base your composition. Bearing all of this in mind, here is a sequence of steps that I suggest you should take when it comes to writing the exam essay.

Step 1: Do the comprehending section first. You will then be very familiar with at least *two texts*, which will help when it comes to choosing your essay. You will also know exactly how much *time* you have left for the composing task.

• Remember though, that both sections carry *equal marks* and that you would be well advised to spend at least an hour on the comprehending task.

Note: You have two hours and fifty minutes overall for this paper. If you complete the comprehending section in one hour, I suggest you allow one hour thirty minutes for the composing task, *including* planning time. Use the remaining twenty minutes of exam time to review *all* of Paper 1. Timing your work in this way is vital. Leaving even a little space for re-reading, and possible rewriting, could make a real difference to your marks overall.

Step 2: Take five minutes to read all seven composition titles carefully, underlining the key words in each title.

Step 3: Take five minutes to identify the predominant genre in each essay, while allowing for elements of other genres that are appropriate to the task. Make some short notes, underneath the titles, as follows:

1. Write a speech you would make ...
Compose an argument for or against ...
Note: *Language of Argument.*
Elements of Information and Persuasion.

2. Imagine that you are in the world of ...
Write a personal essay ...
Write a series of diary entries ...
Write an account of ...
Note: *Aesthetic Use of Language.*
Elements of Narration and Information.

3. Write an article ... attempt to persuade ...
Compose a persuasive article ...
Write a clear letter outlining your response to ...
Note: *Language of Persuasion.*
Elements of Information, Argument and Narration.

4. Write a short story prompted by one of the images in Text 4 ...
Write a narrative similar in style to ...
Note: *Language of Narration.*
Elements of the Aesthetic Use and Information.

5. Write a factual account of ...
Write an informative piece on ...
Write a news report on ...
Note: *Language of Information.*
Elements of Narration and Argument.

The above are guidelines only, intended to help you clarify for yourself the most appropriate genre for the task. They are not intended to restrict you in any way. Genres mix and mingle all the time, but **coherence** and **clarity of purpose** are terms the examiner will use when judging your composition. So be aware of that.

Step 4: *Choose the composition*, allow five minutes for this task.
• Select an essay title that allows you to write in your preferred genre, the one with which you feel most comfortable.
• Consider choosing an essay based on a text you have *already* read for the purpose of answering Question A or Question B in the comprehending section. You will be familiar with these two texts and can therefore more easily identify the link(s) between title and text.
• If choosing a title inspired by a text you haven't read, then you must allow yourself extra time (ten minutes) to read this text carefully, as you are encouraged to *engage* with your chosen text and will be rewarded for doing so, by the examiner.

Step 5: *Draw up a plan*, allow fifteen minutes for this task. Steps 2, 3, and 4 should have taken just *fifteen minutes – excluding* time required to read a text not read previously in the comprehending section.
• Step 5 allows fifteen minutes to draw up an **overall plan** for your composition. Do not stint on this time. Do not be tempted to plunge straight away into any essay, through fear or panic. If you use this fifteen minutes to structure your thoughts into a set of coherent paragraphs, you will write a much better essay.

- Remember that you will still have one hour in which to write your essay. If necessary, you can use some of the twenty minutes, which you have allowed for, at the end of the exam period.
- Having a **plan** in front of you, as you write, will give you confidence and ensure a sense of continuity and consistency in your writing.
- In terms of the *layout* of your essay plan, let me refer you back to:

Unit 1, Section C, *Planning the Composition*   Unit 3, Section C, *Engaging with the Text*
Unit 2, Section C, *Starting the Essay*   Unit 4, Section C, *Concluding the Essay*

Finally, here are the seven composition titles for Unit 5. In this last Unit, I am not giving you any notes on these titles. Consider writing one of them as a test style essay, without assistance from your teacher or your book. If in doubt about any *individual* title, however, you should refer to my notes on essays from previous Units. As in Units 1–4, the essay titles that follow reflect the format of the exam.

The Titles – Theme: Journeys and Change

Task: Write a composition on any one of the following. Each composition carries 100 marks. The composition assignments below are intended to reflect language study in the areas of information, argument, persuasion, narration and the aesthetic use of language.

Essay 1

'I felt doomed, and of all things wonderful.' (Text 3)

> Write a narrative similar in style to the author's story in Text 3.

Essay 2

'Gaelscoileanna believes in the right of every child to be educated through the medium of Irish, regardless of where he/she might live.' (Text 1)

Write a speech you would make in a school or public debate for or against this motion.

Journeys and Change 225

Essay 3

'I always wanted to travel in India.' (Text 2)

Write an account of your experience of a journey that you had always wanted to make, and finally did. The account is to appear in a popular magazine for older teenagers.

Essay 4

Write a short story prompted by one or more of the images in Text 4.

Essay 5

'We began to shrug off the valley and look more to the world …' (Text 3)

Write a personal essay in which you explore your sense of 'shrugging off' your adolescence and moving into adulthood.

Essay 6

'If you listen to people with a disability and you hear them, that's the first step.' (Text 2)

Write a letter to the Minister for Education and Science in which you attempt to persuade the Minister to facilitate the entry of disabled students into all our schools.

Essay 7

'This is my life …' (Text 1)

Imagine you are one of the four students featured in Text 1. Tell your story.

SECTION D LANGUAGE SKILLS

Efficiency of Language Use 5

> 'Developing language awareness means helping students to become conscious of what they already know about language and then attempting to build on that.'
> (*Draft Guidelines for Teachers of English*, Dept. of Education and Science)

To the student

In Section D of Units 1–4, we have been working on exercising language, according to the 'Criteria for Assessment' for Leaving Cert. English. 'Accuracy of Mechanics' (ten per cent) and 'Efficiency of Language Use' (thirty per cent) have been our focus. In this final Unit, we will be looking at how you can **avoid repetition** in your work and how to **write more concisely**. In 'Grammatical Patterns', we will be exercising the *active and passive voice*. In 'Punctuation', we will be concentrating on making sense of texts with little or no punctuation, and in 'Spelling' on some combination vocabulary/spelling exercises, as in Unit 3.

Avoiding Repetition

Repetition is a major flaw in students' work. You can avoid it by:
- *Substitution* i.e. replacing the word with a pronoun and/or verb
- *Ellipsis* i.e. reducing the number of words in a sentence
- *Using a Synonym* (see Unit 3, Section D)

Let's look at how substitution and ellipsis work.

Substitution

Example: 'Do you think Denis will win?'
'No, I don't think *Denis will win*.' (repetition)
'No, I don't think *he* will.'

Here we have substituted a pronoun (he) for 'Denis', and there is no need to repeat the verb 'win'.

Exercise 1

Substitute <u>one word</u> for the underlined parts of the following sentences, and then re-write the sentence in the space provided.

(a) 'I used to watch *The Simpsons*, but I don't watch <u>The Simpsons</u> any more.'
_____

(b) 'Have you got a DVD player?' 'Yes, we've just bought <u>a DVD player</u>.'
_____

(c) She misses Paul a lot. She writes to <u>Paul</u> every Friday.
_____

(d) 'Is that my Maths book?' 'No, it's <u>my Maths book</u>.'
_____

(e) He writes poems all the time. He's writing <u>some poems</u> about childhood at the moment.
_____

(f) 'Do you think *The Third Man* is a good film?' 'Yes, I think <u>The Third Man</u> is a good film.'
_____

(g) She was going to the shops, but when she got <u>to the shops</u>, they were closed.
_____

(h) Donnacha said he would succeed and he <u>succeeded</u>.
_____

(i) If Aileen said she will phone, she <u>will phone</u>.
_____

(j) 'Do you promise to love, honour and cherish her?' '<u>I promise to love, honour and cherish her</u>.'
_____

Ellipsis
Note: Do not confuse this term with *Points of Ellipsis* or *dots (...)* as used in punctuation. Ellipsis means **the omission of a number of words from a sentence**, in order to avoid repetition and to **reduce the number of words overall**.
Example: Liam was good at English, Teresa was good at Maths, and Cathy was good at French. (16 words)
Using ellipsis: Liam was good at English, Teresa at Maths, and Cathy at French. (-4 words)
Using ellipsis in this way will result in tighter, sharper writing, it also forces you to **eliminate repetition**, where possible.

Exercise 2
Reduce these sentences by *removing* the suggested number of words, then rewrite the sentence in the space provided.
Note: You cannot *change* words. You can only *remove* them. This is not as easy as it looks!

(a) Tina is studying and at the same time she is bringing up two children. (-2)
    Reduced sentence _____
(b) We decided we would encourage the girls exactly as we would encourage the boys. (-1)
    Reduced sentence _____
(c) She never finished the course though now she wishes she had finished it. (-2)
    Reduced sentence _____
(d) Mum takes the girls to the pool and Dad takes the boys to the pool. (-4)
    Reduced sentence _____
(e) People believe in the right to educate their children and fight for the right to educate their children. (-6)
    Reduced sentence _____
(f) Seán was excellent at Spanish, Peter was excellent at Business Studies, and Gráinne was excellent at everything! (-4)
    Reduced sentence _____
(g) Girls can be provided with the same educational and career opportunities, and must be provided with the same educational and career opportunities as boys are provided with. (-12!)
    Reduced sentence _____

Writing More Concisely

'Only the hand that erases can write the true thing.' (Meister Eckhart)

To the student

On the Higher Paper, in the exam, you are usually required to write Question B answers within 150–200 words. It is important that you respect this word limit. You will be penalised if you go significantly over – say by thirty words or more. It is difficult to write well under pressure, but if you get into the habit of rough drafting and editing your work for homework, it will really pay off on the day of the exam. Here is a suggestion for an exercise that will help you to write more concisely.

Mini-Saga

Note: This is a complete story written in no more than fifty words. It's a real challenge! Read this example, then attempt the exercises that follow.

> *Donna's story of how her father proposed to her mother*
> Exams over, John set off to request Rose's hand. At the pub, he met his best friend, who confided: 'I'm going to propose to Rose!' John said nothing, but arrived first

and was accepted. Told years later, Rose said 'I have always loved only you!' But had he behaved honourably? (50 words)

Note: It is quite difficult to write so concisely. The first draft was considerably longer. Here it is, for comparison.

When John passed his exams, he set out to request the hand of Rose, the woman he loved. On the way he stopped at a pub, where he met his best friend. As they were drinking together, his friend confided that he intended proposing to Rose. John said nothing but hurried out of the pub. By the time his friend reached Rose's house, John had already proposed and she had accepted. When she was told what happened many years later, she said 'I had always loved only you!' But John often wondered if he had done the right thing, and never had quite the same relationship with his best friend again. (114 words)

Exercise 1
Study both versions of the story. What details have been changed or left out to make the mini-saga shorter? Which version do you prefer? Why?
(a) Write a first draft of a mini-saga about a family, or a friend, or an incident in your own life, in about 120 words. Then reduce it to fifty words in the second draft.
(b) Write a mini-saga inspired by one of the images in Text 4 of Section A (Comprehending) from any of the Units in this book.

Note: This is excellent practice in the craft of writing. It's a discipline that will certainly ensure you keep within the word limit in the exam and improve your writing skills overall.

Grammatical Patterns
Active v. Passive Voice
Depending on their structures, all sentences can be described as being in either the active voice or the passive voice.

Example: Active Sentence
    The burglar attacked the man.
    Syntax   1. subject/agent = burglar
                      2. verb/action = attacked
                      3. object = man

Example: Passive Sentence
    The man was attacked by the burglar.
    Syntax   1. object = man

2. verb/action = was attacked
3. subject = by the burglar

Note that in the passive sentence – the **syntax**, or order of the words, has been inverted, and some new (auxiliary) words added, i.e. was, by.

Student: When should I use the active and when the passive?

Good question. Here's the general rule.

Rule: Active sentences are used most of the time, because they are more direct and energetic. In personal writing they should be used as much as possible.

However, when you need to be impersonal, and to write in a formal context, then passive sentences can be more appropriate. For example, the passive is often used in newspaper reports in order to emphasise an event or an action, and to make it sound more formal and the report more objective.

'The sense of devastation and despair that followed the bombing of the World Trade Center in New York, on 11 September 2001, was felt throughout the world.'

Whether you use the active or passive voice is clearly related to an appropriate style of writing. Here are some exercises on changing active sentences to passive and vice versa. They are intended to help you to familiarise yourself with the elements of both formal and informal styles of writing.

Exercise 1 Active to Passive

Rephrase the following sentences beginning with the word(s) given underneath each sentence. (i.e. from active to passive). Take care to keep the correct *tense*, and remember that the *syntax* (order of words) may change considerably. The first one *may be used* (passive!) as an example.

(a) They announced a delay.
   A delay ...
   Passive: A delay *was announced*.
(b) The computer made the error.
   The error ...
   Passive: _____
(c) They didn't force the students to attend the ceremony.
   Students ...
   Passive: _____
(d) They are building a new factory there.
   A new factory ...
   Passive: _____

(e) In Italy, they use pasta as the main ingredient of many dishes.
   Pasta ...
   Passive: _____
(f) Is someone collecting the data?
   Is the data ...
   Passive: _____
(g) You must keep the records in the vault.
   The records ...
   Passive: _____
(h) Somebody wants you on Ward 5.
   You ...
   Passive: _____
(i) He could not move the body.
   The body ...
   Passive: _____
(j) The police are watching him closely.
   He is ...
   Passive: _____

Exercise 2 Passive to Active

Rephrase the following sentences beginning with the word(s) given underneath each sentence. (i.e. from passive to active) Take care to keep the correct *tense*, and remember that the *syntax* (order of words) may change considerably. You may use the first one as an example.

(a) The car will have to be sold.
   I ...
   Active: *I will have* to sell the car.
(b) It is said that money cannot buy happiness.
   They ...
   Active: _____
(c) I wasn't fooled by her story.
   Her ...
   Active: _____
(d) The machine was overloaded.
   They ...
   Active: _____

(e) The new cabinet has been announced by the Taoiseach.
     The ...
     Active: _____
(f) The street was flooded by the river.
     The ...
     Active: _____
(g) Are you being brought to the station?
     Is ...
     Active: _____
(h) Will Man. United be beaten by Liverpool on Saturday?
     Will ...
     Active: _____
(i) The summit will be reached by midnight.
     They ...
     Active: _____
(j) The final will be won by Tipperary.
     Tipperary ...
     Active: _____

Exercise 3
Try writing a short paragraph (75–100 words) or a Question B style answer (150–200 words) in two distinctly different styles of writing, and genres i.e.
   formal – using the **passive** voice
   informal – using the **active** voice.
Use any of the comprehending texts or composing titles from this Unit for inspiration.

Punctuation

'Those dots, strokes and squiggles may appear physically insignificant on a page of print ... but without them all would be chaos ... Any piece of writing will fall apart without the nuts and bolts of punctuation.'
(Graham King, *Collins WordPower Punctuation*, Harper Collins Publishers)

To the student
Units 1–4 contain lots of practice in the main punctuation marks needed to help your teacher and the examiner to understand your work. In addition, if you have a problem with *apostrophes*, you will find work on these in Unit 3, and on *quotation marks* in Unit 4.
Note: Remember that the bottom line with all of your written work is *care*. You need to

allow time in the exam to re-read your Question A and Question B answers in the comprehending section, and your essay, and to check your punctuation and spelling. This should not be regarded as a waste of time, but rather as an intelligent use of your time, which will ensure that you submit your best possible work, thereby maximising your chance for higher marks.

In this final punctuation exercise, you will find extracts from the opening pages of five novels on your Leaving Cert. course. You are required to replace the main punctuation marks, indicated at the top of each extract. This exercise is intended to heighten your awareness of good punctuation, but also, I hope, to encourage you to read the novels!

1. An extract from *Reading in the Dark* by Seamus Deane.

    Replace: capital letters   quotation marks
                   full stops   question marks
                   commas   apostrophes

on the stairs there was a clear plain silence

it was a short staircase fourteen steps in all covered in lino from which the original pattern had been polished away to the point where it had the look of a faint memory eleven steps took you to the turn of the stairs where the cathedral and the sky always hung in the window frame three more steps took you on to the landing about six feet long

dont move my mother said from the landing dont cross that window

i was on the tenth step she was on the landing i could have touched her

theres something there between us a shadow dont move

i had no intention i was enthralled but i could see no shadow

theres somebody there somebody unhappy go back down the stairs son

> i retreated one step howll you get down
> ill stay a while and it will go away
> how do you know
> ill feel it gone
> what if it doesnt go
> it always does ill not be long
> i stood there looking up at her i loved her then she was small and anxious but without real fear

2. An extract from *The Homesick Garden* by Kate Cruise O'Brien.
   Replace: capital letters   quotation marks
   full stops   apostrophes
   commas

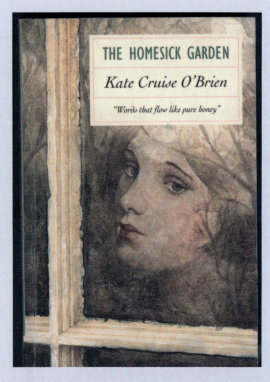

aunt grace came in out of the rain shivering trembling and sneezing like a wet dog it was sunday morning in our house – everywhere else too i suppose – but sunday morning in our house is not the time to pay a call they were in bed dad in the big bare front room and mum in the small squashed back room they had had a quarrel they usually do quarrel on a saturday night there was a lot of door-slamming and talk about drinking (mums) and indifference (dads) and when i passed mum on the stairs she was crying but i noticed she had a small glass in one hand and her cigarettes and lighter in the other i didnt go into the kitchen where dad was because i knew hed just point a finger at me and say out in that tight voice he has so dad stayed up late and read the papers at the kitchen table and mum went to bed early with the brandy and the fags and a big pile of books she used to read when she was a girl when i was a girl like you she said once with a smile only i never was a girl like you i was something between a coward and a goody-goody and i still read books that are safe and small its comforting mum needs a lot of comfort one way or another what with the cigarettes and the brandy and the books but then im not afraid of dads tight voice and mum is so saturday night is the reason that no one in their senses would care to call at my house on a sunday morning and aunt grace has a lot of sense aunt grace is my best friend and mentor

3. An extract from *The Grass is Singing* by Doris Lessing.
   Replace: capital letters   3 examples of quotation marks
             full stops   commas

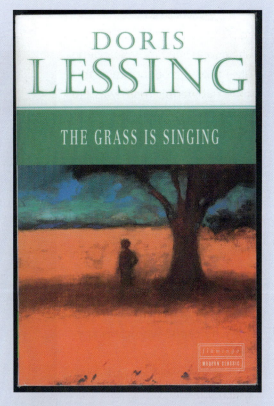

mary turner wife of richard turner a farmer at ngesi was found murdered on the front verandah of their homestead yesterday morning the houseboy who as been arrested has confessed to the crime no motive has been discovered

it is thought he was in search of valuables

the newspaper did not say much people all over the country must have glanced at the paragraph with its sensational heading and felt a little spurt of anger mingled with what was almost satisfaction as if some belief had been confirmed as if something had happened which could only have been expected when natives steal murder or rape that is the feeling white people have

and then they turned the page to something else

but the people in the district who knew the turners either by sight or from gossiping about them for so many years did not turn the page so quickly many

> must have snipped out the paragraph put it among old letters or between the pages of a book keeping it perhaps as an omen or warning glancing at the yelowing piece of paper with closed secretive faces for they did not discuss the murder ; that was the most extraordinary thing about it it was as if they had a sixth sense which told them everything there was to be known although the three people in a position to explain the facts said nothing the murder was simply not discussed a bad business someone would remark ; and the faces of the people round about would put on that reserved and guarded look a very bad business came the reply – and that was the end of it

4. An extract from *Amongst Women* by John McGahern.
   Replace: capital letters   quotation marks
   full stops   apostrophes
   commas

> as he weakened moran became afraid of his daughters this once powerful man was so implanted in their lives that they had never really left great meadow in spite of jobs and marriages and children and houses of their own in dublin and london now they could not let him slip away
>
> youll have to shape up daddy you cant go on like this youre giving us no help we cant get you better on our own
>
> who cares? who cares anyhow?
>
> we care we all care very much
>
> they all came at christmas after christmas mona the one girl who had not married came every weekend from dublin sometimes sheila got away form her family to come with her and she drove

down for a few hours as well now and again in the middle of the week the air fare from london was too expensive for maggie to come regularly michael their younger brother had promised to come from london at easter but luke the eldest still would not come all three girls planned to revive monaghan day they had to explain to their stepmother rose what monaghan day was she had never heard of it in all her time in the house

the end-of-february fair in mohill was monaghan day mcquaid came every year to the house on monaghan day he and moran had fought in the same flying column in the war mcquaid always drank a bottle of whiskey in the house when he came

if we could revive monaghan day for daddy it could help to start him back to himself monaghan day meant the world to him once

5. An extract from *Great Expectations* by Charles Dickens.
    Replace: capital letters   apostrophes
                 full stops   quotation marks
                 commas   question marks

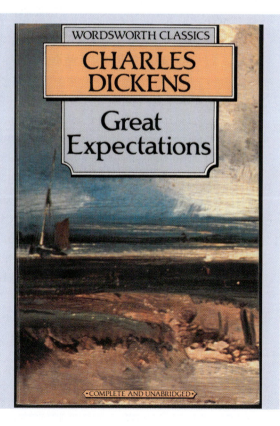

as we were going with our candle along the dark passage estella stopped all of a sudden and facing round said in her taunting manner with her face quite close to mine:

well

well miss i answered almost falling over her and checking myself

she stood looking at me and of course i stood looking at her

am i pretty

yes; i think you are very pretty

am i insulting

not so much as you were last time said i

not so much so

no

she fired when she asked the

> last question and she slapped my face with such force as she had when i answered it
>
> now said she you little coarse monster what do you think of me now
>
> i shall not tell you
>
> because you are going to tell up-stairs is that it
>
> no said i thats not it
>
> why dont you cry again you little wretch
>
> because ill never cry for you again said i which was i suppose as false a declaration as ever was made; for i was inwardly crying for her then and i know what i know of the pain she cost me afterwards

And finally ...

> ### A Victorian Schoolmistress's 10 Golden Rules of Punctuation
>
> Sentences begin with a *Capital letter*,
> So as to make your writing better.
>
> Use a *full stop* to mark the end.
> It closes every sentence penned.
>
> The *comma* is for short pauses and breaks,
> And also for lists the writer makes.
> *Dashes* – like these – are for thoughts by the way.
> They give extra information (so do *brackets*) we may say.
> These two dots are *colons*: they pause to compare.
> They also do this: list, explain, and prepare.
> The *semicolon* makes a break; followed by a clause,
> It does the job of words that link; it's also a short pause.
> An *apostroph*e shows the owner of anyone's things,
> And it's also useful for shortenings.
> I'm so glad! He's so mad! We're having such a lark!
> To show strong feelings use an *exclamation mark*!
> A *question mark* follows What? When? Where? Why?
> and How?
> Do you? Can I? Shall we? Give us your answer now!
> "*Quotation marks*" enclose what is said,
> Which is why they're sometimes called "speech marks" instead
>
> (Graham King, *Collins Wordpower Punctuation,* Harper Collins Publishers)

Spelling

'Do you spell it with a 'V' or a 'W'?' inquired the judge.
'That depends upon the taste and fancy of the speller, my Lord,' replied Sam.
(Charles Dickens, *Pickwick Papers*)

To the student

In Units 1–4 you were given a list of the ten most frequently misspelled words at the end of Section D.

In this Unit, you will find your final list of words, followed by a **Test Yourself** exercise. If you have *not* learned the spellings in the previous four Units, this test will give you some idea of how good or bad your spelling really is, and may serve as a warning to do some work in this area. If you *have* studied the lists, then you should perform well in this test, and have a real sense of improvement – and confidence, in your spelling ability.

Most frequently misspelled words

Word	Spell it	Short sentence
1. alr<u>ea</u>dy	---------	_____
2. beautifu<u>l</u>	---------	_____
3. cons<u>c</u>ience	---------	_____
4. brou<u>gh</u>t (bring)	----------	_____
5. immediat<u>e</u>ly	----------	_____
6. <u>k</u>nowledge	----------	_____
7. o<u>cc</u>ur	----------	_____
8. rel<u>e</u>vant	----------	_____
9. rh<u>y</u>thm	----------	_____
10. s<u>u</u>rprise	----------	_____

Exercise 1 The 50 Word Test

Frequently misspelled words

A. Circle the correct spelling:
   1. biginning   beginning
   2. description   discription
   3. sceene   scene
   4. goverment   government
   5. allways   always
   6. poetry   peotry

240 Write Now!

    7. speach   speech
    8. argument   arguement
    9. truely   truly
  10. necessary   nesessary

B. Here is a list of adjectives. Spell the noun.

    Adjective   Noun
     1. thoughtful
     2. conscious
     3. knowledgeable
     4. rhythmic
     5. occasional
     6. responsible
     7. literary
     8. environmental
     9. critical
    10. eternal

C. Here are some nouns. Spell the adjective.

    Noun   Adjective
     1. fascination
     2. humour
     3. dominance
     4. evidence
     5. beauty
     6. relevance

D. Here are some nouns. Spell the verb.

    Noun   Verb
     1. belief
     2. exaggeration
     3. appreciation
     4. teaching ** past tense
     5. portrayal
     6. persuasion
     7. occurrence
     8. surprise

E. Fill in the blanks with the appropriate adverb. The first letter of the adverb and the number of letters in the word are given to you.
1. Susan was e ---------------------------- (9) angry.
2. Donnacha was a --------------------- (7) there.
3. Aileen was q --------------------------- (5) worried.
4. Hubert was contacted i ---------------------------- (11).
5. 'Yours s -------------------------------- (9).'

Eleven words remain from the lists of ten given at the end of Section D in each Unit – six nouns, three adjectives and two verbs. Can you guess which ones they are from the definitions given below?

F. **Definition**   Word

   Nouns
   1. a public notice or announcement   _____
   2. the collective qualities that distinguish a person or thing   _____
   3. figurative illustrations as used by an author for particular effect   _____
   4. the relative nature or kind of character of a thing   _____
   5. the legal union of a man and woman   _____
   6. the act of breaking the continuous progress an action, speech,
      a person speaking, etc.   _____

   Adjectives
   7. readily visible or perceivable, seeming   _____
   8. having a position on the other or further side facing, or back to
      back   _____
   9. unusual or remarkable   _____

   Verbs
   10. produce an effect on, touch the feeling of   _____
   11. past simple of the verb 'to bring'   _____

N.B. If you scored forty or more in this test – well done! If not, then you need to do some more work on your spelling.

Revise the words over a period of time – say ten per week. Then do the test again. It's worth the effort, remember. Good Luck!

Last Words

To the student

In Section C (Composing) I suggested using **quotations** as a possible starting or concluding point for your essays. Here is a list of quotations on a number of themes and issues suggested by the literature on your course, which may also occur as general themes for Paper 1. They are in alphabetical order for easy reference.

1. *Art*

    'Art is meant to disturb, science reassures.' (Georges Braque, 1882–1963)

2. *Betrayal*

    'Is it possible to succeed without any act of betrayal?' (Jean Renoir)

3. *Childhood*

    'There is always one moment in childhood when the door opens and lets the future in.' (Graham Greene, *The Power and the Glory*)

    'Childhood is the Last Chance Gulch for happiness. After that, you know too much.' (Tom Stoppard, playwright)

4. *Death*

    'Dying is an art, like everything else.' (Sylvia Plath, 'Lady Lazarus')

    'Excuse my dust.' (Dorothy Parker's own epitaph)

5. *Education*

    'Education is not the filling of a pail, but the lighting of a fire.' (W.B. Yeats)

    'I have never let my schooling interfere with my education.' (Mark Twain)

6. *Evil*

    'The world is evil.' (A fireman attending victims of the attack on the World Trade Center, 11 September 2001)

    'We ... here in Britain stand shoulder to shoulder with our American friends in this hour of tragedy and we, like them, will not rest until this evil is driven from our world.' (Tony Blair, British Prime Minister, September 2001)

    'To respond to evil by committing another evil does not eliminate evil but allows it to go on forever.' (Vaclav Havel, President of the Czech Republic)

7. *Family*

    'The family – that dear octopus form whose tentacles we never quite escape.' (Dodie Smith, novelist and dramatist, 1896–1990)

8. *Freedom*

    'No-one's free – even the birds are chained to the sky.' (Bob Dylan)

9. *Friendship*
   'Friends are relatives you make for yourself.' (Anon)
   'What is a friend? A single soul dwelling in two bodies.' (Aristotle)
10. *Future*
    'I never think of the future. It comes soon enough.' (Albert Einstein)
    'The future is a convenient place for dreams.' (Anatole France)
    'We're not only going to rebuild. We're going to come out stronger than we were before.' (Mayor Rudolf Guiliani of New York City, September 2001)
11. *Journeys*
    'Any road will lead you to the end of the world.' (Carlyle)
    'As a child I was haunted above all things by the school room atlas. I thought of it as sort of one's back-door.' (Bruce Chatwin)
12. *Language*
    'Language is like a cracked kettle on which we beat out tunes for bears to dance to, while all the time we long to move the stars to pity.' (Unknown)
13. *Love*
    'Four be the things I'd been better without:
    Love, curiosity, freckles, and doubt.' (Dorothy Parker)
    'Love set you going like a fat gold watch.' (Sylvia Plath, 'Morning Song')
    'What will survive of us is love.' (Philip Larkin, 'An Arundel Tomb' 1964)
14. *Politics*
    'Politics is war without bloodshed while War is politics with bloodshed.' (Mao Zedong)
    'Politics are too serious a matter to be left to the politicians.' (Charles de Gaulle)
15. *Power*
    'Power tends to corrupt, and absolute power corrupts absolutely.' (Lord Acton)
    'You cannot have power for good without having power for evil too.' (George Bernard Shaw)
    'What power have you got?
    Where did you get it from?
    In whose interests do you exercise it?
    To whom are you accountable?
    How do we get rid of you?'
    (Questions habitually asked by Tony Benn, British Labour politician, on meeting somebody in power)
16. *Racism*
    'There are no "white" or "colored" signs on the foxholes or graveyards of battle.' (President John F Kennedy)

'I think: "Where do I sit? At the front? In the middle? At the back?" and when I see someone who looks like an Arab, I get off.' (Ms Na'ama Binyamin, sixteen, on assessing the risk from suicide bombers while travelling by bus in Israel)

17. *Society*
'Society needs to condemn a little more and understand a little less.' (John Major, Conservative Prime Minister 1990–97)
'A free society is a society where it is safe to be unpopular.' (Adlai Stevenson, US Democratic politician, 1900–65)

18. *War*
'We've just seen the first war of the 21st century.' (President George W. Bush, 15 September 2001)
'After each war there is a little less democracy to save.' (Brooks Atkinson, US journalist and critic, 1894–1984)
'My subject is war, and the pity of war. The poetry is in the pity.' (Wilfred Owen, English poet, 1893–1918)

19. *Women*
'I expect that woman will be the last thing civilised by man.' (George Meredith)
'Instead of rocking the cradle, they rocked the system.' (Mary Robinson, President 1990–97, in her victory speech, paying tribute to the women of Ireland, *The Times*, 10 November 1990)

20. *Words*
'Words are, of course, the most powerful drug used by mankind.' (Rudyard Kipling, 1865–1936)
'All books are either dreams or swords: you can cut, or you can drug with words.' (Amy Lowell, poet, 1874–1925)

21. *Youth*
'Youth would be an ideal state if it came a little later in life.' (Henry Asquith, English Prime Minister, 1908–16)
Youth is something very new: twenty years ago no one mentioned it. (Coco Chanel)
'Being young is greatly overestimated ... Any failure seems so total. Later on you realise you can have another go.' (Mary Quant, fashion designer, 1996)
'People ought to be one of two things, young or old. No – what's the use of fooling? People ought to be one of two things, young or dead.' (Dorothy Parker, American wit in the 1930s)

Glossary of Terms used in the Exam

The following glossary of terms used in the examination papers may be of some help to you in clarifying the tasks set for you to do.

PAPER 1 (ORDINARY AND HIGHER) COVER PAGE

1.	'familiarise'	To browse, look quickly through the texts to get the general gist of what they are about and to help you make choices about the questions you would like to answer. Pay attention here to the Title given to each text, the short introduction provided and the images that accompany the 'written' texts.

PAPER 1 ORDINARY AND HIGHER LEVEL

2.	'Write a letter'	Look through the Department of Education and Science Sample Papers to see the different kinds of letters that have been set – 'a letter home', 'a letter to Phoebe', 'a letter to a politician', 'a letter to a newspaper', and so on. Think about how these letters are different from each other. It is not necessary for you to worry unduly about getting the correct format or layout for the letter. Take the letter printed in the Higher Level paper (on page 9) as your guideline in that respect.
3.	'Imagine you are the narrator'	Remember that you are being asked to write <u>from the point of view</u> of a person in the text. Write your answer to the task in the first person.
4.	'Compose diary entries'	Remember that you do not have to use conventional punctuation here. The diary is a 'private' document; the writer is also the reader of the document. [Saturday morning – got up at eleven – went to town with friends saw 'you-know-who' and so on] Of course, you may write in a more conventional format if you judge that that would be more effective or suitable.

5.	'Write a clear description of an image'	What you are being asked to do here is to describe clearly and accurately what you see in the image you have chosen. There is no need to dwell on what the image suggests to you.
6.	'Write a short report for a news programme'	Here you are free to use conventions such as a headline and sub-headlines to give your writing the appearance of a newspaper report. Equally, you can write your answer as the text that would be spoken by a radio or television reporter.
7.	'What general conclusions do you draw'	The task here is not the same as writing a summary of the points made in the text. You should try to distill down the material into a series of short, general statements that you can support by illustration from the text.
8.	'explaining... and encouraging'	Note that some questions will set you more than one task.

From *Assessment Advice for Students,* Leaving Certificate English CD-rom, Department of Education and Science

Marking Criteria for Leaving Certificate English

APPENDIX 1

LEAVING CERTIFICATE ENGLISH
CRITERIA FOR ASSESSMENT

| Clarity of purpose

P	Engagement with the set task	e.g. relevance, focus, originality, freshness, clear aim, understanding of genre	Percentage weighting 100 50 30 15
Coherence of delivery

G | Ability to sustain the response over the entire answer | *Where appropriate:* continuity of argument, sequencing, management of ideas, choice of reference, use of examples, engagement with texts, control of register and shape, creative modelling | 30   15 |
| Efficiency of language use

L | Management and control of language to achieve clear communication | e.g. vocabulary, syntax, sentence patterns, paragraph structure, punctuation appropriate to the register, use of lively interesting phrasing, energy, style, fluency *appropriate to the delivery of the task* | 30   15 |
| Accuracy of mechanics

M | Spelling

Grammar | e.g. levels of accuracy in spelling *appropriate to the delivery of the task* grammatical patterns appropriate to the register | 10   5 |

From Leaving Certificate English CD-rom, Department of Education and Science

Acknowledgments

For permission to reproduce copyright material in this book, grateful acknowledgment is made to the following:

Greenwood Publishing Group for extracts from *Living By the World* by Alice Walker;
Faber and Faber Ltd for lines from 'Little Gidding' (*Four Quartets*) by T.S. Eliot and for an extract from *Amongst Women* by John McGahern;
Penguin Books for extracts from *How Many Miles to Babylon?* by Jennifer Johnston and *Death of a Salesman* by Arthur Miller;
Bloomsbury Publishing for an extract from *Cat's Eye* by Margaret Atwood;
Time Warner Books UK for an extract from *I Know Why the Caged Bird Sings* by Maya Angelou;
Anvil Press Poetry for 'Her Blindness' by Thomas McCarthy;
Carcanet Press for 'The Black Lace Fan My Mother Gave Me' from *Collected Poems* by Eavan Boland;
Bloodaxe Books and Brendan Kennelly for 'Poem from a Three-Year-Old' by Brendan Kennelly;
Methuen Publishing Ltd for an extract from *Shirley Valentine* by Willy Russell;
David Higham Associates for an extract from *Under Milk Wood* by Dylan Thomas (published by J.M. Dent);
The Random House Group Ltd for extracts from *Reading in the Dark* by Seamus Deane published by Jonathan Cape, and from *The Illustrated Cider with* Rosie by Laurie Lee published by Hutchinson (originally published by Hogarth Press);
Poolbeg Press for an extract from *The Homesick Garden* by Kate Cruise O'Brien;
HarperCollins for an extract from *The Grass is Singing* by Doris Lessing;
The *Irish Times*; *Time* magazine and *National Geographic* for various extracts.

Photos:

Rex Features; Frank Spooner/Gamma; The *Irish Times*; Vivant Univers; Derek Speirs/Report; Metro Eireann; Imagefile; The Art Archive; BBC Picture Archives; Anthony Crickmay/Candoco Dance Company; Bridgeman Art Library/estate of Sir Sidney Nolan; The Kobal Collection; Trinity College Dublin; Photostage/Donald Cooper; Martyn Turner.

The publishers have made every effort to trace copyright holders, but if they have inadvertently overlooked any they will be pleased to make the necessary arrangements at the first opportunity.